Contemporary States and the Pandemic

This volume elaborately studies the challenges posed and impact made by the Covid-19 pandemic. Through detailed case studies, it presents ethical, political, economic, medical, logistical, and social impediments faced by contemporary states in the EU. The book focuses on the short- and long-term consequences of the economic shock caused by the COVID-19 pandemic and covers issues concerning the world economy, the EU economy, as well as the Visegrad economies.

The chapters in this volume:

- Probe into the response of states to the economic phenomena resulting from the pandemic and analyses the institutional framework of the resulting crisis, lapses in social communication, social protests and the decline in democratic standards in countries such as the Czech Republic, Poland, Slovakia, and Hungary;
- Discuss issues related to state security under conditions of the pandemic, the effectiveness of state and self-government administration, the transition of states from an external controllability to an internal controllability model of power, as well as challenge related to security in the digital space;
- Present policy actions at three basic levels, i.e. at the global, regional and sub-regional, and investigates strategies of the UN, WHO, the EU and the Visegrad Group as they play the most important role in the fight against COVID-19.

This insightful and timely volume will be of great interest to scholars, researchers and anyone inquisitive about political theory, public policy, public health and social care, international relations, governance, security studies, and public administration.

Jolanta Itrich-Drabarek is Professor, University of Warsaw. She is a political scientist and holds Ph.D. with "habilitation" in social science and is Member of the Scientific Excellence Council of the 1st term.

Contemporary States and the Pandemic

Edited by
Jolanta Itrich-Drabarek

Routledge
Taylor & Francis Group
LONDON AND NEW YORK

First published 2023
by Routledge
4 Park Square, Milton Park, Abingdon, Oxon OX14 4RN

and by Routledge
605 Third Avenue, New York, NY 10158

Routledge is an imprint of the Taylor & Francis Group, an informa business

British Library Cataloguing-in-Publication Data
A catalogue record for this book is available from the British Library

ISBN: 978-1-032-00726-7 (hbk)
ISBN: 978-1-032-40591-9 (pbk)
ISBN: 978-1-003-35380-5 (ebk)

DOI: 10.4324/9781003353805

Typeset in Sabon
by Deanta Global Publishing Services, Chennai, India

Contents

Illustrations

Figures

Tables

Contributors

Jolanta Itrich-Drabarek is Professor and has a Ph.D. on "habilitation" in social science, Vice-Dean for Development, Faculty of Political Sciences and International Studies, University of Warsaw, political scientist.

Marcin Górnikiewicz has a Ph.D. on "habilitation" in social science/security studies and is Vice-Dean for International Affairs & Development, at the Faculty of Security, Logistics and Management of the Military University of Technology.

Tadeusz Klementewicz is a Polish political scientist, professor of social sciences, lecturer at the Faculty of Political Science and International Studies at the University of Warsaw, and is a specialist in the field of political theory and methodology of social sciences.

Katarzyna Kołodziejczyk has a Ph.D. on habilitation in political science (2014), is a scholar at the Faculty of Political Science and International Studies, University of Warsaw, and is Supervisor of Studies in National Security, secretary of the Political Science Committee at the Polish Academy of Sciences.

Wiesław Lizak is a holder of a post-doctoral degree in social science in Faculty of Political Science and International Studies at Warsaw University, and is the author of several publications featuring problems of security and stability in Africa and the Middle East, i.e. issues such as reasons and consequences of regional conflicts.

Stanisław Mazur is Professor at the Krakow University of Economics, Rector of the Krakow University of Economics, former Dean of the College of Economy and Public Administration, Head of the Department of Public Policies, Graduate of the Faculty of Law and Administration at the Jagiellonian University.

Magdalena Mikołajczyk has a Ph.D. on habilitation in political science. She is Assistant Professor at the Institute of Political Science of the University of Wroclaw. She specialises in Political Theory and Political Sociology, and conducts research on political discourses and their visual representations.

Andrzej Misiuk is Professor of humanities, head of the Department of Security Science at the Institute of Political Science, University of Warsaw. He is the author of 60 compact works and over 200 scientific articles in the field of security, history and public administration.

Kamil Mroczka holds a Ph.D. in political science, is Assistant Professor at the Faculty of Political Science and International Studies of the University of Warsaw, and is a graduate of the Executive MBA programme offered by the International Management Center at the University of Warsaw. He was Member of the Supervisory Board of Bank from 2017 to 2019.

Artur Nowak-Far is Professor of law (tenure, SGH-Warsaw School of Economics), Ph.D. economics, advisor to the Senate of the Republic of Poland, 2007–2013 member of the Collegium of the Supreme Chamber of Auditors, 2003–2005 advisor to the Minister of Agriculture (EU law).

Grzegorz Rydlewski is Professor of humanities in political science, Head of the Department of State and Public Administration, University of Warsaw. After 1990 Secretary of Council of Ministers, Head of the Chancellery of the Prime Minister, Head of the Advisers to the Prime Minister, OECD consultant in Paris.

Joanna Starzyk-Sulejewska holds a post-doctoral degree in social sciences and is Vice-Dean for science at the Faculty of Political Science and International Studies at the University of Warsaw.

Marzena Walkowiak holds a Ph.D. in social science/security studies for International Affairs & Development, at the Faculty of Security, Logistics and Management of the Military University of Technology.

Jacek Wojnicki is Professor of social science, Head of Department of Political Systems at the Faculty of Political Sciences and International Studies, University of Warsaw. His areas of interest include the political and administrative systems of Central and Eastern European countries in comparison with Poland.

Introduction

Jolanta Itrich-Drabarek

The pandemic of the coronavirus SARS-CoV-2 causing COVID-19 disease has once again made it necessary to discuss the role and function of the state. A state that has assumed responsibility for the health and lives of its citizens, for their safety and well-being. Announced on 11 March 2020 by WHO, the pandemic has become a new experience for the rulers and societies worldwide. Governments, public administrations, law enforcement, and medical services of countries of the affluent North and the poor South have been forced to face its course. The state has faced many cataclysms in its history: from natural disasters to man-made ones in the most tragic form – the war. In the 21st century, the age of technology, it has become apparent that we, as mankind, are but a tiny part of nature, and the first global cataclysm of this century was a pandemic which, as it spread, showed once again the different face of the humanity: a mixture of cynicism and heroism, greed and noble, selfless acts.

The studies of epidemics and pandemics in the past have focused on their history, the search for their impact on economic development or stagnation, the mechanisms of transmission of the contagion and its effect on collective behaviour, the impact on the development of medicine and methods of containment. The results of this work allow us to understand the causes of pandemics, the methods of their prevention in Europe and worldwide, and to see the specificities of social mobilisation in difficult times. However, there has not been a political science study that points to the specific role of the state during a pandemic and the challenges faced by policymakers during its course. The main research objectives of this book are to examine the political-legal framework of political actors in the fight against a pandemic and to analyse the risks and effectiveness of the measures taken. That is, to conduct an analysis of the methods used by contemporary states in the face of pandemic challenges and to seek answers to the fundamental question of why states took different actions despite a common threat and political values. Investigating the sources of the diverse behaviour of individual states and the differences in the ways in which pandemic restrictions are justified is important from the perspective of the political scientist. The subjects of the study are all political actors who: participated in preventing and combating

DOI: 10.4324/9781003353805-1

the effects of the pandemic, took part on the side of the government in its containment, anti-restriction protests and other forms of collective action, and were involved in collective politics as representatives of the state apparatus (police officers, firefighters, politicians, public sector employees, civil servants, and public media journalists). The type of regime (democracy or authoritarianism), the type of leadership, the relationship between central and local government, the way public policies are organised and financed (including the organisation of crisis management, health and social policies), the ability of the state to organise and control health services and public administration are seen as determinants of observable types of responses to pandemic governance. Another question, albeit one without a single right answer, is whether power relations have changed (and are still changing) during the SARS-CoV-2 pandemic. At what level, if any, is their change advanced and irreversible? The impossibility of drawing general conclusions on this question is linked to the diversity of political systems, political cultures, and resources available to state authorities in the period immediately following the WHO's declaration of an epidemic emergency.

The book attempts to explain the extent of political violence committed during the times of the pandemic. It draws attention to the extent to which and how politicians' attitudes differed in behavioural paradigms during the different phases of the pandemic, but also what exactly contributed to the differences in their behaviour in particular countries. This book, therefore, is the first attempt to systematically define and explain the behaviour of political actors in different pandemic contexts, to identify similarities and differences between countries using Central Europe as an example, and to identify the sources and outcomes of these critical features.

The authors of this study posed a number of research questions. Was and is the state sufficiently prepared for disasters? Has the modern state done its job well, and has its action contributed sufficiently to minimising the effects of the pandemic? Does the state system influence the pandemic control model and to what extent? What models of pandemic control have emerged during the course of the pandemic? To what extent do the mass media and information in cyberspace influence government and public attitudes towards the pandemic? How has the pandemic been used instrumentally for current political purposes? What is driving the politicisation of the pandemic? Is there a link between the fight against SARS-CoV-2 and the ruling parties' policies on migrants, legal changes restricting human and civil rights but unrelated to the pandemic? Will the effects of the pandemic strengthen the position of China, Germany, and the European Union; weaken France; strengthen the institutions of the state in Sweden, or vice versa, and by how much? Why has the moral dilemma of who to save first not broken through in public discourse?

The essential question for political scientists is whether the political systems of states, their systems constructed on the basis of monistic or plural centres of power, with the supremacy of the executive or its absence, the principles of separation or cooperation of powers, a whole range of other constitutional and extra-constitutional solutions, are a significant variable in the circumstances of the disease determining social life. In other words, did/does the state system play a significant role in impeding the spread of the virus, if only through the existence or lack of inhibitions in the use of coercive measures and, conversely, did the SARS-CoV-2 pandemic deepen the process of de-democratisation (deconsolidation of democracy), deepen the crisis of state institutions, demonstrate the dysfunction of public services organised and financed in various ways?

The book formulates a number of research hypotheses. Firstly, the authors assume that the response of the authorities during the pandemic did not change despite the passing of centuries and historical experience, because the state authority is not sufficiently prepared for a pandemic, its decisions do not keep up with the development of events, and the main threat is perceived from outside the state, rather than in the disease itself and its consequences.

Research methods have been used in this study, including systematic, historical, comparative, and forecasting methods. The Pearson correlation technique has been used to determine the type and strength of linear correlations between explanatory indicators and indicators to be explained. The results of the research are analysed and elaborated using observation of the causal process of the construction of the descriptive systems method. The neo-institutional method is used to analyse specific hypotheses based on theory.

The authors of the individual chapters, based on a systematic review of the relevant literature, attempt to characterise the nature of the pandemic crisis. Using a comprehensive set of methodological assumptions, they systematically and critically analyse the current specialist literature on this category, the organisational and legal framework in which modern states have to operate, the indicators explaining the essence of the pandemic, and the classification framework of the category. They attempt to assess the impact of major epidemics on the fate of the state in world history, the attitude of authorities and rulers during the pandemic, and analyse the international conditions of the modern state during the pandemic. This allows for an assessment of the extent to which contemporary states understand the challenge they face.

The authors define the basic category that is the paradigm of the state during challenges brought by a pandemic, which are defined by temporal, subject and object indicators. They then formulate a conceptual framework for the return of the state and its boundaries with the concept – "War for Health," which includes: the political actors that use state violence, the extent of coherence between the power to use political violence arising from developments in times of a pandemic and its actual use and the mutual acceptance of policy by political structures within the framework of the relationship between parliament and the executive, central and local government, and finally government and citizens in times of the pandemic.

The book discusses the impact of the SARS-CoV-2 pandemic on economic processes. The analysis covers issues relating to both the global economy and the economy of the European Union, including the economies of the Visegrad Group countries. It also addresses the nature of the economic shock caused by the COVID-19 pandemic and presents its short- and long-term consequences.

The book is also an attempt to design models of pandemic control in order to maintain the validity of identification and comparisons between different countries. By establishing the similarities and differences between the various models, it develops a typology of pandemic control that emerged in countries during the pandemic.

The first chapter, entitled "The Essence of the Pandemic Crisis," by Jolanta Itrich-Drabarek, defines the concept of a pandemic, epidemic, and presents its essence. The author assumes that a pandemic, having the character of a rapidly spreading infectious disease on a large scale over a large geographical area that crosses national borders, may significantly increase the morbidity and mortality of people and cause significant economic, social and political disruption, and may also cause stigmatization and search for the guilty, which results from the sense of threat, disinformation, panic reactions of society, the instinctive desire of individuals to survive. A pandemic (and an epidemic – on a national scale) is a type of crisis (with multiple threats), to which the state is obliged to respond according to the available tools provided for in the constitutional order. The author attempts to build models of combating pandemics based on the pragmatics of functioning of individual states. She points to the challenges faced by the state during a pandemic, emphasising their ethical character.

In the second chapter, "Models of the Fight against a Pandemic," the author Magdalena Mikołajczyk focuses on analysing the correlation between the state system and the effectiveness of public health decisions during the SARS-CoV-2 pandemic and looks for factors that influence the destabilisation of the countries or go beyond the conditions of a state of emergency (not necessarily proclaimed). It tries to find an answer to the question whether the systems of states, their systems constructed on the basis of monistic or plural centres of power, with the supremacy of the executive power or its absence, the principles of separation or cooperation of powers, a whole range of other constitutional and extra-constitutional solutions, are a significant variable in the circumstances of a disease determining social life. It examines whether power relations have changed (and continue to change) during the SARS-CoV-2 pandemic; at what level, if any, their change is advanced and irreversible.

In the third chapter, "State Economic Problems during the SARS-CoV-2 Pandemic," the author Stanislaw Mazur points to the specificity of the economic crisis caused by the COVID-19 pandemic and characterises its manifestations: disruption of global supply chains, reduction of international mobility, and decline in international financial remittances. The author assumes that the specific supply-demand nature of the SARS-CoV-2 pandemic made it necessary to take exceptional measures –in terms of both their nature and scale. The ways in which national governments responded to the economic problems arising from the pandemic were similar to each other and generally involved the pursuit of unconventional monetary and active fiscal policies. The author emphasises that the experience of the COVID-19 pandemic and the struggle to deal with its economic consequences have triggered a lively discussion about revising the dominant theories of neoliberal economics and its rudimentary assumptions, and predicts that the contours of a new economic order are becoming increasingly clear.

In the fourth chapter, entitled "SARS-CoV-2 Pandemic: An Economic Analysis of Regulatory Intervention," author Artur Nowak-Far assumes that the response of states to economic phenomena resulting from the SARS-CoV-2 pandemic consisted of a shift by states from an extraterritorial to an intrinsic model, in which the locus of control was placed in a position characterising actors operating under conditions of greatly reduced rationality. The initial response of the states to the SARS-CoV-2 pandemic was fairly standardised, and characterised by a significant level of imitativeness; as time passed and the transition from an external controllability to an internal controllability model took place, the means of regulatory intervention became highly differentiated. The differentiation of regulatory intervention measures was strongly determined by the state's ability to activate its internal and external resources; the intervention scenario with respect to the economy, on the other hand, was strongly determined by (a) what the state used as measures to combat the pandemic in the external controllability phase and (b) the influence of the external environment, the strength of the impact of which was determined by the strength of the links of the states' economies with the world (i.e. on the level of openness of these economies).

The fifth chapter, entitled "State Security and the Pandemic", by Andrzej Misuk, Grzegorz Rydlewski, Jacek Wojnicki, Kamil Mroczka, and Tadeusz Klementewicz, discusses the problem of state security during a pandemic. The authors assume that from a strategic point of view there is a chance that the pandemic crisis will become an opportunity to eliminate ineffective solutions, burdened with deficiencies and limitations from the security systems. They point to key elements influencing the formation of state security and analyse such areas as central versus local government, cyberspace, and the role of large corporations in the crisis.

The sixth chapter, entitled "The Impact of the Pandemic on the Development of International Relations," by Marcin Górnikiewicz, Katarzyna Kołodziejczyk, Wiesław Lizak, and Marzena Walkowiak (intercollegiate team), discusses the impact of the SARS-CoV-2 pandemic on international cooperation, including transatlantic relations during the most difficult period of the global pandemic. The impact of the pandemic on the development of the New Silk Road in Eurasia and Africa and the situation in Africa and Latin America (Global South) during the pandemic are also analysed.

In the seventh chapter, Joanna Starzyk analyses the main instruments and forms of action applied so far by selected international institutions in combating the SARS-CoV-2 pandemic against the background of their powers in this dimension. The choice of the UN, WHO, the EU, and the Visegrad Group is not accidental, as these are the institutions which play the most important role in the fight against SARS-CoV-2, and represent activity at three basic levels in this field, i.e. at the global, regional, and sub-regional levels.

The author assumes that the pandemic period is an important test of the effectiveness of the functioning of international organisations and their relations with Member States and other international organisations, which points to potential opportunities and problems of their operation during similar crises in the future. She also assumes that during the current pandemic crisis international organisations have only partially fulfilled their role as crisis managers and supporters of Member States in this regard.

The summary reveals the results of the research and introduces directions for future research on the role of the state in extraordinary situations related to a pandemic. In particular, it assesses the importance of hypothesis verification, discussing and summarising the arguments for and against the validity and reliability of the final conclusions. Importantly, it demonstrates the theoretical framework developed in the research process as a result of verification and generation of theory. Finally, it comments on the very nature of the diversity and similarities among pandemic control models, with particular focus on the specificities of Central and Eastern European countries, identifies their sources, and analyses the risks associated with restriction management during a pandemic. At the same time, it opens a discussion on the role of the state in combating pandemics, explains the problems faced by political power and society, points to the dangers of abuse of power during the existence of an extraordinary situation, and indicates the need to define the limits of state power in situations calling for extraordinary measures.

The extensive literature review reflects the fact that the problem of pandemics has become very relevant, but described in a causal or fragmentary way. Although most of the works analysed are neither widely cited nor generally known, their reading has made it possible to discern a wide range of scientific approaches to the characterisation of this problem. The analysis of definitions, models, and explanatory frameworks, given that it is an explanatory indicator or an indicator that needs to be explained, has revealed challenges for researchers who may wish to use them effectively in their work.

1 The essence of the pandemic crisis

Jolanta Itrich-Drabarek

1.1 Pandemic concept

A pandemic is a rapid large-scale spread of an infectious disease over a large geographic area that crosses national borders, which can significantly increase human morbidity and mortality and cause significant economic, social, and political disruption. Pandemics arise from epidemics, which are disease outbreaks confined to one part of the world, such as one country. The definition of a pandemic according to the World Health Organisation (WHO) is the spread of a new disease throughout the world. It is noteworthy that after 2010, WHO, responsible for announcing the existence of a pandemic, abandoned the emphasis on the fact that its immanent characteristic is a large number of deaths as a possible consequence. The risk of a pandemic cannot be eliminated, as with any other type of natural phenomenon, and its occurrence is influenced by anthropogenic changes in the natural environment. The extent of the spread of a disease depends on many determinants, starting with the degree of infectivity of the agent causing the disease, but also those constituting the effect of civilisation development. The probability of a pandemic outbreak increases with the effects of civilisation changes, including population growth, increasing urbanisation, development of mass tourism and international and global trade, expansion of demand for animal protein, loss of habitat, climate change, but also with increased human–animal interactions, changes in land use, and finally with changes in the extent and nature of human use of the natural environment (uncontrolled and predatory exploitation). The intensification of pandemics is favoured by factors of diverse nature: large population centres, extreme poverty (e.g. in slums, favelas), inefficient healthcare systems, poor sanitation (low level or lack of adequate infrastructure), non-compliance with sanitary-hygienic safety rules by societies, ageing of population, coexisting diseases, and antibiotic resistance.

Infectious disease outbreaks can cause stigmatisation and blame-seeking due to a sense of danger, misinformation, panicky social reactions, and a desire to survive on a biological level. In 1918, a rumour was spread that the Spanish flu was intentionally spread by German submarines reaching the

DOI: 10.4324/9781003353805-2

shores of the United States. The Spanish flu got its name because Spain, as one of few countries in the world, did not censor the press and wrote about the epidemic directly. On the other hand, in the United States, Great Britain, and France, where the flu had occurred earlier, censorship was introduced and publications on the subject were not allowed. However, before the name "Spanish flu" was adopted, Brazilians called it the German flu, Senegalese – the Brazilian flu, Poles – the Bolshevik flu. Contemporary epidemics have also seen forms of discrimination, such as avoidance and fear, directed at ethnic minorities or professional communities associated with outbreaks; for example, Africans in Hong Kong, China, have signalled social isolation, anxiety, and economic hardship due to fear of association with the Ebola virus; Chinese in Italy have been blamed for the spread of the SARS-CoV-2 coronavirus that causes COVID-19 disease; and Polish doctors and nurses have faced boycotts from neighbours and vendors. Since 2015, WHO has banned the use of adjectives that stigmatise the source of the virus. It should be noted that during the COVID-19 pandemic, the use of the term "Chinese virus" was generally discontinued fairly quickly in the public space (Itrich-Drabarek, 2021).

A pandemic (and an epidemic – on a national scale) is a kind of crisis (with multiple threats), to which the state is obliged to respond in line with available tools provided for in the constitutional order.

Different countries use different solutions, based mainly on crisis management models, but also extraordinary measures. According to the International Center for Not-for-Profit Law (ICNL), which systematically monitors government responses in terms of the impact on civil liberties and human rights, there have been 110 instances where states faced with a pandemic have made decisions considered by ICNL to be *emergency declarations*. These included states of emergency as well as various states of public calamity, natural disaster (including, for example, a public health emergency), and a state of epidemic emergency (which was applied in Poland) (ICNL, 2021).

Both the management of preparation for a pandemic and the response to it during its course are very complex processes because it is handled by many actors at different levels – on a global or continental scale by international organisations, and on a national scale by the government, public administration, local government, and many services functionally responsible for specific sectors (health, security, etc.). The complexity of these processes in the case of the COVID-19 pandemic is also due to the fact that its consequences affect very different levels of the functioning of the society and the economy, also the functioning of public institutions, and finally the lives of citizens in many dimensions. The state – as in the case of any crisis situation, especially occurring throughout its territory – was and is obliged to counteract the threats, to protect citizens and to create new organisational, legal, and financial solutions. Many of these actions can be categorised as broadly defined internal security policy and health policy, which focus on identifying and limiting emerging outbreaks of diseases that can lead to pandemics and on ensuring the availability of primary healthcare, the organisation of quarantine and isolation procedures and generally on the internal and external readiness of the state to respond, coordinate, and mobilise forces to fight the pandemic. Inherent in the state's actions should be what is known as situational awareness, that is, having an accurate, up-to-date picture of potential or current infectious disease threats and the status of resources (human, financial, informational, and institutional) available to manage those threats. Situational awareness supports policy decisions by monitoring the course of the pandemic and the effectiveness of interventions.

Strategies for preventing and combating a pandemic include pandemic prevention, the ability to detect the presence of the pandemic agent, combating the course of the pandemic, and mitigating its effects. The ability to detect the presence of (and control the course of) the pandemic requires epidemiological scientists and health professionals to recognise the disease and have the technical and laboratory capabilities to identify the pathogen (or exclude known pathogens) and respond quickly to influxes of clinical samples. Rapid identification reduces the risk by allowing infected individuals to be isolated and receive appropriate clinical care. The fight against the pandemic involves both medical interventions, i.e. reducing the infectivity of symptomatic patients, for example, through appropriate treatment and infection control practices, reducing the susceptibility of uninfected individuals, e.g., through vaccination (when vaccines are available), and limiting interactions among the sick and the uninfected, e.g., through patient isolation, quarantine (the practice of quarantine began in the 14th century in response to the plague, known as the "Black Death"), and social distancing (a ban on mass gatherings was first introduced during the 1918 influenza pandemic).

During the COVID-19 pandemic, one of the control methods is the so-called lockdown, i.e. general isolation; drastic limitation of social interaction; limiting the possibility of citizens' movements outside their houses/flats; obligatory closure of all kinds of educational, cultural and service facilities/institutions; etc., as well as many other specific restrictions, e.g., in trade and transport (air, rail, public, urban, etc.). Lockdown has been applied in most countries, as recommended by WHO, and has been combined with the closing of national borders, and in the European Union, with the reintroduction of border controls in the Schengen Area. The extent to which these restrictions were applied (as well as the types and duration) varied from country to country, with the most far-reaching bans applied in China, and to a much lesser extent than average in Sweden. In view of the fact that the year 2020 was the first time when mass restrictions (lockdown) were applied on such a scale, it is difficult to assess their validity and the extent of their economic impact, such as the announced general economic crisis.

The effects of a pandemic are multiple and, in fact, affect all areas of life. A pandemic affects the sense of personal safety, is perceived as a threat to both life and health, and to economic security (individual and general) and social security, and may cause individual and social changes in behaviour. At the macro level, the pandemic may lead to an increase in morbidity and mortality, affect the state of the economy, leading to recession or economic crisis, the impoverishment of societies, as well as deteriorate the political stability of individual countries, create and strengthen social conflicts (including protests, riots, and political tensions) (Itrich-Drabarek, 2021). In its face, the necessity of political science's reflection on both pandemic and post-pandemic time, on the role of the state and the individual in this specific crisis situation is obvious.

1.2 Challenges faced by governments during a pandemic

In the 21st century, which – it would seem – is dominated by technology, it has become apparent that humanity is but a small part of nature, and the end of the second decade will be remembered as a period of global cataclysm due to the pandemic caused by the SARS-CoV-2 coronavirus resulting in COVID-19 disease. As it spread, the pandemic brought out the old face of the world: a mixture of cynicism and heroism, greed and noble, selfless acts.

The pandemic affects individuals, families, communities, nations, continents; it leaves its mark on the private, public, financial, economic, and political spheres. Above all, the state is responsible as the central point of reference; it is expected to remedy and relieve the disaster, and at the same time the assessment of its actions is often critical. Opponents of its omnipotence are naturally silenced or drowned out because the problems brought about by the pandemic crisis effectively crowd out or relegate almost all others to the background. The democratic state, the authoritarian state, the welfare state, the privatised state, the night watchman state, or the minimal state – each becomes, in an instant, the state that should have in its possession the tools and resources adequate to the scale of the drama. The pandemic revealed

> the intersection of (at least) two contradictions – namely the one between the *desire for the state* and the (often all-too-justified) *fear of the state*, on the one hand, and between the (momentary) *primacy of the state* and the (structuring) *primacy of the economic*, on the other.
>
> (Toscano, 2020)

The fear it incited caused people to naturally turn to the state, expecting its help.

States and societies have been in the pandemic crisis officially since January 2020, although its symptoms appeared earlier. The causes of the crisis are complex. First, they stem from the chaos and fear created by the very rapid global spread of the coronavirus, second, from the apparent ostensible preparedness of states for a pandemic crisis, and finally, from the delayed response of policymakers. Even if we assume that the pandemic disaster can be considered the result of unforeseen circumstances (although there have been occasional voices saying that it is inevitable and it is only a matter of time before it erupts), the politicians at the helm of power are overwhelmingly responsible for its course and consequences.

Protagoras, the founder of the school of sophists, claimed that the state and society came into being because of fear of the power of nature, fear of its forces. If Protagoras was right, and he probably in part was, then we have become convinced in modern times of the legitimacy of the existence of the state – for it was the state that took action to protect communities from the effects of the spread of COVID-19. This is also what Alberto Toscano argues when he writes:

> the legitimacy of the modern state has largely hinged on its [...] capacity to secure the reproduction of the biological bases of political life, a function that has been repeatedly crystallised and augmented in historical encounters with pandemics. The legitimacy of the modern age and of the modern state is in great part a biopolitical and an epidemiological legitimacy.
>
> (Toscano, 2020)

Governments around the world have thus organised and are organising – in different ways – new ways of the functioning of the state, the economy, the society and of every citizen from the point of view of the overarching goals: first, to defeat the COVID-19 pandemic, and, second, to counter its effects (ubiquitous and far-reaching). Once again, it has become apparent that from time to time, proponents of market-based solutions must be challenged to answer the question of how to solve a crisis that affects entire societies, economies, and basically all spheres of the functioning of the state? There is only one answer, which is symbolically reflected in the statement of the above-quoted professor of economics at New York's Columbia University:

> I have free-market views and in normal times I am not inclined to automatically rely on the government to solve problems [...] no one can protect themselves against such a crisis. Only the state can insure us against something like this.
>
> (Toscano, 2020)

One level of the discussion that swept through Europe centred on the polemic over who was more effective in acting against the pandemic – the states and the European Union or the private sector. It appears to have been settled in favour of the state and an integrating grouping like the EU. Without the support of publicly funded research, the vaccines would not have been developed so quickly (Pfizer, BioNTech, and AstraZeneca received about USD 5 billion in public aid).

The state has repeatedly faced large-scale challenges in many parts of the world, such as the great economic crises of 1929 and 2008, waves of terrorism, and successive migration crises from Africa to Europe. Today, countries have to overcome the effects of the coronavirus pandemic. The new challenges brought on by the fight against the pandemic took governments and public administrations in most parts of the world by surprise, yet it was up to the wisdom of leaders to determine the scale of the surprise, how quickly countries went on the offensive, whether administrations proved sufficiently mobile, and whether the plans adopted to manage the pandemic crisis proved effective – and whether they will continue to prove so. The scale of the threat in this regard is illustrated by the unequivocal phrases of the leaders of each country: the Italian prime minister Giuseppe Conte – "our war against coronavirus," the French president Emmanuel Macron – "we are at war," the German chancellor Angela Merkel and the Austrian chancellor Sebastian Kurz – "we are facing the biggest challenge since World War II," the Spanish prime minister Pedro Sánchez – "it's like being at war." In turn, leaders such as then U.S. president Donald Trump and British prime minister Boris Johnson initially saw the coronavirus as part of a political fight and tried to treat it as harshly as they did their political opponents – which was brutally verified by the pandemic reality.

The fight against coronavirus involves coordinating the efforts of many thousands of people acting on behalf of the state. First and foremost, those on the front line, i.e. healthcare workers (including auxiliary workers), especially emergency medical services and personnel of the separate "COVID sector." New challenges due to the specificity of threats in public spaces have been faced by sectors such as social and geriatric care or education. In addition, as mentioned above, the fight against the pandemic included a variety of restrictions and prohibitions related to lockdown, resulting in, among others, the implementation of new technical and organisational solutions (public offices, education, etc.), the spread of remote working on an unprecedented scale, as well as the closure of entire sectors – tourism, gastronomy, sports, culture, etc. Therefore, equally important are the actions of the structures responsible for the functioning of individual areas of social and economic life under the conditions of the epidemic, including the protection of jobs, the implementation of solutions to support individual sectors that either had to undergo rapid organisational and technical changes or were simply closed. Thus, it was necessary, for example, to launch a rapid processing of applications from entrepreneurs to be provided with financial assistance, to implement substantive and organisational support for distance learning (access to equipment and the Internet for children and teachers), to ensure the supply chain for the production or sale of essential medicines (not only for COVID-19, but also for many other diseases, including cardiovascular or oncological ones), to ensure the efficient functioning of the social welfare system under drastically changed conditions (care for the disabled, including lonely seniors, and counteracting domestic violence).

The challenges faced by governments during the pandemic are multifaceted and varied in nature – ethical, political, economic, medical, logistical, social, and related to human resources.

Ethical challenges – in the face of the massiveness of the pandemic, it becomes necessary to find solutions that will eliminate the need to make dramatic choices – whose life to save first, who has a preference in the care of the sick or access to life-saving measures, access to "better" and "worse" vaccines. The ethical challenge is to answer the question of what values guide the state in its chain of relations with public administration and specialist services, with health services, with interest groups, with social groups, with migrants, or with business representatives. It is about upholding standards in law-making, information policy, the quality and safety of patients, the challenges of information and communication technologies, and, finally, the use of the involvement of social groups that are willing to fight the pandemic and the cooperation of local governments. Equally important in times of the pandemic is how governments function in terms of political promotions and demotions, project financing, remuneration of politicians and heads of state-owned companies, public procurement, lobbying, corruption, etc. In a nutshell, in the time of the COVID-19 crisis, which has the character of a natural disaster resulting in an impending economic crisis, national governments have to make a choice whether to act in accordance with the recommendations of Global Ethics and cooperate to defeat the coronavirus, bearing the costs in solidarity, or to place these costs on weaker states or weaker social groups. The challenge is the level of control given to the government over healthcare decisions for individual citizens. However, this issue is also fundamental to the discussion of individual freedom and state intervention in the health choices of the individual. In the debate over increased state control in the realm of individual health, the "against" argument appeals to the value of individual autonomy over health choices, while the "for" argument appeals to the importance of paternalism and the prevention of harm. This is crucial in the context of the pandemic, as an individual's views on these issues influence their decisions and behaviours regarding both quarantine and vaccination policies. This is all the more so because the pandemic-related restrictions are actually at odds with the existing system of law, ethics, and policies regarding freedom of choice in healthcare (Hancocks, 2020).

Political challenges – associated with new priorities and difficult decisions, re-evaluation of the principles of political action, alliances, building a strategy of action. The pandemic forces leaders and their party and state support to make difficult decisions, often unpopular and in conflict with the interests of various social groups. Governments and leaders are challenged with the task of separating current political expediency from taking responsibility for the health and lives of citizens. The situation requires avoiding the temptation to seek cheap political applause in favour of hard work that does not always produce results, pursuing policies that are transparent and effective. Populist leaders may try to use the pandemic for instrumental purposes to strengthen their position; they may use emergency powers to weaken the role of the parliament, the opposition, and civil society. The challenge is for politicians and experts (virologists and epidemiologists, mathematical modelling specialists) to work together in managing the crisis, especially in terms of accountability for decisions made and defining a long-term strategy. Since the beginning of the pandemic, political challenges were related to the problem of cooperation of countries, among others, in obtaining and distributing vaccines and working out appropriate (effective) solutions. The challenge is to establish responsibility for the race against time to develop and produce a vaccine that effectively counteracts COVID-19 disease. The challenge is to choose one of many vaccines, with full knowledge of their "better" and "worse" performance.

Economic challenges involve not only launching additional funds in the budgets of the states for the purchase of equipment to save the health and lives of people (ventilators, masks, protective and disinfecting agents, etc.), but also closing entire branches of the economy, related to, for example, tourism, gastronomy, or services. Whether and how to protect jobs – this has become one of the key questions for the economy.

Challenges in the medical sphere – in the broadest sense they concern the creation of simulations of the course of the pandemic, forecasting its duration. And also development and implementation of effective therapies, ways and methods of treatment, the effectiveness of protective vaccinations, determining the scope and forms of recommended/mandatory restrictions, including, for example, the selection of appropriate measures of social distance, creating the so-called health protocols.

Logistical challenges – concern many areas affected by the pandemic, but mainly health services. They are related to providing a sufficient number of specialist hospital wards (properly secured), quick access to them, efficient medical emergency services, a network of testing and vaccination points, as well as acquisition and distribution of vaccines. This is accompanied by increasing problems with personnel, equipment, etc. – to provide an adequate number of hospital beds, life-saving equipment, medical services, medicines, protective and auxiliary equipment.

Challenges in the social dimension – are the result of multiple effects of restrictions of contact, limited accessibility to a variety of facilities (including medical care) or their closure, immediate introduction of distance learning at all levels of education. It became necessary to ensure adequate (institutionally organised) support for social welfare homes, seniors' homes, orphanages, as well as support for the homeless. New problems include dealing with fear, the feeling of helplessness, isolation, but also appropriate management of attempts to actively support the state in the fight against the pandemic. In all these aspects it is necessary to build logical communication with the public.

Challenges in the human resources dimension – mobilisation and management of human resources in healthcare, in public administration and more broadly in the public sphere (police officers, teachers, the military) to build a logical chain to fight the pandemic. The pandemic-related crisis has shown how important the role of the state is, how important is the professionalism of its staff and the efficiency of the institutional system – their low level can have negative effects for citizens in terms of the efficiency of the above-discussed solutions (challenges), as well as prolong the duration of the state of emergency. The World Bank expert Zahid Hasnain, using the example of personnel and civil servants employed in the public administration, showed why the priority of the state should be to protect jobs – in both the public and private sectors. He argues that the administration is the one fighting the pandemic, so restructuring during the pandemic could prove fatal to efforts to contain it. Instead of dismissing, the expert also recommended redeploying employees to where they are needed most (Hasnain, 2020).

As part of socio-economic challenges, organisation and protection of jobs have come to the fore. The change in working styles, the shift to working remotely, and the resulting constraints (social isolation, a new style of human resource management, the task-based, rather than time-based, nature of work), but also the new challenges for employees (separating work and leisure zones and family life at home) and the new dimension of professional (continuing) education, upskilling and training – all these became part of the new challenges faced by both employees and employers. However, it is job protection that has become the key issue. Many companies have disappeared from the economic map, some have re-branded, and this was connected not only with the closure of individual industries themselves, but also with the spillover of the effects of lockdown into related industries (service, supply, etc.). Many governments as well as international organisations applied the policy of duty of care, i.e. the principle of taking care of employees in crisis situations. Some companies and institutions not only did not lay off employees, but developed plans on how to protect the so-called daily staff, i.e. people who are hired on an hourly basis, operate cafeterias, and cooperate with the organisation as needed (e.g. translators). Since working from home has proven to work well in many industries, it seems pointless to continue building or renting large office buildings. But at the same time, the new widespread manner of work during the pandemic has sparked a discussion about working conditions at home, ergonomics, utility costs, and sufficient working space.[1]

The science and education sector has felt the pandemic reality in many ways – as constraints and as challenges. It should be recalled that public universities and representatives of the world of science have often been

1 Many of the effects of the changes introduced by the "pandemic solutions" overlap and intersect – e.g. working from home plus the closure of school and childcare facilities causes a collision of simultaneity of work and childcare.

discredited, both by undermining and disregarding research, and by the limitations of budget cuts, primitive economisation of the education sector accounted for profit, instead of in terms of fulfilling the mission assigned to this sphere. Meanwhile, it turned out once again that it is the world of science that bears the responsibility for developing recipes and solutions to rescue societies and economies from various threats – not only for the invention of a vaccine that gives protection to health and life and a chance to return to a sense of security, but also to provide answers to a number of questions and doubts, such as how to mitigate the losses associated with the recession, how to defend human and civil rights during a pandemic, how to protect culture, and how to conduct elections. The pandemic crisis has become both an opportunity and a necessity for the world of science to enter the digital space, to develop (many new ones) forms of exchange of ideas and best practices, to intensify cooperation – intra-sectoral, inter-university, and with businesses, government, local government, as well as on an international scale. It appeared that when the situation became uncertain and the future unknown, scientists and researchers were perceived as people with passion that escapes rigid political and economic rigours.

Wider collaboration in the post-pandemic world of science is inevitable, especially to address global challenges such as unemployment, poverty, migration, local wars, climate change, or more pandemics. Science knows no limits – neither cultural nor formal. Today, it is global. The fight against the SARS-CoV-2 coronavirus that causes COVID-19 disease is further proof of the importance of sharing data and results openly. The crisis has highlighted the importance of research and innovation, e-learning and ITC tools, and the problem of funding science at an appropriate level concerns not only national budgets but also the long-term EU budget.

Changes in learning principles obviously impose new challenges, but also constraints. The effect of the pandemic could be the increase of the disparity between wealthy students and those from poorer backgrounds, resulting in reduced opportunities for the latter, and a government looking to make savings in education is a misguided government. Contrary to the common perception that the higher education system and universities should educate students primarily and directly to meet the needs of the economy, it turned out that modern education should, especially in times of pandemic, provide students with personal development, skills, and competencies to meet the changing socio-economic and cultural conditions in which they have come and will come to live.

Remote learning requires access to computer equipment and the Internet; it is an opportunity to develop skills with technology, but it is also a threat.[2] Online courses and exams reduce some of the costs of schools and universi-

2 The impact of the pandemic on children and young adults, of both the state of emergency and the isolation itself, is a broad separate topic and a research task.

ties (e.g. renting of lecture halls, less administrative support of buildings) and students (rent of premises, the cost of staying in a place other than the place of residence). Of course, the issue of education quality in these new conditions must not be overlooked, but this is a separate and broad topic (previously, this quality also varied widely, although now the range of factors determining its level has widened). Providing a high level of online education is costly and requires thoughtful investment. The experience of the pandemic verified the organisational efficiency of schools and universities, which in the future may result in their better flexibility of operation. Therefore, the efficiency of operation in completely different technological conditions is also subject to verification of teaching and research staff. As some scholars have suggested (e.g. Helen Fletcher-Kennedy, Eugene Sebastian, and Martijn van der Kamp), pandemic conditions have increased inequality and academic patriarchy. In addition, women are more likely to face structural, social, cultural, and financial obstacles and are less likely to collaborate internationally in research work (Fletcher-Kennedy et al., 2020). This raises the question – how do we create a level playing field and build more inclusive international research teams?

The role of the Internet during the COVID-19 pandemic has significantly increased in learning processes, in the management and day-to-day operation of companies, and in everyday life (e.g. communication, online shopping). The use of modern technologies designed to support learning at home has increased, but accessibility is an issue. For example, in Canada in one of the provinces it was calculated that over 30% of students do not have access to the Internet or digital devices at home. With the economic crisis deepening, many families who have lost their livelihoods will have to choose between maintaining Internet services and meeting their family's existential needs. The world of science, business, and politics must understand that the time has come – and the corona crisis has only accelerated this process – for more innovative solutions, which should be the work of modern academia and universities developing new products, technologies, etc. The social role of universities and their involvement in helping companies to reduce the financial impact and socio-economic damage caused by the pandemic, in supporting public health and in protecting society from the negative effects of the pandemic are expected to grow. The new situation also made all concerned aware of the role of science and the "tension between evidence-based policy and policy driven by political interest groups" (more: Itrich-Drabarek & Mazur, 2021).

1.3 Models of the pandemic control

It is probably difficult for advocates of democracy to agree with the notion that authoritarian states can be more effective at suppressing pandemics than fully democratic states, but in some respects recent experience has shown this tendency. This is, of course, because civil rights and freedoms are more easily curtailed in societies already enslaved. In the face of the need to quickly implement, and in fact impose, restrictions and rigours, the authoritarian state thus wields resources more effectively through proven mechanisms. On the other hand, semi-democratic states or the so-called façade democracies deal with pandemics differently, depending on the severity of the threats and the nature of the problems, but also on the political calendar – a populist attitude does not allow the full truth about the pandemic to be communicated to citizens (especially during the election campaign and elections themselves), while at the same time, painful deficiencies in the functioning of healthcare are covered up by sham and ineffective actions (such as the construction and furnishing of temporary hospitals, in which the quality of equipment and security of appropriate medical staff are not always sufficient, e.g. beds come from demobilised resources, or ventilators do not meet the standards). Populist governments have tried to pursue a policy of balancing corona-sceptics and anti-vaccinationists with the implementation of projects to prevent the spread and impact of pandemics. Unfortunately, COVID-19 has actually brought to the forefront the anti-vaccine movement, which has become one of the more popular social movements, while exacerbating conflict situations in society.

It is difficult at this stage to indicate clear models of combating the pandemic, but by analysing the methods of action against the spreading coronavirus, one can be tempted to create some outline of them, distinguishing three models: restrictive, participatory, and hybrid. However, it should be noted that the challenges and specifics of each successive wave of the pandemic caused changes in some countries, and their governments sometimes departed from previous plans and strategies in search of a more effective method of preventing the effects of the pandemic.

1. Restrictive model – responsibility for combating the pandemic is assumed by the central state authority, and political decisions in this area are made by the close leadership of the ruling party; crisis management is carried out through the implementation of restrictions in the form of limited or total lockdown, closure of certain sectors of the economy overnight. Closed educational institutions and sectors of tourism (hotels), gastronomy, sports and fitness, culture, and other services, orders to wear masks in public places, maintaining social distance, in the case of an exacerbation of the disease, among other things, restrictions on movement in public spaces, mass testing, checking the health of children in schools (if open), in some public places measuring people's temperature, wide availability of containers with liquid hand disinfectant. Strict control over the stay of citizens through the so-called health code – each user has a record of the last two weeks of stay. Prohibition of political demonstrations. Using the pandemic to introduce legal solutions unrelated to the pandemic, but limiting the

rights and freedoms of citizens. The government communicating with the public in the form of a one-sided message, without the possibility of feedback. Building temporary hospitals through the economies of scale. This model, in its broadest sense, was mainly characteristic of Asian countries such as China, India, and Thailand for most of the pandemic's duration, although some of its features are also found in European countries (e.g. Central Europe). In the restrictive model little or no attention is paid to the policy towards vulnerable or socially excluded groups (e.g. the homeless).

2. Participatory model – the central point in the fight against the pandemic is specialised state services, the participation of parties and political leaders is minimal, the observance of restrictions by citizens is carried out mainly through their self-control, the principle in the management of the pandemic crisis is the use of medical advice at the stage of decision-making. The government's communication with the public takes the form of explaining and clarifying government decisions, with the possibility of feedback. There is social support of the government in actions to prevent the spread of the virus from different social groups (business people, neighbourhood groups, local communities, self-organising groups, people with disabilities). Organisation of hospital places without economies of scale (Italy). Features of such a model can be found, for example, in Canada or Germany. An extreme variant of the participatory model is the Swedish model – the pandemic was managed by representatives of public administration, not politicians, no lockdown was announced, the focus was on social distance and the development of herd immunity, the assumption was made that beds for patients with severe forms of coronavirus will be sufficient for all, so there is no need to introduce a national quarantine.
3. Hybrid model – the most frequent, its basic feature is the variability covering, in fact, all aspects of the pandemic control: strategies, management structures at the central level, information policy, relations with the expert-scientific community and the extent of its use, etc. The central crisis management centre went through phases from a decidedly party-state character to the acceptance of expert-medics and other specialists in crisis management. The chaotic and contradictory information policy gradually shifted to a communicative version, conveying to the public relevant information important in an increasingly prolonged pandemic situation. This model shows a shift from politicising the pandemic and using it for current political purposes – to a united front on vaccine policy. It should be noted that in Central European societies this is accompanied by low trust in state institutions and politicians on the one hand, and in the world of science on the other (scientists as part of the elite, a position often reinforced by those in power), which translates into distrust of vaccination.

In none of the models was there a discussion in the public space about the ethical strategy of the state during the fight against the pandemic that would transparently answer the question of who to protect first, who to save first, and whether to introduce the principle of equal access to vaccinations, as well as how to achieve the key goal of optimising vaccination, stopping the number of deaths, infections, hospitalisations, calculations of economic, social, and psychological costs.

Politicians, who were eager to speak (albeit often in general terms and with little substance) on simple questions of procedures of protective measures or promotion of vaccination, avoided responsibility at times of intensifying waves of the pandemic for the current dramatic decisions in overburdened hospitals, with inadequate staffing and equipment, in effect placing this responsibility on doctors and other healthcare workers. Thus, medical procedures were used to select patients according to the severity of their injuries and possible prognosis, but in Spain and Italy, for example, another criterion was added – the social utility of the sick person (a socially useful person is one who provides the best reproductive opportunities for the species).

As the philosopher Vaclav Nemec proclaims, values such as democracy, human dignity, and human rights disappeared from public consciousness during the pandemic. The pandemic revealed the inability of people to follow rules, the inability of marketing politics and populism to solve real problems. He is horrified that sometimes leaders are politicians who do not consider moral dilemmas. They are not empathetic to others in any way (Člověk, 2020).

Undoubtedly, the state is responsible for how effective the fight against the pandemic is, how effective the efforts to extinguish it are. But the COVID-19 pandemic has also shown once again how important the individual is and how he or she behaves in the face of threat, and therefore how important it is to reach as many individuals as possible with information and actions – citizens, communities, individual environments, so that counteracting this specific disaster could be effective. It is the individual who is the carrier of the disease and macro-scale actions will not succeed if they "bounce off" the reluctance, ignorance and disbelief in the effectiveness of solutions introduced by states and international organisations. And this is what differentiates the restrictive model from the participatory one, as the prescriptive mode does not appeal to understanding, but to obedience, and does not provide for a dialogue.

Another level of difference between the two models is the problem of human rights and freedoms. Many scholars have emphasised the fear of excessive surveillance and control by the state. The discussion of the dilemma of the individual versus the general interest, respect for basic human and civil rights versus the survival of society has gained new dimensions.

1.4 Conclusions and projections from the pandemic

The SARS-CoV-2 coronavirus causing COVID-19 pandemic has caused many re-evaluations of both perceptions of the contemporary world and predictions of a post-pandemic world. According to some philosophers, it is possible to build a different community than the "nightmare of the neoliberal state of nature." Statements by Catherine Malabou, Slavoj Žižek, and Judith Butler indicate that the world will change irreversibly for the better. Butler believes that just as people turned to rebirth after the Black Death in the Middle Ages, a new community will emerge based on the elimination of extreme inequality and discrimination in access to medical resources and vaccinations. Slavoj Žižek, on the other hand, believes in the coming of global communism, based on a real alliance of the masses and not on oligarchic cronyism. Tomasz Stawiszyński emphasises that "all [of them] in fact revolved around the same basic recognition," which is that "the pandemic suspension of the seemingly inevitable rules of the world's functioning, of laws that we considered impossible to replace, revealed for a moment their contingency" (Stawiszyński, 2020).

Optimists assume that the economy will be based more on pro-ecological thinking, and the world will withdraw from the destruction of the environment. In contrast, Giorgo Agamben is pessimistic, stating that the state has exploited human fear for biological survival so that it can legalise a "permanent state of emergency," but unfortunately Italians are willing to sacrifice "normal living conditions, work, friendship, religion, and political beliefs just to avoid the danger of infection." Agamben asks the rhetorical question, "What is a society in which there is no value other than the desire to survive?" – and recognises that people easily came to terms with the restrictions because they were already ready for such living conditions, and the epidemic was merely an excuse to accept them (Agamben, 2020). In response to such a position, one has to conclude that a society which wants to survive sometimes has to depart from the established canons of behaviour. It is a pity, however, that Agamben did not ask questions about how people are to live in post-pandemic times – whether they will demand that national governments roll back restrictions, or how to make people want to recognise as valuable what they have given up in the name of protecting biological life. The Polish philosopher – Piotr Nowak commented on human indifference to the victims of the pandemic as follows:

> Inhabitants of Paris, London, Moscow or Warsaw will smile, drink latte, eat meringue, taste Italian or Spanish wine. At the same time, at night, trucks from the local 'Bergamo' will transport the corpses by the thousands to anonymous, mass, lime-whitened pits.
>
> (Nowak, 2020)

Thus, it can be assumed that not only will the world not change the direction of development, but may reinforce the existing trends. In post-communist countries, authoritarian tendencies that limit the rights and freedoms of citizens may further strengthen. New fortunes will grow on the ruins of the pandemic, and the emerging social solidarity (shopping for neighbours, masks, singing on balconies, applause for doctors) will be overshadowed by the current pursuit of the material delusion of the world. We need to remember, as the ethicist Roman Kubicki emphasises, that

> Man is humane only in humane conditions, as Gustaw Herling-Grudzinski said. What we are capable of, we already know. [...] When millions of people lose their jobs, run out of savings, and hunger peeks into their eyes, the worst instincts may come to mind.
>
> (Kubicki, 2020)

Undoubtedly, the pandemic exposed the weakness of the nation-state, as none of the countries in the world was able to cope with its effects independently, but it also revealed the awakening power of national egoisms and attempts to build new spheres of influence (China, Russia, the United Kingdom). The pandemic crisis has been repeatedly used by politicians for purposes related to the struggle to gain and maintain power in the state (elections in Poland, the Czech Republic, Slovakia, France); governments have repeatedly, under the pretext of countering the pandemic, initiated actions related to both institutional and legal transformations and blaming the opposition for any failures related to its spread and effects. It is difficult to assess what the reversibility of pandemic-related changes will be (also under the pretext of the fight against it), which on the example of Central European countries can be described as undermining the democratic system. Fears of perpetuating pandemic rigours and hastily implemented "special norms" are also justified by what the 19th-century British thinker Lord Acton once said, i.e. that power corrupts, and absolute power corrupts absolutely.[3]

The political impact of the pandemic is manifold, and the specificity of the situation in individual countries can be noted. Britain, boasting of the success of universal vaccination, emphasises the rightness of Brexit and freedom from the EU bureaucracy. France is uncomfortable about not having developed its own vaccine. In Poland, Slovakia, or the Czech Republic, populist politicians have discovered that they can perpetuate their rule by effectively suppressing public protests under the guise of "spreading the infection" and relying on ignorance and fear reinforcement.

3 However, it is worth adding context to this famous quote – as Lord Acton emphatically stated that all people without exception, regardless of their office or position, must abide by universal moral principles.

It could be considered a paradox that this crisis is strengthening the populists in Central Europe, despite the fact that so ineffective have their actions often been that the pandemic, which was not properly contained, has brought much suffering and death to hundreds of thousands of people. However, let us recall what the essence of populism is:

> It is offering simple diagnoses (or rather just observations, since they are very rarely accompanied by any reliable statistics and deeper analyses) and simple, not to say simplistic prescriptions for solving the world's complex problems, for the use of usually plain, so-called ordinary people.
> (Anioł, 2020, p. 138)

Populists, relying on disinformation, fear, and lack of elementary knowledge of citizens, strengthened and confirmed their electorate in the belief that they cope according to the circumstances, and if they do not cope, it is due to objective reasons and not as a result of wrong decisions. Before the COVID-19 pandemic, all Visegrad countries were experiencing symptoms of democratic decline, but this crisis provided an opportunity for populist leaders to further undermine liberal democracy (Guasti, 2020).

To put in order the changes that occurred in different spheres as a result of the COVID-19 pandemic, a set of conclusions (that can be considered fundamental) is presented below.

1. Subversion of faith in the existing crisis management strategies, as it turned out that none of the countries was sufficiently prepared for a pandemic crisis, and the effects of the fight against coronavirus were determined by their overall resources, the structures of their healthcare organisations, and the wisdom and consistency of their leaders.
2. Consolidation of the existing structural inequalities and international divisions, revealing the lack of effective procedures for interaction both internally and internationally, the lack of mechanisms for effective cooperation among countries, the lack of mechanisms for the exchange of knowledge and information, inappropriate solutions for international financial policy. The pandemic showed once again the inconsistent legal solutions in the international space and the lack of adequate infrastructural resources. Irresponsibility of China, which concealed key information about the coronavirus, in the first days or weeks of the pandemic, and the U.S decision to withdraw from the World Health Organisation in the middle of the pandemic are just the more prominent examples of the problems in international relations during this period.
3. A very strong negative impact on both the global economy and national economies. The economic shock caused by the pandemic had, and still has, a variety of consequences, such as global food price increases, rising inflation, unemployment, and the redefinition of supply chains to

ensure the health and economic security of nation states and communities such as the European Union.[4] The response of national economies varied across the EU countries. Countries with stricter blocking measures experienced greater economic collapse, and the subsequent withdrawal of rigour was not enough to offset the economic collapse. The extent of the negative effects also depended on how much tourism and hospitality contributed to the economy. But most importantly, it depended on what the efficiency of governance in the country was. Factors such as the extent of lockdown, the percentage of tourism in the economy, and the quality of governance explain the nearly 60% difference among the EU countries in terms of the economic impact of the pandemic (Sapir, 2020).

4. The revealing of additional factors of international competitiveness, such as access to key components of medicines or electronic equipment, sanitary safety, or job protection. In addition, the pandemic vividly demonstrated the indispensability of specialists to overcome various types of emergencies, further strengthening their role. The pandemic also caused an excessive increase in profits for technology giants and those companies that produced the resources needed to fight the pandemic.
5. Exposition of shortcomings and problems in the relationship between the worlds of science and politics. It has become apparent that in many countries policymakers do not view the output of scientists as having a significant substantive impact in the decision-making process. The results of work presented by the scientific world, which are considered incompatible with the goals and interests of policymakers, are questioned or rejected as false. This, in turn, gives the public permission to question the findings of science. This problem has taken on a particular dimension especially in the context of the activities of anti-vaccine movements. The pandemic has also exposed the poor quality of public education, which is reflected in many conspiracy theories about the genesis of the pandemic, its effects, but also the effects of preventive measures.[5]

4 As a result of the Covid-19 restrictions, the labour market has been disrupted, and, according to the International Labour Organisation, in 2020, 8.8% of global working hours were lost compared to the fourth quarter of 2019, an equivalent to 255 million full-time jobs. Losses of working hours were particularly high in the Americas and the Caribbean, Southern Europe, and South Asia. The loss of working hours in 2020 was about four times higher than during the global financial crisis in 2009 (ILO, 2021).

5 Examples of absurd opinions recorded in Poland include: "wearing masks causes the brain to shrivel," "wearing masks is a symptom of coronoparanoia," "rags without attestation," "the rest of the world are covidiots." Polish researcher Malgorzata Kossowska points to another phenomenon, which is Poles' complacency about their own health and belief that the coronavirus SARS-CoV-2 pandemic causing Covid-19 poses minimal risk, a sense of self-efficacy in reducing the threat juxtaposed with the level of trust in science and politicians, and that small inconveniences in accessing vaccination cause hesitation about whether to vaccinate at all (Winiecki, 2021).

6. Deepening of the traditional divisions in the European Union – the North–South conflicts (the financially disciplined rich versus the indebted poor) were joined by a new one – the countries holding a common vaccine front versus the minority contesting the current policy. Hungary, Denmark, Slovakia, Austria, and Italy broke away from the united EU front (e.g. in Slovakia and Hungary the use of the Russian vaccine Sputnik was allowed, although it was not approved for the EU market by the European Medicines Agency).
7. Disclosure of the scale of ruthlessness in the face of misfortune, and worse – also of wickedness and greed in the structures of power, as the source of using the fight against the pandemic to get rich. The scale of corruption in government procurement of essential supplies for the fight against the pandemic (ventilators, gloves, disinfectants, etc.), and letaprivation involving the creation of laws or the exploitation of legal loopholes to seize public assets under the pretext of the pandemic control, is not fully known. Drastic examples include the passing of a series of laws and regulations accepting irrational pandemic-related purchases. This group also includes cynical manipulation for political gain, such as the fictitious opening of a hospital for media use (the case of the Polish town of Kielce). In the group of attitudes indicative of cynicism and ruthlessness, one should also note the breaking of the rigours binding the society (sometimes ostentatiously) by politicians from the top echelons of power (Polish examples include: a visit by the president of the ruling party to a cemetery that was closed to others; ski slopes were closed in lockdown, but were open for the deputy prime minister and her children).
8. Disclosure of the scale of ineptitude and helplessness of the authorities, surprised and unable to cope with the challenge in the face of the pandemic, as well as the consequences of this, in the form of mismanagement, excessive spending, chaotic decisions, and lack of consistency. An example of absurd solutions ordered by the Polish authorities is a ban on entering forests, but only the state-owned ones.
9. Deterioration of health conditions (both physical and mental) in many societies, and exposure of deficiencies in healthcare systems. Studies in Poland show that during the pandemic there has been an increase in health problems, e.g. overweight and depression. Closing access to health facilities, stopping treatments – these are well-known problems especially during the height of the pandemic. There was also a widening scale of problems of exclusion and lack of organised support among the oldest seniors (especially the single ones), the disabled, the homeless (unfortunately, the scale of volunteer assistance was insufficient).
10. Lack of coherent policy towards migrants in Central European countries in the face of the pandemic, which resulted, among others, in the fact that they remained largely unvaccinated.

The above list probably does not exhaust all the problems, as the pandemic has in fact affected almost every sphere of public and social life. One must agree with the statement that

> The COVID-19 pandemic poses a double challenge to public health and democracy. It is an opportunity for democratic collapse because extraordinary measures greatly expand executive power and allow for temporary restrictions on civil liberties in the name of public health. It is also an opportunity for democratic resilience if four conditions are met: there is a free press critical of the information provided by the government; independent courts ensure that mitigation measures and restrictions remain within the constitutional order; an effective parliamentary opposition controls/ supervises the actions of those in power; and an active civil society mobilises to defend democracy.
>
> (Weyland, 2001)

Among the positive aspects of the pandemic processes, it is important to point out that attempts to find a culprit were muted rather quickly, resulting in the fact that the term "China virus" was not used in the public space. Another plus is the European Union's strategy of jointly procuring vaccines, which has yielded some positive results. The European Commission has launched a European data platform to share research results and data among scientists working on combating the virus – this is the first part of the "European cloud for open science." And third – the pandemic proved once again how important technological and information tools are in the functioning of societies and economies of the world, which were used not only for work, but also in remote learning. And, finally, it should be emphasised that in the public space, the evaluation of the strategy aimed at protecting the population from disease and death, as well as methods of dealing with the consequences of the pandemic concerned the state and its bodies, that is, the responsible entities. The history of social, economic, financial crises of the modern era shows unequivocally that government interventions are absolutely necessary.

It is possible that the pandemic of the SARS-CoV-2 coronavirus causing COVID-19 is preparing the world for another change – a shift away from consumerism towards a world of values, or vice versa – preparing the world for economic and social change. Research on the pandemic in Central Europe indicates that it is being used by politicians to consolidate declining power and confirms Italian philosopher Agamben's thesis that the current state of affairs serves politicians who, using fear and anxiety about uncertainty, impose orders and bans in order to gain even more power in the future. Does the COVID-19 pandemic represent a turning point in human history? Will it shake up the world enough to bring about irreversible changes like the Black Plague did? Or is it just a brief episode that will be pushed out of memory with time? Given the two historical pandemics: the Black Death and the Spanish influenza, we can predict that the effects of the COVID-19 pandemic will also be far-reaching.

Thus, when analysing the circumstances of the functioning of the state during the pandemic, one is faced with a problem, which is well known to political scientists, i.e. the problem of assessing the role of the state in countering and combating the effects of the pandemic. As researchers, we are obliged to make an analysis that will help us understand whether the modern era is ending before our own eyes and whether we are "entering a new era that requires a 'theory' of a new beginning." Its symptom would indeed be the pandemic. The new beginning would be expressed – in this positive version – by a change in the way of thinking about power, the state and the world, and by a change in the character and way of life of both individuals and social groups; and also through the return of such values as friendship, neighbourly support, care for the surroundings and the environment, and freedom. But perhaps nothing will change for the better, as the world will accelerate in its pursuit of wealth and the satisfaction of every need, towards an ecological and humanitarian disaster.

References

Agamben, G. (2020). *Lo stato d'eccezione provocato da un'emergenza immotivata. Il Manifesto*. 26.02.2020 (Polish version: Stan wyjątkowy wywołany nieuzasadnioną sytuacją kryzysową, trans. Ł. Moll). Available from: https://www.praktykateoretyczna.pl/artykuly/stan-wyjatkowy-sytuacja-kryzysowa/, accessed: 12.10.2021.

Anioł, W. (2020). *Trzecia Rzeczpospolita w trzech opowieściach. Wokół polskich przemian 1989–2019*. Dom Wydawniczy ELIPSA.

Člověk, jenž o lidských životech uvažuje jako handlíř, nemůže stát v krizi v čele země, říká filozof | Plus (rozhlas.cz), accessed: 30.12.2020.

Electronic source: https://www.jstor.org/stable/422412

Fletcher-Kennedy, H., Sebastian, E., & van der Kamp, M. (2020). *Smashing Barriers for Women in International Science*. University World News, 30.05.2020. Available from: https://www.universityworldnews.com/post.php?%20story=20200529085407898, accessed: 17.10.2021.

Guasti, P. (2020). The Impact of the COVID-19 Pandemic in Central and Eastern Europe, The Rise of Autocracy and Democratic Resilience. *Democratic Theory*, 7(2), pp. 47–60. https://doi.org/10.3167/dt.2020.070207

Hancocks, T. (2020). *Government in a Pandemic: How Coronavirus Caused a Dramatic Shift in our Relationship with The State*. The Conversation, 8.10.2020. Available from: https://theconversation.com/government-in-a-pandemic-how-coronavirus-caused-a-dramatic-shift-in-our-relationship-with-the-state-147679, accesssed: 10.09.2021.

Hasnain, Z. (2020). *What about Public Sector Wage Bill Cuts to Finance Coronavirus Response?*Worldbank. Available from: https://blogs.worldbank.org/governance/should-public-sector-wages-be-cut-finance-coronavirus-response, accessed: 17.10.2021.

ILO (2021). *International Labour Organisation, ILO Monitor: COVID-19 and The World of Work*. Seventh Edition Updated Estimates and Analysis, 25.01.2021. Available from: https://www.ilo.org/wcmsp5/groups/public/---dgreports/---dcomm/documents/briefingnote/wcms_767028.pdf, accessed: 10.09.2021.

INCL (2021). *ICNL, International Center for Not-for-Profit Law - COVID-19 Civic Freedom Tracker*. Keep Civic Space Healthy. Available from: https://www.icnl.org/covid19tracker/?location=&issue=5&date=&type=, accessed: 12.10.2021.

Itrich-Drabarek, J. (2021). Pandemia. In A. Misiuk, J. Itrich-Drabarek, & M. Dobrowolska-Opała (Eds), *Encyklopedia bezpieczeństwa wewnętrznego*. Dom Wydawniczy ELIPSA. Available from: https://encyklopedia.wnpism.uw.edu.pl/ebw/pandemia, accessed: 12.10.2021.

Itrich-Drabarek, J., & Mazur, S. (2021). Experience of (for) Science and Higher Education in Times of The Coronavirus Crisis Causing COVID-19 Disease. *Studia Iuridica*, 88, pp. 136–150. https://doi.org/10.31338/2544-3135.si.2021-88.7

Kubicki, R. (2020). *Nie wiemy czy płyniemy na Titanicu, czy lecimy Tupolewem*. Głos Wielkopolski, 11.04.2020. Available from: https://plus.gloswielkopolski.pl/filozof-z-uam-o-pandemii-koronawirusa-nie-wiemy-czy-plyniemy-na-titanicu-czy-lecimy-tupolewem/ar/c1-14908008, accessed: 18.10.2021.

Nowak, P. (2020). *J'accuse...!* Teologia Polityczna, 14.04.2020. Available from: https://teologiapolityczna.pl/piotr-nowak-j%E2%80%99accuse%E2%80%A6, accessed: 18.10.2021.

Sapir, A. (2020). *Why has COVID-19 Hit Different European Union Economies so Differently?* Bruegel, 22.09.2020. Available from: https://www.bruegel.org/2020/09/why-has-covid-19-hit-different-european-union-economies-so-differently/, accessed: 21.11.2020.

Stawiszyński, T. (2020). Koronawirus i (nie)konieczność filozofii. *Dwutygodnik*, 285. Available from: https://www.dwutygodnik.com/artykul/9008-koronawirus-i-niekoniecznosc-filozofii.html, accessed: 18.10.2021.

Toscano, A. (2020). The State of the Pandemic. *Historical Materialism*, 28(4), pp. 3–23. https://doi.org/10.1163/1569206X-12342804

Weyland, K. (2001). Clarifying a Contested Concept: Populism in The Study of Latin American Politics. *Comparative Politics*, 34(1), pp. 1–22. https://doi.org/10.2307/422412

Winiecki, J. (2021). *Polscy antyszczepionkowcy*. Polityka, 23. 4.06.2021. Available from: https://www.polityka.pl/tygodnikpolityka/spoleczenstwo/2120645,1,polscy-antyszczepionkowcy.read

2 Models of the fight against a pandemic

Magdalena Mikołajczyk

2.1 Introduction

Today's 40- and 50-year-olds, aspiring to important public roles or forming the power elites of many modern states, may have enjoyed computer games like Civilisation, Age of Empires, or SimCity during their childhood. The creation of a prosperous state or city required patience, strategy, and correct decisions to achieve a kind of balance, for example through moderation in expenditure and care for different segments of the community, the right balance of conflict and stagnation. The creators of the game took into account the complexity of the structures of societies at the time, the variety of institutions, the relatively frequent external conflicts, and randomly occurring natural disasters or pestilences, which eliminated previous efforts. The devastation of fields by locusts was in this optic less severe than an epidemic decimating the population which is something unexpected, unpredictable in terms of beginning and end. Black swans, as Taleb (2010) calls such "falling from the sky" cases, were included in the scenario. The metaphor of such a game has many implications for the world, including being in a situation currently observed and analysed by policymakers, by political cabinets of experts, and by academics motivated yet differently.

Firstly, the algorithm inherent in the above-mentioned computer games always takes into account the possibility of returning to *equilibrium*, repair, and reconstruction. The trajectory of the economic and social processes imagined in them does not have a linear course, and the agency and control of the playing field by the players, most often personifying the rulers, are only effective at certain moments. Researchers focusing attention on the many social aspects of the SARS-CoV-2 pandemic are aware of the lack of data on which phase the process is observed. They reserve the possible difference between results obtained during the study and later, at the time of publication. They are aware of how temporal variables determine the ways in which the effects of change are perceived and evaluated, as Fernand Braudel or Ralf Dahrendorf, for example, have taught. Publicists, popularisers of science, often emphasise the probability of such effects appearing, which will make hitherto ways of existence impossible. This does not refer

DOI: 10.4324/9781003353805-3

to one threat but to many occurring in parallel, not invalidated by the occurrence of another. It is peculiar that repair and reconstruction must go on without the end of the threat being announced. This perspective underlines the probability of the need for a change of mindset, of accepting that a phenomenon, however extensive, once incidental, may in the future become the common experience of humanity. This implies, among other things, the need for a different normalisation of actually different subsystems, not only the law. However, some politicians present, or at any rate they did in the first half of 2020, the optics appropriate to a computer game – the epidemic continues, will peak and subside. This has not escaped the attention of critical philosophers and sociologists (Žižek, 2020, p. 44; Krastev, 2020, p. 24). In turn, the initiation by governments of institutional transformations (normative, structural, related to the organisation of the state apparatus), conditioned by the circumstances of the pandemic, in countries such as Hungary or Poland results in the question about the reversibility of changes made "under the pretext," which destroy the democratic system step by step.

Secondly, metaphors used to illustrate the non-linearity, aleatoricity, discontinuity, or multilinearity of processes are present (apart from myths co-constituting European identity and narratives specific to other societies) in many political analyses. Huntington's waves of democracy are an example that illustrates this well, and is useful in the argument that follows. The process of arriving at this type of regime, whether it concerns a state, a region, or is observed on a transcontinental scale, has, like the tides of the sea, its ebbs and flows – which means that it surges and retreats. Among the conditions favouring the consolidation of democracy, the length of past experience with democratic institutions, the level of economic development, the influence of foreign actors, and the international environment in general have been mentioned. The sources (endogenous or exogenous) and the time associated with the introduction, institutionalisation of democratic principles, do matter (Huntington, 1991). In the cited comparison and explanation of pathways to democracy, not only institutional (structural and normative) changes were taken into account. Determinants of a cultural nature and the strategies of political actors (parties, interest groups, leaders) were considered as equally important. It is worth noting here that countries such as the Czech Republic, Poland, Slovakia, and Hungary joined the liberal democracies in a noticeably stable way after 1989, which, incidentally, only one third of the countries emerging from real socialism at that time managed to do (McFaul, 2002, p. 227).

In describing the course of the SARS-CoV-2 pandemic, the metaphor of waves or cycles is equally valid. The danger of sudden surges and situations of relative calm are perceived. The virus is still present, mutates, and spreads again. The determinants mentioned in the case of democracy – experience, economic and other resources, ability to draw on knowledge and assistance from external actors – are similarly relevant in a pandemic. Here, too, attention must be paid to strategies and actions taken by state bodies and leaders, their initiative or inertia, and the whole range of variables that determine policy effectiveness in the crisis of 2020–2021. In management science, another metaphor as useful as waves is turbulence (Goetz & Sindbjerg, 2021).

Thirdly, the perception, diagnosis, description of the causes, course, and effects of the pandemic (from the detection of individual cases of the disease in various places, the announcement made on 11 March 2020 by the WHO, to the analyses carried out on an ongoing basis) are associated with different research strategies and methods. The diversified scientific fields and disciplines are paradoxically united by the object of research. However, the intensification of scientific efforts is accompanied by the acceleration of views far from rationality, otherwise also studied. Without questioning the usefulness of quantitative methods, statistics, and mathematical modelling – so crucial for studying the spread of the disease – it can be shown that the representatives of social sciences, assessing the processes determining our contemporary existence, also notice "The Relativist Turn," drawing attention to the "truth," which is extremely difficult to define, the presence of many "perspectives" (determined by geographical, political, economic, organisational, cultural, social, and temporal criteria), and the impossibility of pointing to exceptionless or permanent correlations. Referring here to the project of the methodological approach proposed by Simon Susen for the study of post-modern society, numerous analyses of pandemics have already emphasised the need to minimise the inevitable uncertainty, to respond flexibly, to adapt, and to anticipate (prevent) in any actions aimed at combating the virus and the multisystemic effects of the crisis. The relative equality of existential experiences coexists with a diversity of solutions. A phenomenon of global dimensions affects to the greatest extent the most "globalised" parts of the world, populated, urbanised, with an intensity of social contacts. However, various anomalies and peculiarities can be observed in local, peripheral spaces. The neglected, although famous for its modernity, "society-as-a-project" has been replaced by the non-identical "projects-in-society" (Susen, 2015, pp. 175–1780). Their construction depends on the pool of resources available to the players (rulers), their skills and social capital. Ambiguity constitutes *signat tempora*.

Another important premise follows from the above. The analogy to an imagination-stirring computer game causes the proper effect of participation, also in the processes associated with the fight against the virus, to be the learning of the subjects involved, the possibility of using mainly their own, but also other people's experience. What counts is flexibility and adaptation; in some situations precise standardisation of actions has proved to bring better results, in others (like vaccines) – innovation. Past experience has resulted in faster and more efficient implementation of medical and social procedures and those serving to maintain social distance. It is obvious that all crises are a testing ground for countries and institutions involved in designing and implementing public policies. Each wave of a pandemic is like moving to the next level, with a new mutation of the virus, but also new variables, such as the introduction of vaccines, vaccinations, and vaccination rates. It is difficult not to see it and not to take it into account in the search for factors shaping the remedial models of the states in the crisis caused by the SARS-CoV-2 pandemic. Hypotheses formulated on the basis of this type of rationale refer, for example, to the higher resilience of communities, states, and regions with memories of the effects of previous struggles with rapidly spreading viral diseases. However, learning is, it is worth adding, to a large extent, a function of the communication available and used (the communication system, the modes of communication, the educational institutions, and media mediating these processes). Undeniably, we live in an era in which information (including scientific information) spreads very rapidly and global multimedia and financial networks are highly interconnected. The conversion of knowledge into outcomes relevant to public health is reflected upon by scientists operating in the media space, also considering the poorly perceived and indirect effects of pandemics, e.g. on freedom of an individual, increasingly under surveillance "under the pretext" (Harari, 2021). However, in the numerous statements evaluating ways of dealing with the effects of the pandemic and attempts to implement strategies to counteract the intensification of illness and death, it was not large corporations but states that came to the fore. The network of power constructed around states and political systems turned out to be irreplaceable once again, as in the crisis of 2008, when government interventions proved in the end to be absolutely necessary. This is related to the existing institutionalised forms of action, the fulfilment of coordinative, regulatory and stabilising functions by the state, and the legitimate monopoly of violence inherent only to the state (Castells, 2013, p. 418).

Taking the above inspirations and assumptions into account, analysing the discourse consisting of statements of published scientific analyses, statements of a journalistic nature, reports of organisations recording data on the course of the SARS-CoV 2 pandemic, as well as reports containing indicators which make it possible to position countries according to the democratic (or not) features of their systems, I want to verify the hypothesis on the cause-and-effect link between the crisis caused by the virus and the lowering of democratic standards in three dimensions – institutional, communicative, and related to the expression of political opposition. The problem is related to the reflection on political change – an area which can be treated very broadly – as a change of the state and intra-state relations, and narrowly – as a change of certain institutions, of a less permanent character, with "corrective" potential, when, for example, the issue concerns the centralisation of the decision-making process, restriction of media pluralism, or repressiveness towards citizens who gather and demonstrate their beliefs. Limiting the analysis to Central European countries, I stipulate that the attempt to search for features determining the model of actions taken at the time of an epidemic threat against the disease, in connection with the disease, under the pretext of the disease, and indifferent to it but accepting the benefit of distraction, must be set in a broader context. For the countries in question, this context is at the same time linked to the universal need for solutions based on a regional framework, linking national systems to decisions from the level of the European Union. It should be added that, when placed in the field of research, the practices undertaken by state governments to combat the pandemic and to limit its direct and indirect effects, the parameters characterising the initial situation are extremely important. The state system can be treated as an independent variable when we are interested in the type and subsequent effectiveness of public health decisions, and as a dependent variable when we want to find out whether the SARS-CoV-2 pandemic is affecting the destabilisation of the state or the actions exceeding the conditions of a state of emergency (not necessarily proclaimed).

2.2 Power and rulers in times of the pandemic

The questions worth asking again, the hypotheses that are formulated and are still being verified after many months of the pandemic, most often still concern the most relevant medical and epidemiological aspects of SARS-CoV-2. The questions of virus mutation, availability, and effectiveness of vaccines remain at the forefront. Representatives of social sciences, on the other hand, are concerned with the interdependence of the processes observed, with emphasis on the economic and social impact of interventions undertaken by governments or international organisations. The European Citizens' Initiative, an appeal signed by scientists, artists and other citizens to make the COVID-19 vaccine a common good for humanity, is a unifying gesture, symbolic, and counter-hegemonic at the same time. The initiative is original, with civil society acting as David against the Goliath of the market, corporations, intellectual property, and patent law (*Right to Cure*, 2020). An example of an initiative that crosses continental and disciplinary boundaries is the 22 May 2021 manifesto "Work. Democratise, Decommodify, Remediate" (2021).

Not without significance is the internal aspect and the way in which states, state governments, and their leaders have dealt with the now permanent crisis situation. Here, researchers examine what resources had been available to the state before the pandemic, what solutions for the crisis were provided by the constitution and the legal system in general, what legitimacy governments and the parliamentary majorities supporting them enjoyed, how radical or less radical measures were motivated, how government information was incorporated into the existing communication system, etc. Intentionally, when confronted with the circumstances for the first time, we try to find out what type of decisions, or even personal leadership, is conducive to the desired behaviour by triggering trust, and which, on the contrary, escalates social opposition. Publicists have not ceased in their search either, criticising the irrationality of certain actions, exaggerated image orientation, wondering about more original than political variables differentiating decision-makers, such as age, gender, applied rhetoric. Women's management style has not been left without reaction, including the scientific perspective (Purkayastha et al., 2020; Dada et al., 2021; Garikipati & Kambhampati, 2021).

Ultimately, we want to find out who and why did best during the first waves of COVID-19, which country achieves satisfactory results in terms of health, social, and economic policies on a temporary or continuous basis. The first comparative studies are being published with evaluations of public policies, assessments of results, forecasts of social or economic consequences, together with a package of remedial actions (Joyce et al., 2020; Greer et al., 2020). The political aspects of the pandemic are not ignored. The ability of state authorities to make effective decisions relevant to the protection of human life and maintenance of the stable functioning of all institutions was and is crucial in any emergency situation. Each of such decisions, and all of them together, have, in the long run, significance for the social structure, income differentiation of social groups and categories, deepening inequalities, status of minority and disadvantaged groups. It is an impulse to redefine the nature of the state, even though these projects may not subsequently be implemented, as evidenced by the forecasts of reconstruction and reorganisation of the institutional order after 2008 (Touraine, 2013). Many publications of a contributory nature bring reports depicting strategies and instrumentation used as a response to threats in different states and regions or, for example, for business, labour markets, education.

The cardinal question is whether state regimes, their systems constructed on the basis of monistic or plural centres of power, with or without executive supremacy, principles of separation or cooperation of powers, and a whole range of other constitutional and extra-constitutional solutions, are a significant variable in the circumstances of a disease which significantly affects social life. In other words, whether the state system played/is playing a significant role in inhibiting the spread of the virus, if only through the existence or lack of restraints in the use of coercive measures and, conversely, whether the SARS-CoV-2 pandemic has deepened the process of de-democratisation (deconsolidation of democracy), the crisis of state institutions, and demonstrated the dysfunction of public services organised and financed in various ways.

The type of regime (democracy or authoritarianism), the way in which public policies are organised and financed (including the organisation of crisis management, health and social policies), political institutions, and the capacity of the state to control health services and public administration are seen as determinants of observable types of responses/reactions to pandemics by governments, authorities, or, more personally, political leaders and elites (Greer et al., 2020).

Another question, albeit one with no single right answer, is whether power relations have changed (and continue to change) during the SARS-CoV-2 pandemic. At what level is their presumptive change advanced and irreversible? The impossibility of generalising on this issue is related to the diversity of political systems, political cultures, and resources available to state authorities at the time immediately following the WHO declaration of an epidemic emergency. The existing legal and constitutional arrangements have repeatedly proved inadequate and the possibility of rapid constitutional revision – often politically unrealistic. The need for quick response and the often inconsistent interpretation of the situation within the parliamentary majority itself or even within the government's close circle have been obstacles. The need to involve experts in the decision-making process was as much necessary as burdensome – the latter because of the not always coherent position of those with medical expertise and because of their high potential for media influence, for influencing public opinion, to some extent competing with politicians, taking the opportunity to assume the role of saviour or statesman.

Compiled and published once a month by the Bloomberg Agency, *The Covid Resilience Ranking* ranks countries according to several important indices classified as Covid Status, Reopening Progress, and Quality of Life (*The World Finally Reopens*, 2021). Among them, there is no positioning by regime type. Among the indicators of the first type, the number of infections per 100,000 people, the mortality rate, the number of deaths per 1 million inhabitants of the country, and the percentage of positive test indications are taken into account. Other parameters concern the possibility of reactivation, reopening of the economy to the world, and return to pre-2020 activity, understood in new terms, i.e. the vaccination rate of the population, the severity of lockdown affecting the social, and economic activity of individuals, restoring communication with the world in real spaces. The ranking, in this category, takes into account the resumption of travel by comparing the flights in 2019 to those opening (or stopping) in the following months and the range of potential bidirectional routes (exit and entry to different countries of the world) for the vaccinated. Extremely important, composed of many sub-categories, is the indicator on overall health service efficiency. The correlation of all scores with the Human Development Index is illustrative of the rather trivial thesis that educated societies, countries not destroying the sphere of public services in the last decades, are doing better; however, the possibilities to influence multidimensional resilience are limited. For the sake of argument, it should be added that the ranking takes into account 53 countries with advanced economic development, and no country has occupied any position in the ranking on a permanent basis during the year. The instability of positions is a result of decisions made by governments and factors beyond their control, such as seasonal drops in temperature. Fewer infections and hospitalisations result from greater isolation, which is influenced by the severity (strictness) of lockdowns and regulations on human gatherings, from assemblies to social and family gatherings, participation in religious services, etc. The analysed resilience only temporarily makes some states the front-runner, while others are the disgrace of the hypothetical rivalry.

2.3 States of liberal democracy, populist or already authoritarian

The crisis of democracy and, more specifically, the dismantling of its institutions by legally elected authorities (government, parties forming a parliamentary majority) did not begin in 2020, nor do they concern only Central European countries, although it is not difficult to notice that many researchers use the example of Hungary, Poland, or the Czech Republic in a deliberately selected sample (Mancosu et al., 2021; Löblová et al., 2021). The interest in the "turning astern" of the third wave of democracy, in deconsolidation, in transition in an unknown direction, is not something accidental. In addition to spectacular titles, in every language foretelling disillusionment, erosion, disengagement or ultimately the twilight and end of democracy, publications of the early 21st century renewed reflections on the state of the principles organising political systems on all continents and abound in constructions resembling or illustrating the paradoxes of the democratic system.

The first paradox is related to the openness of democratic systems, not limiting but, on the contrary, creating channels for articulation of interests for subjects of various kinds, including minority representation. Social inclusion is, however, perceived as growing and complicating reality. Pluralism and diversification work against each other. Instead of creating a comfortable framework for participation, they cause a lack of understanding, an aversion to complexity, and ultimately distance potential participants from the decision-making process (Dahl, 2000, pp. 35–36; Canovan, 2007, p. 58; Antoszewski, 2016, p. 33). The sense of excess or chaos, the inability to effectively criticise the mainstream information, create a silent, passive, yielding to pressure and mostly uncritical majority. Not only uneducated citizens abstain from voting, also educated ones who do not perceive the attractiveness of the offer of existing political parties and leaders. This results in the activation of cartel parties or populist forces, using anti-establishment rhetoric, operating on the edge of the system, and being de facto anti-systemic. Leadership, in turn, is associated not only with spectacular statements, media popularity, personalised and image politics, but even with more advanced information and propaganda technologies than political marketing. The potential opposition, most often split into a number of parties with different ideological profiles and electorates with different interests, does not present an equally attractive and competitive offer as the ruling formation. Even if one of its groupings has the potential to produce an alternative programme, interesting solutions for public policies, it is unable to break through the mainstream of promises constructed for the benefit of those in power in the public media. Social media are full of protesters who only have enough energy to create a few humorous memes. Demonstrations are often nothing more than a flash mob; even when they concern important issues fundamental to the state (such as courts of law) or the rights of any social category (such as women), they are not effective, at the utmost slowing down the decision-making process or causing a temporary split within cabinet coalitions. The problem of representation or the effectiveness of defining and solving social problems takes on a fairy-tale character in this context. The deficit of the principle of representation, with universal suffrage, can be seen more broadly as the exhaustion of the advantages or viability of democratic systems (Wieviorka, 2020).

Other types of paradoxes are derived from the necessary but insufficient mutual trust of citizens and rulers, and of citizens in their mutual relations. The creation of the culture of trust will be fostered in democratic societies – normative certainty, transparency of social organisation, stability of social order, responsibility (with transparency of actions) of the rulers (Sztompka, 1998). For the Polish sociologist Piotr Sztompka, who presents in his works successive paradoxes of a system derived from the rule of the people, the whole is completed by the enforcement of rights and the imposition of obligations as an alternative to powerlessness and the omission of sanctions against transgressions, and – not identical to the previous one – the enforcement of obligations and the fulfilment of duties. The state and its relevant government institutions, authorities, and administrations are expected to act in favour of the dignity, integrity, and autonomy of every member of society. However, it is a paradox in democratic systems that trust is generated through distrust. The established control mechanisms, checks and balances, and deliberative practices are part of democratic strategies. A paradox of a different kind is the need for restraint, refraining from tinkering with the existing mechanisms of control and security (Sztompka, 1998). The fragility of democratic principles and institutional constructs, repeatedly disregarded in history, has become the cause of staggered shifts that annihilate principles while leaving nominally only democratic institutions in place (Levitsky & Way, 2010, p. 27). It is also a paradox that, in contrast to authoritarianism equipped with mechanisms that prevent abdication or replacement of rulers, the immanent property of democracy is a suicidal predisposition (Antoszewski, 2016, p. 33).

Larry Diamond's comparative research from developing countries back in the 1990s identified another three contradictions: between *conflict* and *consensus*, *representativeness* and *governability*, *consent* and *effectiveness* (Diamond, 2005, pp. 40–41). Each of these, despite being the product of theoretical generalisation of many cases, existing long before the SARS-CoV-2 pandemic, makes itself known even at this time. The dilemmas of contemporary management are situated in these three fields. The need for consensus, which at least hypothetically increases the chances of minimising the loss of life, health of citizens, and resources at the collective's disposal, must collide with the complexity of contemporary societies, the reconfiguration of old class structures, reactivated tribalism, and sociopolitically driven polarisation. In the latter case, electoral results observed in many places indicate differentiation between centre and periphery, activation of nationalisms and conflicts related to politics of difference, escalation of worldview and religious disputes. This is reflected in new political parties, alliances within coalitions previously seen as impossible. For parties and leaders coming from factions that are in opposition to the government, the opportunity for criticism is created, of course, by extra-procedural moves, interventions of those in power in the sphere of civil rights and freedoms, inaccuracies in the information provided, omissions involving any of the social groups, incompetence of any kind. The limitation of representativeness in democratic systems means, according to Diamond, that the authorities inhibit the claims of all interest groups, the ability to negotiate and mediate (2005). However, a thin line distinguishes attempts to limit representativeness from over-representing groups identified as the social base of the factions that make up the government, at the same time failing to act and dismissing the problems inherent in the supporters of competing actors. The third contradiction in this theory of democracy is presented by pointing to the need to legitimise democracy more than any other system. This is the paradox most clearly evident in contemporary politics. Gaining support to win the next election, through spectacular, often costly, programmes or investments, annihilates the chances of development in the long term, beyond the generation. Politics is not conducted with future generations in mind, but its effects are calculated as benefits for those in power (in personal, party, and political clientele terms). In presenting this paradox, Diamond used the example of Central and Eastern Europe, countries in need of structural reforms after 1989, beginning their economic transformation. His assertion from the distance of three decades turns out to be accurate. He argued, using a metaphor of "you can use a small spoon to satisfy your hunger," that economies reformed in a sustainable way, investing in the human capital of the poor, enabling everyone to meet their basic needs, maintain growth. The collapse of the economy, the collapse of a democratic political system are unfavourable, but not unforeseeable, transitions. Two important circumstances account for the post-transition ability of states and societies to cope with the epidemic threat. On the side of the state we will place the organisation and expenditure on public healthcare, on the side of society we will place the education, innovation, and adaptability of all its members, also remaining in connection with the financing of education, culture, media that do not need commercial advertising, including patronage offer from the government, to sustain themselves. Education, as it ultimately turns out, is not just something that can be shown by presenting a diploma. The SARS-CoV-2 pandemic is, above all, a litmus test, a poker "check," testing previous investments and outlays in healthcare, the number of professional medical staff, the competencies of administrative staff in many fields, such as logistics, and additionally the level of functional illiteracy.

The parallel of the viral spread is used by analysts of democracy, depicting its shrinking, increasing number of authoritarian states noticeable in 2020-2021 (Nazifa et al., 2021).

The countries that are cited in the discourse and show an unexpected resilience (such as Taiwan until spring 2021) are examples of quieting political conflict, increasing representativeness by inviting specialists to participate in decision-making (e.g. extending political decision-making circles to include representatives of doctors, medical staff, and healthcare managers), and consenting to unprecedented surveillance for the duration of the pandemic, forced by fear for health. The analysis of examples from different continents allows one to formulate a thesis of very high generality that the probability of an effective fight against the virus is influenced by three variables: state capacity, social trust, and political leadership (Fukuyama & López-Calva, 2021). If we take into account the state system, extreme solutions, i.e. liberal democracies and consolidated authoritarianisms work.

The situation of the four Central European countries – Hungary, Poland, the Czech Republic, Slovakia – show as many similarities as differences. They all transformed their political systems with the third wave of democratisation, after the collapse of the communist bloc and after 1989. The transition process was peaceful, initiated by the Round Table talks (Poland) and the Triangle Table (Hungary), and names like the Velvet Revolution (Czechoslovakia) reflected their character. Among the many features they have in common, the formation of the sub-regional Visegrad Group by the countries, their accession to the European Union at the same time, and their similar experiences of simultaneously leaping to the metaphorical two depths – capitalist economy and post-modernity (post-industrial and information society) – are equally significant. All have a parliamentary-cabinet type of system, constitutions from the 1990s, except Hungary which, not insignificantly, enacted its constitution (replacing the 1949 act) only in 2011. In the Polish case, it is accurate to say that the constitution is invisible. If the political forces in parliament were more favourable to the ruling party, its amendment would be initiated. Those in power seem at times not to notice that this change has not taken place.

The disillusionment with democracy, the resuscitation of movements with a nationalist and populist orientation, and the rise of right-wing authoritarianism in this part of the world have their own original explanations. More complex and more difficult to prove, they are linked to a more deeply embedded heritage than the contemporary one, and refer to resentments from the last half-century, the aforementioned processes of transformation and modernisation. The authors point to the instability of democratic patterns and the lack of their internalisation, the presence of "anti-political politics" characteristic of past dissidents, and a sense of deprivation. Not insignificant for the transformation of marginal movements into dynamic ones capable of seizing power is the use of rhetorical figures of a "stolen revolution," a "crushed majority" (Mudde, 2007). For Tismaneanu, their activity, including escalating at many crucial moments, was already a remedy for the trauma of transformational change in the 1990s; he derived the vitality of nationalisms in this part of Europe from a constellation of symbols, emotions, and ideas, creating a redemptive language of liberation for groups long subjugated or humiliated (Tismaneanu, 1998).

In the optics of Ivan Krastev and Stephen Holmes, populisms in this part of the world are an emanation of social rebellion against the perceived necessity, also in the realities of the 21st century, to conform to the liberal and democratic patterns of the rich Western countries (Krastev & Holmes, 2019). In a more universal dimension, disillusionment with democracy is rooted in a psychological sense of epistemic threat (when the world becomes incomprehensible), existential threat (when one anticipates the loss of livelihood, status, competitiveness or even the ability to act), and third, associated with affiliation, loss of community, lack of groups providing support in the normative and behavioural dimension. The rise of populist offers and the subsequent increase in support for them are also often located in the non-transparency of organisations (global, European, domestic), the crisis of the politics of recognition of individual identities, the longing for community (collective identities), the financial crisis, and the deficit of control (Drozdowski, 2017).

Populism is also explained by new technologies, affecting the social structure now and in the future, by the need to change the organisation of the world of work, by the increase in economic inequality and the accompanying sense of disempowerment, as well as by the cultural backlash. According to this theory, the rise in support for populist parties is a reaction to profound changes in worldview, so significant that they are felt as a threat to the status of previously dominant groups (Inglehart & Norris, 2019). However, the threat of secularisation moves Polish and Hungarian populists rather than Czech populists, who are more likely to be motivated by the anti-EU arguments, seeing threats both in the dominance of liberal elites from Brussels and in the increasing presence of immigrants.

The rhetoric of the parties conquering the political scenes of Hungary, Poland, the Czech Republic, and Slovakia in the second decade of the 21st century clearly identifies populist elements, more often conservative than social democratic, with the promise of a strong causal state, carrying out more welfare functions (especially towards the family) and public tasks, assertive in international and economic relations (Kornai, 2015; Héjj, 2017; Kovács & Tóth, 2021; Kubát & Hartliński, 2019; Wojtas, 2011). Anti-establishment slogans, critical of the governments of the past, demonstrating their incompetence and corruption, emancipatory and dignifying the ordinary citizens, are shared by leaders of different ideological provenance, i.e. Victor Orban (FIDESZ), Jarosław Kaczyński (PiS), Andrej Babiš (ANO), Igor Matovič (OL'aNO). The first of them, present on the political scene for over a decade, is a metaphorical Patient Zero for populism in this part of Europe. The last one won the election virtually on the threshold of the first wave of the pandemic. His party managed to win a third of the seats in the unicameral (and very divided parliament), ousting the previously ruling party SMER, more due to a change in Slovak political sympathies after the murder of investigative journalist Ján Kuciak and his fiancée Martina Kušnírova than due to showy happenings. A year later, he was replaced as prime minister by another leader of the same party, Eduard Heger. Of the above, only Jarosław Kaczyński was not prime minister in March 2020, yet he exercised actual political leadership. He assumed the position of deputy prime minister, with Mateusz Morawiecki as prime minister, in October 2020, which makes his political responsibility at least minimally plausible. Andrej Babiš stands out in this group of leaders for his wealth, clearer self-interest orientation, and pragmatism, which, complemented by stronger checks and balances than in Poland, allow the Czech Republic to remain among the more stable electoral democracies (Pehe, 2018). In the analyses of the circumstances of gaining power by the aforementioned leaders and parties, it is interesting to note the argument about the transformation of early party (or personal) defeat into later victory and the indifferent material, national, family status of the leaders, often not confirming the flagship slogans of their political formations.

Discussions on the case of Hungary or Poland, evolving systems leaving somewhere behind the model of Western liberal democracy, were initiated before the pandemic began. The mode of political organisation of society, the state system can be characterised by indicating their (a) liminality; (b) broad, popular, communitarian exclusiveness; (c) patronage or – looking at the relations of power from a different angle – clientelism; (d) axiological pressure with eclecticism of the programme offer; (e) demonstration of the omnipotence of the state, (f) channelling of the information, i.e. controlling the message in the public media through one-sided pro-government propaganda.

A liminal system is one that still has the characteristics of a liberal democracy, but in some respects is no longer one. The more complex indices are able to capture this subtle change, while others, considering competitive elections as a basic condition, fail to see the symptoms or signs of a farewell to democracy. A façade, for example, is provided by NGOs, accepted if they support the existing type of regime, distance themselves from politics, not accepted if they do not, and – on the contrary – engage in criticism of the government and have foreign sponsors. Indicators of change are not typical. Following the Polish discourse, one can cite statements pointing to the existing paradox, such as the title of an article by the doyen of regime historians – Marian Kallas – "The parliamentary majority as an anti-system opposition in Poland" (2018).

In the typology of fractured democracies or hybrid regimes, two models are worth noting – illiberal democracy and competitive authoritarianism. The first concept popularised in the literature by Fareed Zakaria (2004) is eagerly used by Victor Orban to accentuate the difference (Lendvai, 2019).

Features of this type of regime are also identified in post-2015 Poland. Among them, the marginalisation of individual freedoms, the subordination of all actions of state institutions to national interests, the usurping of exclusive rights to patriotism, or the monopolisation of the right to express national interests by the winning party are of particular importance. In Central European states, elaborate propaganda instruments are used for this purpose – with historical politics, re-vindication discourse, the stimulation of fears and hostility.

The second type of political system, competitive authoritarianism, is characterised as a defection from authoritarianism *sensu stricto*, i.e. one in which elections or multiparty elections that would allow a government to emerge are not held at all, or opposition parties are excluded from elections, elections are rigged, and a system of repression is created that prevents opposition parties and civic movements from functioning (Levitsky & Way, 2010). In a model of competitive authoritarianism, elections are not fair, individual freedoms and rights may be violated, rivals have an uneven playing field. This means that elections take place, but there are indicators of their unfairness, such as: exclusion of any of the contenders, confirmation by independent centres of electoral malpractices inspired or tolerated by those in power, obstruction of campaigning for rival parties or candidates, rationing of access to the media and other public resources unfavourable to competition. In the second category, government actions limiting freedom of speech or association, creating a sense of threat and inhibiting opposition or civic activity, political attacks on the media, are indicative. The media also form a "playing field." Unequal access to them, bias in favour of the government side, media's financial dependence on state sponsorship, as well as politicisation of state institutions, abandonment of their impartiality form a catalogue of indicators confirming (by the presence of any of them) the competitive authoritarianism (Levitsky & Way, 2010).

Communitarianism and exclusiveness only seem on the surface to be an antinomy. Each of the previously mentioned governments will point to the legitimising support of the electorate. Regardless of whether the electoral system is designed to give a bonus to the leading group, the distribution of the obtained seats creates a constitutional majority, or, on the contrary, forces a coalition compromise, those in power emphasise acting in accordance with the will of the sovereign, the interest of the nation. The cohesion of the group, of the community, is achieved by exclusion, so that the status of any minority becomes endangered. The existence of one's own people and strangers is not just a rhetorical phrase.

Patronage, clientelism, can be associated in yet another way, bearing in mind the four decades of communist experience in Poland, Hungary, and Czechoslovakia, i.e. with the nomenklatura existing in those regimes. It was a system of privileges belonging exclusively to the Communist Party cadres. This type of comparison is definitely milder than the notion of a mafia state used by Bálint Magyar (2018), a sociologist and former politician who criticises Hungarian realities. The description of a state of this kind, exemplified by the Hungarian system, points to the concentration of power and wealth, the building of a network of connections among entrepreneurs (oligarchs) and the power elite, and to processes culminating in the takeover (political subordination) of institutions of public power and those controlling the executive. The legitimacy deficit of a state organised in this way is overcome by manipulations in the electoral system (the electoral system is tailored to the needs of the party forming the government) and the incapacitation of the media (their organisation in such a way as to exclude criticism of those in power).

An arsenal of ideological means is also used (nationalism, anti-Semitism, racism), among which conservative values such as religion and family most often top the metaphorical banners (Magyar, 2018, pp. 269–323). Systems of this type, identifiable in Hungary and Poland, much less so in the Czech Republic and Slovakia, give permission to the verbal and behavioural expression of the radical right. As there is a link between insecurity and authoritarianism, the use of enemy figures becomes a perfect breeding ground for such attitudes. Just like the relative deprivation experienced by the less educated, those on the margins of the labour market, those with less money, those living in the provinces. Threats are a derivative of modern civilisation with its consumerism, permissiveness, and ethical relativism. The mechanism for controlling threats is faith in God (religion) and in government. It is hard not to add that the unpredictability of the mutation of the virus, the rate of its spread, health issues, and social consequences become a primary source of concern.

For the liminal phase, the transition between democratic and authoritarian systems, all centralisation measures are relevant. By reactivating the value of the state and government, the unrivalled competitiveness of these actors in the provision of goods, services, and security is indicated. The redistributive function of the state is obscured; it is the government that gives all financial aid to those in need, provides protection and assistance.

The antidote to the paradoxes of democracy, the social search for a protective umbrella against an uncertain future in authoritarian solutions can be found in control solutions, their reactivation, or simply their defence. The powers of oversight are parliamentary procedures of control of the executive and investigative powers, the possibility of shaping public opinion in the polarised media space, critical speeches of opposition parties, activities of social movements and civic organisations (Rosanvallon, 2011).

2.4 Models of fighting pandemics in Central Europe

The fight against the SARS-CoV-2 pandemic is regarded as a unique event in the history of modern nations. An unrepeatable event, interesting in every sense. Sociologically, because at the same time it contributes to atomisation and integration, politically, for the reasons mentioned above, pretexts that can be used for quiet and clever institutional transformations, recasting democracies as systems that limit civil rights and freedoms and reduce pluralism. In Europe, this is comparable to warfare, fought not with each other, however, but, as Timothy Garton Ash metaphorically put it, "with Hitler in the bloodstream, Stalin in the lungs" (2021). Despite many repetitive algorithms, resulting in the first period from the need to organise the infrastructure and acquire (production, purchase) or redeploy the resources needed for this extraordinary circumstance, and in the subsequent periods from the strategies adopted, the policies of the states showed significant differences. An attempt to construct a model should be based on a classification of state actions, more specifically state authorities, according to several criteria: speed of response to a threat (fast, slow), resourcefulness (after the occurrence of a threat, with preventive actions), adopted strategy (passive, thus preventive, and active), creativity of solutions (standard actions, innovations). The strategies adopted could also be imitative or autonomous, open to cooperation or not, providing assistance to other states or requiring such assistance.

None of the four countries showed innovative ways forward. Only Slovakia showed originality by deciding in November 2020 to expressly test almost all citizens (in the 10–65 age group). This is not to say that the efforts were completely ineffective or that the actions were purely for image. The successes announced were encouraging, but more often than not the names of Central European countries appeared in the middle quartiles of the ranking.

The peculiarity of the situation favoured the implementation of existing crisis procedures or the creation of new ones (for the SARS-CoV-2 pandemic). The Czech Republic and Slovakia made use of existing solutions and legal states of emergency in their legal systems. This path was not taken by the Polish government, which used solutions not provided for in the constitution (state of epidemic threat, state of epidemic). The deepest legal interventions took place in Hungary, where the basis for action, in addition to the constitution, was provided by the Disaster Act of 2011, amended for the circumstances of the pandemic. The possession of a strong political majority in parliament made it possible to grant extraordinary powers to the Hungarian government, consequently ruling by decrees, the number and quality of which are symptomatic, illustrating the assumption of control in areas irrelevant to human health, a profound intervention in the sphere related to civil rights. The pandemic, irrespective of the state system, implied the need for various types of prohibitions, control and surveillance systems, additionally legitimising interference in the area of civil rights and freedoms.

As early as in the spring of 2020, not knowing the end date of the pandemic, the analysis of governments' decisions of a political and legal nature made it possible to predict the consequences involving changes in the functions of the state, disruption of electoral processes, expansion of executive power, centralisation of decisions, and strengthening of supervision, influence on civilian control of the military, restriction of civil rights (through prohibition of movement, orders of a sanitary-epidemic nature, control of media messages or even control of individual speeches, restriction of assembly, etc.). Taxation, the structure of public spending, the roles and interrelationships of public and non-state actors have also been included in the area of change (Brown et al., 2020; Bolleyer & Salát, 2021).

Successive waves of the pandemic have occurred and are occurring in a situation of measurable and manageable risk, but still in a state that allows abuses of power to be qualified as extraordinary measures beyond the norm, justified by the situation. Restrictions on protesters, their detentions and arrests, and violence during political interventions in the circumstances of the first lockdown in the spring of 2020 and then throughout the pandemic were equally likely in the states categorised by Freedom House as Free, Partly Free, and Not Free. Similarly, there were no clear correlations in relation to parliamentary disruption or restrictions affecting journalists and the media (Freedom House, 2020, p. 4). The need to make quick regulatory and redistributive decisions may have been a justification for the suspension of social dialogue, the centralisation of powers, and, within this framework, the strengthening of clientelist relations, favouring selected local power actors, for example those who show political alignment with the faction(s) forming the government.

The need to reorganise various types of resources for the protection of citizens' health and the protection of economic activity and the labour market could have been (and still is), first, a pretext for strengthening the position of the party or coalition forming the parliamentary majority and the government, and for taking decisions, including those involving law-making and income redistribution. Second, all actions that had to be taken could and did result in legitimising or delegitimising those in power. One might venture to say that the SARS-CoV-2 pandemic, however global and profound its reach, may have been more important for the climate than for halting or stunting democracy at the polls. Creating information messages in an emergency situation was, from the very beginning, a necessity, a duty of the government and other public administrations, as was the even more rudimentary organisation of procurement and logistics concerning the functioning of the public health service, the sanitation service, the deployment of the necessary medical equipment. In the first wave of the pandemic, attention was drawn to shortages of masks, disinfectants, decisions on border traffic, actions using modern technology to trace the contact chains of infected people, decisions on quarantine or subject, object, time, or territorial coverage of lockdown. Citizens' behaviours, from the simplest ones such as stopping certain activities, keeping a distance, disinfection, wearing masks in public, to more complex ones such as undergoing quarantine or getting vaccinated, depended on more or less rapidly established norms, the perception of their rationality, and publicity and education campaigns.

Governments have used the fight against the pandemic to make shifts of a managerial or financial nature, marginalising local authorities, limiting their sources of funding (as in Hungary, for example, by changing the rules on car tax and industrial tax) or in Poland, where relations between the government and local authorities, including financial ones, are conditioned by political alignment. The second area of interference was the media. Interference in this area is gradual, ranging from shifts in personnel to changes (where possible) in concessions and ownership structures. An illustrative example is the takeover by the state-owned oil company Orlen of the publishing group Polska Press (20 regional dailies and internet services) from a German holding, and the attempt to eliminate from the media market the news television TVN 24, critical of the government.

Without the pretext provided by the pandemic, the fluctuating epidemic affecting the number of infected and hospitalised persons, interference which alters the positions of the authorities has continued in Hungary and Poland. The judiciary is treated as a transmission belt for the projects of the executive. The case law of the Polish Constitutional Tribunal is a clear example of this. There is also a similarity in the actions which the Helsinki Committee's report on Hungary presents as the construction of a parallel state. The pre-2020 practices in this diagnosis illustrated the intention to eliminate all institutions capable of controlling the executive, through personnel appointments, regulation of the funding stream, and obstruction of yet another kind. The period of the pandemic facilitated another type of strategy, the creation of new structures, politically linked to the party forming the government, securing the interests of these parties even if they lose the elections (Qualitative changes, 2021).

The reports of the organisations monitoring democracy in all the countries of the world for 2020 are as disturbing as they are unambiguous. The SARS-CoV-2 pandemic is enabling institutional transformations of an undemocratic nature, which may have consequences in the long term. These mainly involve the unlimited use of emergency measures and interventions affecting the media. In addition, attention is drawn to discrimination against minorities, violations of fundamental rights (inalienable rights), excessive use of force, and restrictions on the ability of the legislature to influence the executive branch of the government. Poland and Hungary are examples of states classified by The V-Dem Institute as the third wave of autocratisation (Lührmann et al., 2020).

The answer to the second question about how the state system, during the SARS-CoV-2 pandemic, helped (or may still be helping) to eliminate the threats to human life and the dire economic and social consequences implied by the need to implement the social distance norms, is not clear-cut, even for neighbouring states embarking on the process of democratisation at a similar time. In a broader comparative perspective, pandemic control strategies were more likely to be effective in countries with consolidated democracies, where governments invested in additional, expert forms of communication, abandoning the demonstration of omniscience and including doctors, health personnel, medical managers in the decision-making process, and vice versa, i.e. where full authoritarianism allowed for immediate action to isolate the population under the threat of strong sanctions.

The organisation of the information system and the way to communicate about the actions taken by the government has its institutionalised framework, in which information centres, spokespersons of the government, and individual ministries operate, briefings and press conferences are organised, information is given to press agencies and directly to the media, updated content is prepared for social media. The first months after the announcement of the SARS-CoV-2 pandemic required the organisation of a multidimensional information system, the incorporation of additional reporting entities, a rethinking of communication with citizens so that elementary knowledge of the disease and its control became shared by the general public. The management of information including data on cases, deaths, availability of hospital beds and ventilators in Central European countries, as in other cities of the world, has become part of crisis management. None of the governments in question had a capacity comparable to countries where digital applications made it possible to identify infected people and track their contacts. The European Commission, by the way, had already recommended a common EU approach to solutions of this kind in April 2020, because of standards related to data protection and privacy.

The need for reliable information was at odds with the need to enhance the image of the government and leaders, by highlighting their efficiency, resourcefulness, effectiveness. Image-building activities in this case cannot be perceived solely through ad hoc political expediency for the benefit of leaders and any government agencies. The preparation and implementation of well-thought-out information campaigns influenced public confidence (expressed towards the authorities, towards the policies undertaken and the actions recommended), thus increasing the likelihood of successful coordination actions and social discipline. In each country, there were plenty of spectacular announcements, statements, inspired media performances. The Polish government organised the import of Chinese masks and hazmat suits by hiring the world's largest aircraft – the Antonov An-225 Mriya. Victor Orban and FIDESZ politicians, when the first wave of the pandemic subsided, proclaimed that Hungary had coped magnificently, the radicalism of any action was justified, and the opposition had nothing to offer. It was difficult to argue with any government message in light of the fact that within the controversial 30 March 2020 law on epidemic prevention there was a ban on spreading false information about COVID-19, creating a pretext for sanctioning those expressing an opinion different from that presented by the government. The changing epidemic situation required the activation, within the narrative, of those responsible for failure. In this role it was possible to cast the European Union institutions, other states, in internal relations responsibility could be assigned to a selected professional group (e.g.

doctors, journalists, LGBT+ communities). The successes achieved by those in power in one phase of the pandemic and the accompanying lifting of restrictions resulted in more cases in the next phase. Politicians appearing at press conferences played the role of rational hosts calming down the moods, promoting solutions up-to-date at a given moment, suppressing information that discredited the adopted course of action. Slovakia and Hungary broke out and started the vaccination earlier than the set time for the European Union countries.

Communication aimed at calming the moods, reducing the image of chaos, tuning the image of the government, health ministers, and other persons actually responsible for infrastructures related to the medical service of the population (tests, quarantines, hospitalisation, vaccines) was adversely affected by (a) information discrediting initiatives taken in the authority bodies, demonstrating the absurdity of certain regulations or (b) revealing omissions, ignorance or carelessness; (c) speeches by leaders ignoring the possible effects of the virus; and (d) individual practices undertaken by politicians violating the prohibition in force for all.

An example of the first kind in Poland was the contested ban on entering forests and national parks, with the Ombudsman denying there was legal basis for it. In the Czech Republic, on the other hand, a ban on singing was imposed under a state of emergency in autumn 2020. Decisions of this kind, it would seem, concerned minor things and were easier to show in the media than examples of public money spent on unusable equipment, transactions dictated by rivalry (e.g. in the vaccine race) or concluded in unclear circumstances. Polish authorities were put at a disadvantage when it turned out that the incidence statistics and other data on COVID-19 were compiled by a high school graduate. The painstaking work of a teenager aggregating data obtained from hospitals and local institutions was used by researchers, in projects featuring statistics on a regional and global scale, and may have been relied upon by the government.

Admittedly, none of the Visegrad leaders presented an attitude that explicitly denied the existence of the virus and the possible deadly threat. Several statements from the early stages of the crisis fall into this category. For example, the words of Gergely Gulyás, the Hungarian minister responsible for the prime minister's office, who stated at a government press conference that the virus was harmless to the young and healthy, so journalists could infect each other at will. Slightly more frequent were incidents of politicians breaking epidemic regulations, such as former Czech president Václav Klaus not giving up eating in restaurants even after they had closed. Similar behaviour was presented by the Czech minister for health, Roman Prymula. In Poland, Jarosław Kaczyński's limousine ride to the cemetery on the 10th anniversary of the plane crash that killed his brother, the then president of Poland, was similarly controversial, all the more that the visit took place in full lockdown. Apart from these incidents shaping public opinion, other far more important decisions (such as the purchase of vaccines) influenced the positions of government members. In Poland and the Czech Republic, there was a change of the minister of health, and in Slovakia, after the resignation of the prime minister, the government was reconstituted.

Already in the first months after lockdown was declared, whether or not a state of emergency of any kind was proclaimed, the very need for distance, not just restrictions, was an important element inhibiting the possibility of resistance. Organisations reporting on this state of affairs pointed to the need to shift civic activity to social networks. Online platforms, instant messaging, and groups formed on digital platforms undertook relief, care, production, and distribution activities, supporting local authorities in doing so or filling in the gaps in the system of aid organised by the state (Brechenmacher et al., 2020). The pandemic has challenged and continues to challenge the capacity of mobilising social resistance and protest movements demonstrating in real spaces. The shift of activities to the internet and digital activism are not equivalent in shaping public opinion. In authoritarian states or those experiencing de-democratisation, police intervention and diversity and the size of sanctions have been intensified in addition to, and sometimes in relation to, epidemic risk.

After 2019, which for the countries of Central Europe was a great theatre of social protests, mass protests did not have a comparable scope in the two years that followed, except in Poland, where the unprecedented insolence was the offensive of the government (without any consultation) and the ruling of the Constitutional Court on the unconstitutionality of the norms allowing abortion due to severe irreversible impairment of the foetus, an incurable disease threatening its life. This brought thousands of women onto the streets and led to several days of protests also in small provincial towns. The protests, dubbed the "cardboard revolution" on account of the homemade banners, had no effect on the legal system that was being changed. The regulations on epidemic circumstances were a pretext for arrests and other restrictions affecting, for example, schoolgirls taking part in the demonstrations.

The protests in the Czech Republic and Slovakia have a different character. They are more clearly anti-government than in Poland, with the names of prime ministers appearing here much more often. In the autumn of 2020, demonstrations against the restrictions took place in the capitals of both of these countries. The protesters are often entrepreneurs who are losing their sources of income as a result of lockdown. Hence the slogans "Open the Czech Republic," "Stop the hidden tyranny." Blockades and demonstrations are also organised by other professional groups, such as farmers. The largest collective protest in Hungary during the pandemic was the demonstration against changes to the relatively independent portal Index.hu. Civic protest movements such as the Polish Women's Strike, the Czech Million Moments for Democracy, or the Hungarian Momentum are social capital for better times.

Has the SARS-CoV-2 pandemic contributed to the deconsolidation of democracy, the disruption, or abandonment of norms sustaining such an institutional order, the mutual relations between the rulers and the ruled, thwarted or conversely encouraged protests? The answer to these questions is at the same time a confirmation of the thesis that in extremely complex circumstances, with emotions strongly stimulated by the crises of the 21st century, the financial and refugee crises in Europe in 2015, and anticipated crises of various types of resources (conditioning climate wars and technological unemployment), with a reconfiguration of subjectivity or agency in international relations, the pandemic acted as an accelerator, stimulating processes whose origin was already smouldering before it occurred (Koczanowicz, 2020, p. 16). Existing axiological conflicts were surfacing, although their activation did not appear to be rational. Populist leaders of Central European states could intentionally blame their failures on the European Union institutions, states from across the ocean or neighbouring countries, other mythical enemies (also from citizens' groups). Anti-Europeanism is more significant for the Czech society; in Hungarian and Polish propaganda, oriented towards traditional and conservative hierarchies and norms of social life, world view disputes and hostility towards non-heteronormative people were activated.

In the analysed discourse there is a noticeable presence of forecasts, beliefs of a normative nature, starting with the phrases "it is necessary," "it should be," "it must be," referring to the state and democracy. There are repeated attempts at summaries reactivating the trilemma of the Turkish economist Daniel Rodrik, in which three elements cannot work together – democracy, the global economy, and the nation state (2011). The sequences of different actions needed in the SARS-CoV-2 pandemic strengthened states, and consequently their governments. The need for strengthened border control or competition in the production and distribution of vaccines was a contribution to strengthening thinking in terms of national communities. To paraphrase Mark Twain's *bon mot* – reports of the death of the nation state were greatly exaggerated.

To what extent have states changed? Polish political scientist Mirosław Karwat, in his reflections on the continuity of the state, proposes distinguishing between the *continuity of the existence of the state* (in its full form or in temporary forms), the *continuity of the properties of the state* (where identity, systemic and ideological features are important), the *continuity of the functioning of the state* (this is the problem of whether a new generation creating a new state entity uses the previously existing forms or elements and makes a smooth reformist transition, or on the contrary, the transition is abrupt and the state is created as if from scratch), and the *continuity of the functions of a given state*. In the latter case, the satisfaction of specific social needs (national security, integrity and sovereignty of the territory, economic activity and productivity, protection of heritage and national identity) may change. This aspect makes it possible to state a change in the functions of some European states, which were inclined to accept far greater social obligations after World War II than they do today. The author also mentions the continuity of the state's personnel, again gradual, depending on whether the implementers of the new state system are willing to allow the presence of personnel socialised in different realities, and the legal continuity of the state consisting in accepting and not touching the legal acts previously in force, as well as not questioning the commitments undertaken (Karwat, 2018, pp. 332–333). This proposition lends itself to thinking about observable and potential change concerning the discussed group of states. The SARS-COV-2 pandemic did not catalyse processes of democratic deconsolidation in Hungary, Poland, or elsewhere in the region. However, the need to strengthen certain functions of the state has become a gateway for those in power to smuggle in ideas that would otherwise provoke far greater resistance, not in society, but in the ruling group itself, not necessarily recruited from among the radicals themselves. It has deepened and legitimised the destruction of the rule of law that has already taken place. It has added impetus to activities related to the centralisation of power, the reduction of systemic brakes on the executive or the creation of parallel institutions. It is therefore difficult not to agree with John Keane's assessment: "Contrary to popular fears, there is no historical curse hanging over democracy. Contrary to dominant narratives, it is not democracies that have failed in the face of pandemics, but governments that have previously violated democratic principles" (Keane, 2021, p. 39).

References

Antoszewski, A. (2016). *Współczesne teoria demokracji*. Wydawnictwo Sejmowe.

Ash, T.G. (2021). O reakcji UE na pandemię: Jeden wielki sukces i jedna wielka porażka. *OkoPress*, 9 marca. Available from: https://oko.press/timothy-garton-ash-o-reakcji-ue-na-pandemie/, accessed: 06.06.2021.

Bolleyer, N., & Salát, O. (2021). Parliaments in Times of Crisis: COVID-19, Populism and Executive Dominance. *West European Politics*, 44(5–6), pp. 1103–1128. https://doi.org/10.1080/01402382.2021.1930733. Available from: https://www.tandfonline.com/doi/full/10.1080/01402382.2021.1930733, accessed: 30.06.2021.

Brechenmacher, S., Carothers, T., & Youngs, R. (2020). *Civil Society and the Coronavirus: Dynamism Despite Disruption*. Carnegie Endowment for the International Peace. Available from: https://carnegieendowment.org/2020/04/21/civil-society-and-coronavirus-dynamism-despite-disruption-pub-81592, accessed: 30.06.2021.

Brown, F.Z., Brechenmacher, S., & Carothers, T. (2020). *How will the Coronavirus Reshape Democracy and Governance Globally*? Carnegie Endowment for the International Peace. Available from: https://carnegieendowment. org/2020/04/06/how-willcoronavirus-reshape-democracy-and-governance-globally-pub-81470, accessed: 06.06.2021.

Canovan, M. (2007). Polityka dla ludzi. Populizm jako ideologia demokracji. In Yves Mény, & Yves Surel (Eds), *Demokracja w obliczu populizmu* (pp. 57–82). Oficyna Naukowa.

Castells, M. (2013). *Władza komunikacji*. Wydawnictwo Naukowe PWN.

Dada, S., Ashworth, H.Ch., Bewa M.J., et al. (2021). Words Matter: Political and Gender Analysis of Speeches Made by Heads of Government During the COVID-19 Pandemic. *BMJ Global Health*, 6: e003910. http://dx.doi.org/10.1136/bmjgh-2020-003910

Dahl, R. (2000). A Democratic Paradox? *Political Science Quarterly*. 115(1), pp. 35–36

Diamond, L. (2005). Trzy paradoksy demokracji. In P. Śpiewak (Ed.), *Przyszłość demokracji. Wybór tekstów* (pp. 39–57). Fundacja ALATHEIA.

Drozdowski, R. (2017). Co się dzieje? Między utopią populizmu a poszukiwaniem nowej umowy społecznej. *Ruch Prawniczy, Ekonomiczny, Socjologiczny*, 2, pp. 11–24. https://doi.org/10.14746/rpeis.2017.79.2.2

Freedom House (2020). *Democracy under Lockdown. The Impact of COVID-19 on the Global Struggle for Freedom*. Available from: https://freedomhouse.org/sites/default/files/2020-10/COVID-19_Special_Report_Final_.pdf, accessed: 29.06.2021.

Fukuyama, F., & López-Calva, L.F. (2021). *Pandemics and Political Performance*. Available from: https://www.project-syndicate.org/commentary/pandemic-political-decay-latin-america-caribbean-by-francis-fukuyama-and-luis-felipe-lopez-calva-2021-06, accessed: 30.06.2021.

Garikipati, S., & Kambhampati, U. (2021). Leading the Fight Against the Pandemic: Does Gender Really Matter? *Feminist Economics*, 27(1–2), pp. 401–418. https://doi.org/10.1080/13545701.2021.1874614

Goetz, K.H., & Sindbjerg M.D. (2021). COVID-19: A Dual Challenge to European Liberal Democracy. *West European Politics*, 44(5–6), pp. 1003–1024. https://doi.org/10.1080/01402382.2021.1930463

Greer, S.L., King, E.J., Massard da Fonseca, E., & Peralta-Santos, A. (2020). The Comparative Politics of COVID-19: The Need to Understand Government Responses. *Global Public Health*, 16 (7), pp. 1413–1416. https://doi.org/10.1080/17441692.2020.1783340

Harari, Y.N. (2021). *Lessons from a Year Of Covid*. Financial Time [on-line]. Available from: https://www.ft.com/content/f1b30f2c-84aa-4595-84f2-7816796d6841, accessed: 05.06.2021.

Héjj, D. (2017). Węgry 2010–2017. Ile jest populizmu w reżimie Viktora Orbana? In F. Pierzchalski, & B. Rydliński, *Autorytarny populizm w XXI wieku. Krytyczna rekonstrukcja* (pp. 129–146). Dom Wydawniczy Elipsa.

Huntington, S.P. (1991). *The Third Wave. Democratization in the Late Twentieth Century*. University of Oklahoma Press.

Inglehart, R., & Norris, P. (2019). *Cultural Backlash Trump Brexit and Authoritarian Populism*. Cambridge University Press.

Joyce, P., Maron, F.R., & Purshottama, S. (Eds) (2020). *Good Public Governance in a Global Pandemic*. The International Institute of Administrative Sciences.

Kallas, M. (2018). Większość parlamentarna jako opozycja antysystemowa w Polsce po roku 2015. In R. Balicki, & M. Jabłoński (Eds), *Państwo i jego instytucje. Konstytucja - sądownictwo - samorząd terytorialny* (pp. 222–241). Wydawnictwo Uniwersytetu Wrocławskiego.

Karwat, M. (2018). Metodologiczne aspekty problemu ciągłości państwowej. In M. Pietraś, I. Homan, & S. Michałowski (Eds), *Państwo w czasach zmiany* (pp. 319–343). Wydawnictwo Naukowe Uniwersytetu Marii Curie-Skłodowskiej.

Keane, J. (2021). Desperacja despotów. O ustroju państwa, przywódcach i walce z pandemią. *Polityka*, 1/2 (3294), p. 39.

Koczanowicz, L. (2020). *Wyzwania pandemii a modele demokracji. Opinie i ekspertyzy OE-320*. Kancelaria Senatu. Biuro Analiz, Dokumentacji i Korespondencji. Available from: https://www.senat.gov.pl/gfx/senat/pl/senatekspertyzy/5727/plik/oe-320.pdf, accessed: 30.06.2021.

Kornai, J. (2015). Hungary's U-Turn: Retreating from Democracy. *Journal of Democracy*, 26(3), pp. 34–48. https://doi.org/10.1353/jod.2015.0046

Kovács, K. & Tóth, G.A. (2021). Od niedoskonałej demokracji do niekompletnej autokracji. In A. Czarnota, M. Paździora, & M. Stambulski (Eds), *Nowy Konstytucjonalizm. Polityczność, tożsamość, sfera publiczna* (pp. 175–207). Wydawnictwo Naukowe SCHOLAR.

Krastev, I. (2020). *Nadeszło jutro. Jak pandemia zmienia Europę*. Wydawnictwo Krytyki Politycznej.

Krastev, I., & Holmes, S. (2019). *The Light that Failed: Why the West is Losing the Fight for Democracy*. Pegasus Books.

Kubát, M., & Hartliński, M. (2019). Party Leaders in the Czech Populist Parties and Movements. *Polish Political Science Review. Polski Przegląd Politologiczny*, 7(1), pp. 107–119. https://doi.org/10.2478/ppsr-2019-0007

Lendvai, P. (2019). *Orbán. Nowy model przywództwa w Europie*. Biblioteka Kultury Liberalnej.

Levitsky, S., & Way, L.A. (2010). *Competitive Authoritarianism: Hybrid Regimes after the Cold War (Problems of International Politics)*. Cambridge University Press.

Löblová, O., Rone, J., & Borbáth, E. (2021). COVID-19 in Central and Eastern Europe Focus on Czechia, Hungary, and Bulgaria. In S.L. Greer, E.J. King, E. Massard da Fonseca, & A. Peralta-Santos (Eds), *Coronavirus Politics: The Comparative Politics and Policy of COVID-19* (pp. 413–435). Ann Arbor: University of Michigan Press.

Lührmann, A., Maerz, S.F., Grahn, S. et al. (2020). *Autocratization Surges – Resistance Grows. Democracy Report 2020*. Varieties of Democracy Institute (V-Dem). Available from: https://www.v-dem.net/media/filer_public/de/39/de39af54-0bc5-4421-89ae-fb20dcc53dba/democracy_report.pdf

Magyar, B. (2018). *Węgry. Anatomia państwa mafijnego. Czy taka przyszłość czeka Polskę?* Magam.

Mancosu, M., Vassallo, S., & Vegetti, F. (2021). *Rapporto sulla prima rilevazione per il pubblico italiano. L'opinione pubblica italiana durante la pandemia Aspettative e giudizi sulle istituzioni nel confronto con altri 5 paesi europei*. Istituto Carlo Cattaneo. Available from: https://www.cattaneo.org/wp-content/uploads/2021/04/W1-CovidEPO-Rapporto-Ita.pdf, accessed: 28.06.2021.

McFaul, M. (2002). The Fourth Wave of Democracy and Dictatorship: Noncooperative Transitions in the Postcommunist World. *World Politics*, 54(2), pp. 212–244. https://doi.org/10.1353/wp.2002.0004

Mudde, C. (2007). W imię chłopów, robotników i narodu. Populizm w Europie Wschodniej. In Y. Mény, Y. Surel et al., *Demokracja w obliczu populizmu*. Oficyna Naukowa.

Nazifa, A., Cole, R., Gastaldi, L. et al. (2021). *Autocratization Turns Viral. Democracy Report 2021*. University of Gothenburg: V-Dem Institute. Available from: https://www.v-dem.net/media/filer_public/74/8c/748c68ad-f224-4cd7-87f9-8794add5c60f/dr_2021_updated.pdf
Pehe, J. (2018). Explaining Eastern Europe: Czech Democracy Under Pressure. *Journal of Democracy*, 29(3), pp. 65–77. https://doi.org/10.1353/jod.2018.0045
Purkayastha, S., Maxwell, S., & Bhramar, M. (2020). Are women leaders significantly better at controlling the contagion during the COVID-19 pandemic? *Journal of Health and Social Sciences*, 5(2), pp. 231–240. https://doi.org/10.19204/2020/rwmn9
Qualitative Changes (2021). *Qualitative Changes in Hungary's Illiberal Regime since the Last Article 7 hearing*. Available from: https://helsinki.hu/en/qualitative-changes-in-hungarys-illiberal-regime-since-the-last-article-7-hearing/, accessed: 30.06.2021.
Right to Cure, European Citizens' Initiative number ECI(2020)000005, registered 21.08.2020, https://europa.eu/citizens-initiative/initiatives/details/2020/000005_en, accessed 30 June 2021
Rodrik, D. (2011). *The Globalization Paradox: Democracy and the Future of the World Economy*. W.W. Norton & Company.
Rosanvallon, P. (2011). *Kontrdemokracja. Polityka w dobie nieufności*. Wydawnictwo Naukowe Dolnośląskiej Szkoły Wyższej.
Susen, S. (2015). *The 'Postmodern Turn' in the Social Sciences*. Palgrave Macmillan.
Sztompka, P. (1998). Trust, Distrust and Two Paradoxes of Democracy. *European Journal of Social Theory*, 1(1), pp. 19–32. https://doi.org/10.1177/136843198001001003
Taleb, N.N. (2010). *The Black Swan: The Impact of the Highly Improbable*. The Random House Publishing Group.
The World Finally Reopens. The Covid Resilience Ranking. Available from: https://www.bloomberg.com/graphics/covid-resilience-ranking/, accessed: 29.06.2021.
Tismaneanu, V. (1998). *Fantasies of Salvation: Democracy, Nationalism, and Myth in Post-Communist Europe*. Princeton University.
Touraine, A. (2013). *Po kryzysie*. Oficyna Naukowa.
Wieviorka, M. (2020). Nowe wyzwania dla demokracji. In B. Kerski, & J. Kołtan (Eds), *Solidarność, demokracja, Europa* (pp. 111–122). Europejskie Centrum Solidarności.
Wojtas, K. (2011). *Partie populistyczne w Czechach i na Słowacji*. Wydawnictwo Naukowe SCHOLAR.
Work. Democratise, Decommodify, Remediate. Available from: https://democratizingwork.org, accessed 30.06.2021.
Zakaria, F. (2004). *The Future of Freedom: Illiberal Democracy at Home and Abroad*. W.W. Norton & Company.
Žižek, S. (2020). *Pandemic!: COVID-19 Shakes the World*. OR Books.

3 State economic problems during the SARS-CoV-2 pandemic

Stanisław Mazur

This chapter discusses the issue of the impact of the COVID-19 pandemic on economic processes. It analyses issues relating to both the global economy and the economy of the European Union, including the economies of the Visegrad Group countries. The chapter also addresses the nature of the economic shock caused by the COVID-19 pandemic and presents its short-term and long-term consequences. Moreover, it discusses, for obvious reasons briefly, anti-crisis measures taken in the fiscal and monetary spheres – at the level of both the European Union and some selected countries. The discussion of postulates concerning the revision of the dominant theories of neoliberal economics and its basic assumptions is an important element of this analysis. The chapter is complemented with opinions on the formation of a new economic order in response to the consequences of the economic crisis caused by the COVID-19 pandemic.

3.1 The nature of the crisis caused by the SARS-CoV-2 pandemic

The COVID-19 pandemic crisis is multidimensional, and its consequences have been severely felt, first and foremost in the area of health security (it has caused the deaths of hundreds of thousands of people). It has caused a number of adverse phenomena resulting from social isolation and accompanying psychological problems. The COVID-19 pandemic has also caused powerful economic repercussions resulting in a reduction in global GDP, a slowdown or economic recession in many countries, a radical deterioration in the condition of some sectors of the economy (e.g. tourism, gastronomy), the loss of millions of jobs, and a widening of income disparities in many countries.

The specificity of the economic crisis caused by the COVID-19 pandemic is also determined by the fact that it is a crisis in terms of both supply and demand. It also has a different genesis than the economic crisis of 2006–2009 (Buti, 2020). In the case of the latter, it was speculation and the use of casino logic in economic decisions, fraud, and unethical behaviour that led to turbulence with such severe consequences for the economy. The origin of

DOI: 10.4324/9781003353805-4

Table 3.1 Comparing Crises

	Euro area crisis	*COVID-19 crisis*
Source and nature	Fiscal shock and imbalances of financial sector (endogenous, country-dependent)	Combined demand and supply shock (exogenous and common)
Impact	Serious and country-dependent	Serious and country-sector-dependent
Timing	More than 1 year to unfold	Felt immediately
Recovery	Slow but solid	Fast(er) but fragmentary

Source: Own elaboration based on Buti, Papaconstantinou (2020).

the current crisis lies in the events caused by non-economic phenomena. In order to highlight the nature of the current economic crisis, its features are compared with those of the euro area crisis (see Table 3.1).

3.2 Economic consequences of the crisis caused by the COVID-19 pandemic

The demand-supply nature of the economic crisis triggered by the COVID-19 pandemic implies a number of serious short-term and long-term consequences.

The problems that occurred on the supply side resulted from the violation (disruption) of supply chains, which forced companies to stop production (Inoue & Todo, 2019). In turn, supply-side shock led to severe perturbations on the demand side, including reduced purchasing opportunities, declining workers' incomes, and lowered optimism levels, prompting consumers and companies to abandon consumption and postpone investment decisions (Baldwin & Weder di Mauro, 2020). The economic consequences caused by COVID-19 are briefly discussed below.

As a result of the COVID-19 pandemic, many governments imposed drastic restrictions on doing business and introduced barriers to travel. Almost half of the world's population was affected, and the global economy was negatively impacted. There was a sharp drop in consumption (except for food and medical purchases, for example) and economic sectors such as tourism, transport, and gastronomy experienced a severe recession. Global supply chains were affected or destroyed, with the manufacturing sector hit particularly hard.

The economic crisis manifested itself through three key phenomena: disruption of global supply chains, reduced international mobility, and a decline in international financial remittances (Yeyati, 2021). Over 90% of the global economy experienced a decline in GDP, the highest percentage since the Great Depression of 1930–1933 (Yeyati, 2021). The prolonged pandemic has led to recessions in the US and the euro area, as well as in the global economy as a whole. According to the International Monetary Fund (IMF), global GDP fell by 3% in 2020 instead of the 3.3% growth previously forecast. The crisis has also slowed GDP growth in emerging markets, including China (the International Monetary Fund predicts this could be the lowest growth since the 1970s).

The pandemic has also adversely affected financial markets. In the first quarter of 2020, stock markets around the world collectively lost more than 20% of their value, recording their worst performance since the global financial crisis of 2007–2009. Volatility is also evident in the foreign exchange market. Emerging markets have been hit the hardest, which could threaten the stability of their economies, e.g. in debt servicing.

The COVID-19 pandemic has forced the governments of many countries to face a difficult dilemma – on the one hand, the need to fight the pandemic decisively, including by restricting social mobility and freezing economic activity, and on the other hand, the responsibility to provide income for those who cannot work.

In the case of developing countries, economic difficulties have been compounded by a decline in international remittances of at least 20%, or more than USD 100 billion. Prior to the crisis, remittances operated in a countercyclical manner and have over three times exceeded the official development assistance since the mid-1990s. In 2019, it is estimated that remittances could have exceeded foreign direct investment inflows to low- and middle-income countries. By mid-2020, 120 developing countries had requested access to emergency financial assistance from the International Monetary Fund. Nearly 2.7 billion workers, about 81% of the global workforce, are working and earning less due to the COVID-19-induced recession, with workers in the lower-middle-income range in developing countries losing the most (Jomo & Chowdhury, 2020).

The disruption of global supply chains, in which the key component are workers from countries where wage pressure is relatively low, has caused their sources of income to start shrinking. The primary motivation for shifting labour-intensive work to developing countries has been to reduce labour costs. Employment generated by export-oriented manufacturing is an important item in the economic structure of many developing countries. For this reason, the multiplier effects of reduction of employment have severe economic consequences, threatening to deepen the economic recession in these countries.

One of the consequences of the pandemic has been a restriction of civil liberties. Many governments have imposed strict controls on civil society, arguing for the need to ensure the health security of citizens and invoking the public interest (Kloet et al., 2020). Governments in many countries have closed borders, erecting sanitary cordons, and introduced internal and international border controls in an attempt to control and deter the movement of people infected with COVID-19 (Afsahi et al., 2020). Countries that did not respond early and decisively enough in introducing restrictions to stop the spread of the pandemic, such as the UK (Scambler, 2020), the USA (Thomson, 2020) and Brazil (Malta et al., 2020), saw significantly higher numbers of infections and deaths due to COVID-19 (Gugushvili & Mckee, 2021). Countries where interventions were introduced earlier and using a broad set of restrictions and control measures, such as Taiwan, New Zealand, Vietnam, Australia, South Korea, and Singapore, were much more effective in containing the spread of the pandemic in its early stages (Dalglish, 2020; Afsahi, et al., 2020).

Lessons from the COVID-19-induced economic crisis are likely to change the rules of the global economic game, including a partial retreat from globalisation. The operation of global value chains has contributed to a significant minimisation of production costs. These chains have become an effective instrument for building a competitive position in a globalised economy (Mentzer et al., 2001, p. 2). However, the economic crisis caused by the pandemic has also revealed the risks associated with them.

First, the concentration of production in China has proven to be risky. As a consequence, new manufacturing investments should be expected to be located closer to the target markets. In particular, this is to be expected in economic sectors recognised as critical from the point of view of sanitary safety and public security. This will result in locational diversification of supply chains and their regionalisation (Pla-Barber et al., 2021).

Second, firms are likely to revert to storing parts and components for production in order to be able to continue production despite interruptions in supply chains. So far, the abandonment of parts (product) warehousing has had the effect of lowering firms' operating costs, and a shift away from this practice will likely affect the prices.

Third, the importance of digital services in the economy will increase with the rapidly progressing Fourth Industrial Revolution. Its consequences will include rapid development of digitisation, robotisation, development of technology based on artificial intelligence, autonomous vehicles, 3D printing, learning robots, the Internet of things, and genetic engineering. At the same time, the stream of economic activity and financial and technological resources will move towards building the Green Deal – energy transformation, use of renewable energy sources, and increasing industrial energy efficiency. These processes will trigger radical changes in business models, creating winners and losers.

Fourth, the experience of pandemic times may lead to an increase in public spending on ensuring health security, while at the same time reducing military spending. It seems that in the coming years, citizens' pressure on politicians to ensure and strengthen their health security will increase, becoming one of the key categories around which political debates and election campaigns will focus.

Fifth, public spending on combatting the effects of the pandemic and the stimulus packages being put in place for national economies to avoid recession and return to growth will lead to an increase in state interventionism and a significant increase in global debt, both public and private. This year, this debt is likely to reach a record high of 300%.

Sixth, the economic crisis in the European Union and the USA is creating space for the economic expansion of China. Although the current crisis, unlike in 2007–2009, will significantly slow down the Chinese economy, the relatively quick lifting of restrictions and the start-up of production facilities may cause China to return to the path of rapid economic growth relatively quickly. As a consequence, China may try to rebuild its position as a global supplier of goods and services, while at the same time Chinese investors may actively pursue buyouts of high-tech foreign companies weakened by the economic crisis.

3.3 Actions addressing the economic consequences of the crisis caused by COVID-19

The specific supply-and-demand nature of the COVID-19 pandemic necessitated unique responses – in terms of both their nature and scale. The ways in which national governments responded to the economic problems arising from the pandemic were similar to each other and generally involved the pursuit of unconventional monetary and active fiscal policies.

After the initial shock of the COVID-19 pandemic, governments and central banks injected huge resources into the banking system to provide liquidity. The burden of counteracting the effects of the pandemic fell mainly on governments, which introduced stimulus packages (e.g. the US spent USD 2.2 trillion, Germany EUR 1.1 trillion), and central banks (e.g. the US Fed announced an unlimited buyout, and the European Central Bank prepared an asset purchase programme worth EUR 750 billion, with an option to extend it). In turn, the International Monetary Fund and the World Bank are offering developing countries easier access to financing and are calling on developed countries to suspend debt repayments by the poorest countries.

Measures to combat the negative consequences of the pandemic in the economic sphere include an expansive monetary policy pursued by central banks, such as significant interest rate cuts and purchases of government bonds. Its aim was to mitigate the negative economic and financial effects as a consequence of governments around the world imposing restrictions on work and movement in order to prevent the spread of the COVID-19 pandemic. The policies of the banks were aimed at maintaining liquidity by providing sufficient cash, suspending debt repayments, and providing guarantees so that households could delay payments and workers could be paid even during quarantine or when they temporarily stopped working. At the same time, these policies were intended to prevent mass bankruptcies by providing companies with cash flow to pay workers and suppliers.

A key element of the expansive monetary policy is the near-zero interest rates and implementation of the so-called quantitative easing. The central bank's policy conducted in this way is an anti-crisis measure and may help to mitigate recessionary phenomena. However, as M. Gorynia aptly notes, one should keep in mind the potential adverse consequences of this policy. The cited author draws attention to the following limitations:

a. maintaining low interest rates for a long time may foster the growth of the so-called speculative bubbles;
b. low interest rates and loose monetary policy contribute to an increase in the supply of credit, and, through a demand stimulus, they increase inflationary pressures;
c. low interest rates are generally unfavourable for banks, as they reduce interest margins;
d. low interest rates are unfavourable for holders; they can become a reason for a growing disequilibrium and, thus, another crisis;
e. soft monetary policy increases the pressure on the weakening of the domestic currency against foreign currencies; weakness of the Polish zloty may translate into higher prices of imported goods and higher inflation (Banaszyk et al., 2021).

Taken in response to the COVID-19 pandemic, the global fiscal action reached about EUR 6 trillion in direct budget support in 2020. This amount is more than double the amount of aid provided in response to the global financial crisis in 2007–2009. The fiscal support mitigated the impact of the pandemic on consumption and production, while leading to an increase in the public deficit and debt. Additional spending on the health sector amounted to EUR 800 billion, while direct fiscal support to households and businesses amounted to almost EUR 5 trillion. In addition to the direct fiscal stimulus, governments provided liquidity support measures worth about EUR 5 trillion (about 6% of global GDP) to businesses and households, such as capital injections, loans, asset purchases, or assumption of debt and guarantees. The possible future impact of these commitments on debt and public deficits depends on the extent to which these guarantees are used by the private sector and the extent to which they are activated (Communication from the Commission to the Council, 2021).

The EU is currently going through its third crisis in a decade – following the euro area financial crisis and the migration crisis. In some respects, the potential systemic consequences of the COVID-19 pandemic are even more pervasive than in previous crises (Baldwin & Weder di Mauro, 2020; Fuentes & Moder, 2020).

Real GDP is expected to reach pre-crisis levels in both the EU and the euro area by mid-2022. Most manufacturing sectors started to recover relatively quickly already in Q3 2020, as restrictions on the movement of people, goods, and services began to be lifted. However, there are significant differences in performance among sectors, but also within sectors. Much of the digital industry is performing well, as is the healthcare industry. Sectors such as chemicals, construction, and food and drink are likely to see a V-shaped recovery. Despite the initial bumps, the automotive and textile industries appear to be on a fast recovery path. In contrast, sectors that depend on human contact and interaction, such as the cultural and creative industries and the aerospace industry (due to the decline in mobility and tourism activities), have been hit hard by the crisis and are likely to need more time to return to growth (Jomo & Chowdhury, 2020).

The economy of the European Union is expected to bounce back strongly from the recession this year, and the economies of its Member States are expected to return to growth relatively quickly. Economic growth in the 27 countries of the EU is expected to reach 4.2% this year, a significant increase from the 3.9% forecast in February this year. As EU Commissioner Paolo Gentiloni noted, "The shadow of COVID-19 is beginning to lift from Europe's economy." Next year, the EU economy is expected to grow to 4.4%, instead of the 3.9% projected for February this year, and Member States will also start to see the impact of the first payments from the European Recovery and Resilience Facility (www.business-standard.com).

Among the countries of the Community, the Visegrad countries were the least affected, but they also experienced significant GDP declines in 2020 – from 4.2% in Poland, to around just over 6% in the other three countries of the region. In 2021, recovery is already visible, but due to new mutations of the virus and delays in mass vaccination campaigns, no V4 country will return to pre-crisis GDP levels this year.[1]

The scale of the economic crisis caused by COVID-19 proved so significant that the European Union decided to take action to deal with the consequences of the crisis, disregarding the so-called "ultima ratio" doctrine, according to which EU aid can be provided after a Member State has exhausted its options. By the EU standards to date, these actions have been taken relatively quickly and on a significant scale. At the level of the European Commission, the rapid activation of the general escape clause contained in the provisions of the Stability and Growth Pact has enabled Member States to implement fiscal loosening on a large scale (Communication from the Commission to the Council, 2020). This has been complemented by liquidity measures aimed at protecting companies (relaxation of state aid rules, allowing the activation of national guarantees and combined with an increased overall lending capacity of the European Investment Bank (EIB)), protecting jobs (loans and guarantees provided by the Commission to Member State governments to finance expenditure), and

1 https://visegradinfo.eu/index.php/v4-mirror/617-making-the-most-of-the-recovery-in-visegrad

providing assistance to countries (for the euro area, decisions to support the pandemic crisis under the European Stability Mechanism (ESM)).

This was complemented by liquidity measures aimed at:

- protecting businesses – by relaxing state aid rules, allowing national guarantees to be activated and combined with an increased overall lending capacity of the EIB,
- protecting jobs – loans and guarantees provided by the Commission to Member State governments to finance expenditure,
- providing aid to the Member States – for the euro area, decisions on pandemic crisis support under the European Stability Mechanism (ESM).

A landmark moment was the EU Council decision of July 2020 (European Council, 2020), which introduced a new fiscal framework and financial governance mechanisms. Particularly important was the agreement that read:

> In order to provide the Union with the necessary means to address the challenges posed by the COVID-19 pandemic, the Commission will be authorised to borrow funds on behalf of the Union on the capital markets. The proceeds will be transferred to Union programmes in accordance with NGEU.
>
> (European Council, 2020, p. 2)

The EU's response to the economic crisis caused by the pandemic is NextGenerationEU, a temporary economic recovery facility worth over EUR 800 billion to help repair the direct economic and social damage caused by the coronavirus pandemic. After the COVID-19 pandemic, Europe will become greener, more digital, more resilient, and better prepared for current and future challenges.

The centrepiece of NextGenerationEU is the European Recovery and Resilience Facility, which has a budget of EUR 723.8 billion in loans and grants to support reforms and investments by the EU countries.[2] The aim is to mitigate the economic and social impact of the coronavirus pandemic and ensure that Europe's economy and society are more sustainable, resilient, and better prepared for the challenges and opportunities of green and digital transformation. Member States are developing their recovery and resilience plans to access funding under the Recovery and Resilience Facility.

NextGenerationEU also includes EUR 50.6 billion for the new REACT-EU initiative – as support for reconstruction for the purpose of cohesion and for the European territories. It will make emergency response and recovery measures available to:

2 https://ec.europa.eu/info/strategy/recovery-plan-europe_en

- the European Regional Development Fund (ERDF);
- the European Social Fund (ESF);
- the European Fund for Aid to the Most Deprived (FEAD).

These additional amounts will be made available between 2021 and 2022. NextGenerationEU funds will also contribute to other European programmes and funds such as Horizon 2020, InvestEU, rural development programmes, or the Just Transition Fund (JST). In order to exemplify the abovementioned observations the following data are presented in Table 3.2.

In building the new institutional architecture of the post-pandemic EU, including the economic one, four issues will be particularly important: (a) redefining the boundaries between the state and the market; (b) redefining the principle of subsidiarity; (c) linking the EU policies to the global agenda; (d) learning to respond to long-term structural changes (Buti & Papaconstantinou, 2021).

The COVID-19 pandemic made all countries painfully aware of the importance of well-functioning healthcare systems, as well as the importance of the capacity of national governments and the European community to ensure the health security of citizens. This awareness may open the door to seeking a new arrangement of the relationship between fiscal sustainability and social policy (with higher minimum wages, universal basic income, and more progressive tax systems), as well as provide a stimulus to redefine the concept of economic security of the state and reflect on ways to secure it. Constraints related to global supply chains and the regionalisation of industrial investment, as well as industrial policy per se, will become an important element of this reflection.

The second issue relates to the revision of the interpretation of the principle of subsidiarity. An important aspect, and probably the subject of much controversy, will be to define the boundaries of what belongs to the domain of national policies of Member States and what belongs to the domain of the EU. The pandemic has highlighted the role of coordination at EU level and the need for close cooperation among Member States in crisis situations. One can probably expect a wider shift of competencies in health security

Table 3.2 Money from NextGenerationEU (in EUR)

Recovery and Resilience Facility (RRF)	89.70%
a) of which, loans	47.81%
b) of which, grants	41.89%
React-EU	6.27%
Horizon Europe	0.67%
InvestEU	0.76%
Rural Development	1.00%
Just Transition Fund (JST)	1.35%
RescEU	0.25%
TOTAL:	806.9 billion

Source: own calculation based on https://ec.europa.eu/info/strategy/recovery-plan-europe_pl

policy to the Community, as in the case of large pan-European investment projects – in infrastructure.

The third issue relates to linking the EU's strategic objectives more fully to the global agenda. The lesson of the COVID-19 pandemic points to the need for the EU to actively engage in global policy. In the context of a reshaped geopolitical order, a stronger EU role will be necessary to influence the discussion on global public goods (e.g. health), but also on climate and the digital revolution.

A consequence of a more active EU policy on the global stage will be the necessity to create a situation in which the European single market will have to provide sources of growth and strengthen the sustainability of European value chains. Macroeconomic policies, in turn, will need to reduce dependence on external demand, recognising that persistent current account surpluses are a source of potential risks. Also in this context, consideration should be given to completing the reforms launched with the euro crisis. It also seems necessary to strengthen the international role of the euro, thereby increasing the European Union's influence in the global economy.

The fourth issue is related to responding to long-term changes. The Recovery and Resilience Facility, which assumes the twin transformation, i.e. digital and green, is intended to help with this. In fact, during the pandemic, those sectors of the economy which were characterised by a high level of digitalisation developed dynamically. This requires determination in pursuit of digitisation. At the same time, the dynamic digitisation of social life and the economy raises new challenges regarding regulation, including competition on digital platforms, as well as the issue of protecting employees in the new online environment.

3.4 Economic lessons from the SARS-CoV-2 pandemic

Throughout history, major crises were the turning points for rethinking and reorganising the foundations of socio-economic life, reconfiguring alliances, changing social narratives, and reconfiguring power relations and benefit distribution (Cotula, 2021). It is difficult to say to what extent the economic perturbations resulting from the COVID-19-induced crisis will set in motion a process of redefining the logic of economic operation in its neoliberal form. Certainly, however, in the sphere of both theoretical and practical considerations, there are several issues that can make an important contribution to the revision of the dominant model of the economy. Many of them appeared already in the period before the pandemic, and it only made us aware of their importance, sharpening the dilemmas related to them.

The first of these issues concerns the phenomenon known as ethnonationalism, which refers to *ethno-populism*. Its proponents question the processes of globalisation and the associated neoliberal economic model. The pandemic revealed the growing dysfunctions of the neoliberal economy. Since the world has become more interdependent through the intensification of trade, financial, and communication relations, inequality, uncertainty, and economic asymmetry have increased, while deregulation, privatisation, financialisation, reduction of social benefits, and reduction of spending on social and health security have progressed (Jomo & Chowdhury, 2020). Protagonists of ethno-nationalism emphasise the need to redefine the dominant rules and economic mechanisms towards solutions aimed at building strong national economies, in which public intervention, in both the fiscal and monetary spheres, plays an important role. Manifestations of such views include calls for economic patriotism and recourse to protectionist slogans (protecting jobs, restricting imports through tariff and non-tariff measures, reducing the freedom of capital flows).

The second issue concerns globalisation. For many years there has been an erosion of faith in the reliability of neoliberal solutions in the economic sphere. The undermining of the Washington Consensus and liberal democracy is becoming widespread (Stiglitz, 2002; Rodrik, 2011, 2017). Related to this are calls for deglobalisation of the economy, which were raised long before COVID-19 emerged (Banaszyk et al., 2021). The COVID-19 pandemic added momentum to the criticism of the neoliberal economy. One of its manifestations is redefining the model of supply chains and exposing the need for their geographical diversification to ensure the health and economic security of nation states and communities such as the European Union. At the same time, however, this should not lead to a sustained political drive towards relocation, as this trend may run counter to the need for EU industry to remain competitive internationally. Moreover, both industry leaders and experts point to the limited stability of the investment climate in countries neighbouring the EU and the reluctance to locate (strategic) investments (including R&D) in these countries (De Vet et al., 2021).

The third issue is related to the understanding of international competitiveness. It is considered to be conditioned by the competitive potential of firms in product markets – from the potential of geographical areas and countries to attract mobile factors of production and from the level of labour costs and labour protection policies (Mitschke, 2008, p. 108). As researchers note, the COVID-19 pandemic has revealed additional factors of international competitiveness. These include sanitary security and job protection (Banaszyk et al., 2021). Another observation is related to the confrontation of wage levels of different occupational groups with their hierarchy of social importance. The notion of key professions, the performance of which proves to be particularly important in crisis situations, has become widespread.

The fourth issue relates to the impact of the consequences of the COVID-19 pandemic on the changing balance of economic power globally. China emerges from the pandemic relatively better than the USA. At the same time, however, it is indicated that it will be possible to reduce the role of China as the factory of the world. This is all the more important as, with the passage of time, the likelihood of social unrest, followed by a socio-economic and political crisis, increases in this country. Consequently, and there are many indications of this, a change in the rules of the global economy and the formation of new patterns of economic activity are occurring before our eyes (Banaszyk et al., 2021).

The fifth issue concerns a new way of thinking about the relationship between monetary and fiscal policy. In the realm of monetary and fiscal policy, most countries have pursued similar actions. On the one hand, central banks have injected unprecedented amounts into the private sector through purchases of private and public sector securities and direct credit to the economy. On the other hand, governments are trying to maintain the stability of household incomes through job retention programmes. Central to this new discussion is the combination of fiscal and monetary policy and the role of central banks.

The sixth issue is related to the innovation of the EU crisis response. The European Commission has proposed a EUR 750 billion European Recovery Fund, dubbed NextGenerationEU. This would allow the Commission to borrow in the capital markets on behalf of the EU and to disburse the borrowing to Member States in the form of grants and loans (Skidelsky, 2020). This is a hitherto unknown instrument in the EU history (admittedly, now adopted for a limited time). It may signal new thinking about economic and financial policy coordination from the Community level.

The COVID-19 pandemic had a very strong negative impact both on the global economy and on national economies. The economic shock caused by the pandemic resulted in a number of short-term and long-term consequences for the economy. In response to the economic crisis, which partly took the shape of a recession, international institutions, national governments, and central banks undertook extensive, often unconventional fiscal and monetary policy measures. The experience of the COVID-19 pandemic and the struggle with its economic consequences have triggered a lively discussion on revising the dominant theories of neoliberal economics and its rudimentary assumptions. At the same time, the frameworks of a new economic order in response to the consequences of the economic crisis caused by the COVID-19 pandemic are becoming increasingly clear. Many of them are constructed in opposition to the rules of classical economics and the neoliberal economic model. To what extent they will influence the reconstruction of the global economic order is still difficult to assess, but they will certainly contribute to changes in the way nation states conduct their economic policies.

References

Afsahi, A., Beausoleil, E., Dean, R., Ercan S.A., & Gagnon, J.-P. (2020), Democracy in a Global Emergency Five Lessons from the COVID-19 Pandemic. *Democratic Theory*, 7(2), pp. v–xix. https://doi.org/10.3167/dt.2020.070201

Baldwin, R., & Weder di Mauro, B. (2020). *Economics in the Time of Covid-19: A New eBook*. VoxEU/CEPR Press. Available from: https://voxeu.org/article/economics-time-covid-19-new-ebook

Banaszyk, P., Deszczyński, P., Gorynia, M., & Malaga, K. (2021). Przesłanki modyfikacji wybranych koncepcji ekonomicznych na skutek pandemii COVID-19. Gospodarka Narodowa. *The Polish Journal of Economics*, 305(1), pp. 3–86. DOI:10.33119/GN/132485

Buti, M. (2020). *A Tale of Two Crises: Lessons from the Financial Crisis to Prevent the Great Fragmentation*. VoxEU/CEPR Press. Available from: https://voxeu.org/article/lessons-financial-crisis-prevent-great-fragmentation

Buti, M., & Papacostantinou, G. (2021). *Reshaping Economic Policy in the EU in the Post-Covid World*. VoxEU/CEPR Press. Available from: https://voxeu.org/article/reshaping-european-economic-integration-post-covid-world

Communication from the Commission to the Council (2020). *Communication from the Commission to the Council on the Activation of the General Escape Clause of the Stability and Growth Pact*. Brussels, 20.03.2020. COM(2020) 123 final

Communication from the Commission to the Council (2021). *Communication from the Commission to the Council. One Year since the Outbreak of COVID-19: Fiscal Policy Response*. Brussels, 03.03.2021.

Cotula, L. (2021), Towards a Political Economy of the COVID-19 Crisis: Reflections on an Agenda for Research and Action. *World Development*, 138(February), pp. 105235. https://doi.org/10.1016/j.worlddev.2020.105235

Dalglish, S.L. (2020). COVID-19 Gives the Lie to Global Health Expertise. *The Lancet*, 395 (10231, April 11), p. 1189. https://doi.org/10.1016/S0140-6736(20)30739-X

De Vet, J.M., Nigohosyan, D., Núñez Ferrer, J., Gross, A.K., Kuehl, S., & Flickenschild M. (2021). *Impacts of the COVID-19 Pandemic on EU Industries Policy Department for Economic, Scientific and Quality of Life Policies Directorate-General for Internal Policies*. PE 662.903 – March 2021.

European Council (2020). *Special Meeting of the European Council (17, 18, 19, 20 and 21 July 2020) – Conclusions. EUCO 10/20*. Brussels, 21.07.2020. Available from: https://data.consilium.europa.eu/doc/document/ST-10-2020-INIT/en/pdf

Fuentes, M.N. & Moder, I. (2020). The Scarring Effects of Past Crises on The Global Economy. *Economic Bulletin*, 8, 46–52.

Gugushvili, A., & Mckee, M. (2021). The COVID-19 Pandemic and War. *Scandinavian Journal of Public Health*, https://doi.org/10.1177/1403494821993732

Inoue, H., & Todo, Y. (2019). *Propagation of Economic Shocks Through Supply Chains*. VoxEU/CEPR Press. Available from: https://voxeu.org/article/propagation-economic-shocks-through-supply-chains

Jomo, K.S., & Chowdhury, A. (2020). COVID-19 Pandemic Recession and Recovery. *Development (Society for International Development)*, 1–12. https://doi.org/10.1057/s41301-020-00262-0

Kloet, J., Lin, J., & Chow, Y.F. (2020). We are Doing Better: Biopolitical Nationalism and the COVID-19 Virus in East Asia. *European Journal of Cultural Studies*, 23(4), pp. 635–640. https://doi.org/10.1177/1367549420928092

Malta, D.C., Szwarcwald, C.L., Barros, M., Gomes, C.S., Machado, Í.E., Souza Júnior, P., Romero, D.E., Lima, M.G., Damacena, G.N., Pina, M.F., Freitas, M., Werneck, A.O., Silva, D., Azevedo, L.O., & Gracie, R. (2020). The COVID-19 Pandemic and Changes in Adult Brazilian Lifestyles: A Cross-Sectional Study, A pandemia da COVID-19 e as mudanças no estilo de vida dos brasileiros adultos: um estudo transversal, 2020. *Epidemiologia e servicos de saude : revista do Sistema Unico de Saude do Brasil*, 29(4), e2020407. https://doi.org/10.1590/S1679-49742020000400026

Mentzer, J.T., Flint, D.J., Hult, G., & Tomas, M. (2001). Logistics Service Quality as a Segment-Customized Process. *Journal of Marketing*, 65(4), pp. 82–104. https://doi.org/10.1509/jmkg.65.4.82.18390

Mitschke, A. (2008). *The Influence of National Competition Policy on the International Competitiveness of Nations: A Contribution to the Debate on International Competition Rules*. Springer Science & Business Media

Pla-Barber, J., Villar, C.H.., & Narula J. (2021). Governance of Global Value Chains after the Covid-19 Pandemic: A New Wave of Regionalization? *BRQ Business Research Quarterly*, 24(3), pp. 204–213. https://doi.org/10.1177/23409444211020761

Rodrik, D. (2011). *The Globalization Paradox: Democracy and the Future of the World Economy. Norton and Company*. W.W. Norton.

Rodrik, D. (2017). *Populism and the Economics of Globalization*. AIB Conference, Dubai, 2017.

Scambler, G. (2020). Covid-19 as a 'Breaching Experiment': Exposing the Fractured Society. *Health Sociology Review*, 29(2), pp. 140–148. https://doi.org/10.1080/14461242.2020.1784019

Skidelsky, R. (2020). Economic Recovery in the Age of COVID-19. *Intereconomics*, 55(6), pp. 345–349. https://doi.org/10.1007/s10272-020-0929-6

Stiglitz, J.E. (2002). *Globalization and its Discontents*. W.W. Norton

Thomson, S. (2020). COVID-19 Emergency Measures and the Impending Authoritarian Pandemic. *Journal of Law and the Biosciences*, 7(1, January–June), pp. lsaa064. https://doi.org/10.1093/jlb/lsaa064

Yeyati, E.L. (2021). Social and Economic Impact of COVID-19. Brookings Global Working Paper #158, June, Global Economy and Development program at Brookings, Available from: www.brookings.edu/global

4 SARS-CoV-2 pandemic

An economic analysis of regulatory intervention

Artur Nowak-Far

The pandemic caused by the SARS-CoV-2 virus (hereafter referred to as the "COVID-19 pandemic") is an unprecedented phenomenon in recent world economic history. The novelty of this phenomenon does not arise from the biological scale of the pandemic challenge – the world has dealt with pandemics many times before. What is unique about the COVID-19 pandemic, however, is that it occurred at a time when most of the world's countries had more-or-less efficient health systems and were operating as open economies – with extensive trade relations and large-scale movements of people across borders.

The pandemic was also a signal that the systems which countries had put in place were not fully resilient to large-scale pandemic challenges and that these systems needed to be rebuilt to better respond to such challenges in the future.

In this context, this analysis aims to verify the following hypotheses:

Hypothesis 1: The COVID-19 pandemic highlighted the important role of states and the state-controlled intervention systems operating within them.

Hypothesis 2: The response of states to the economic phenomena resulting from the COVID-19 pandemic consisted of a transition from an external controllability to an internal controllability model, in which the locus of control was placed in a position characterising actors operating under conditions of greatly reduced rationality.

Hypothesis 3: The initial response of states to the COVID-19 pandemic was relatively uniform, and characterised by a significant level of imitativeness; as time passed and the transition from an external controllability to a relatively internal controllability model took place, the measures of regulatory intervention varied strongly.

Hypothesis 4: The diversity of regulatory intervention measures was strongly determined by individual states' ability to activate internal and external resources; in turn, the intervention scenario with respect to the economy was strongly determined by (a) what the state used as measures to combat the pandemic in the external controllability phase and

DOI: 10.4324/9781003353805-5

(b) the influence of the external environment, the strength of the impact of which was determined by the strength of the links of the states' economies with the world (i.e. on the level of openness of these economies).

Hypothesis 5: Countries with relatively open economies had to use tools of more intensive regulatory influence, and not so much because of the adopted lockdown model, but because of the perceived external effects.

The "Covid" policy-mix analysis has a relatively rich literature. One can find literature on policies in individual countries in relation to this issue, as well as comparative studies and those relating to selected specific issues, e.g. mobility or the importance of the governance/management model (Carter, 2020). The analysis model itself has been presented by Nihit Goyal and Michael Hawlett (Goyal & Hawlett, 2021). To a certain extent, it draws rather too far-reaching, because premature, conclusions. Especially the comparative models are arbitrary – they use a criterion of intensity of regulatory intervention (or a similar one) but do not explain exactly the differences in this respect. Therefore, one should treat the regulatory empirical material from this paper with great caution and should limit oneself only to the conclusions that can most safely be drawn from it.

4.1 The model of fighting the SARS-CoV-2 pandemic

An analysis of most of the regulatory interventions of the world's countries in response to the COVID-19 pandemic indicates that none of them were prepared for this highly destabilising external stimulus. At first, social and economic policy authorities were not even aware of the scale of challenge it has produced. However, as the number of people infected rose and caused an increase in the burden on health services to grow very rapidly, the scale of the threat began to be adequately comprehended and assessed. It was at this point that countries began to introduce the first measures, which are now collectively referred to as *lockdown*, but which encompass various public policy measures. In general, lockdown measures aim to radically restrict physical contact among people in order to reduce the possibility of contagion. They therefore include:

(a) a ban on movement;
(b) a ban on private and public gatherings;
(c) closure of establishments that bring people together, especially educational institutions and shops;
(d) drastic restriction of social and economic activities to those forms which are deemed necessary to ensure order and security.

In only a few countries did the lockdown extend to border closures. In many countries, each of the applied lockdown measures had its own modalities, essentially reflecting, on the one hand, the model of functioning of the society before the outbreak of the pandemic, people's habits, as well as the possibility of enforcing specific restrictions, and, on the other hand, the impact of the pandemic. The sheer dynamics of the spread of the COVID-19 virus was also a differentiating factor, as it gave a kind of advantage (time to prepare) to countries that are, in a way, outside the main routes of passenger and cargo traffic, and thus outside the routes of global transmission of viruses such as COVID-19. Such countries include, in particular, those located in the Pacific islands, e.g. Nauru, Palau, and Samoa. In Nauru, the first case of COVID-19 infection was found only in July 2021; in Palau and Samoa, cases of infection have not been found at all, while in most countries of the world, the first officially recorded infections with this virus were recorded within a short time span from January 2020 (when the Chinese health service confirmed that a new, then unknown, virus had emerged in the city of Wuhan) to early April 2020, when it was found in most of the world.

In addition to lockdown, in most countries worldwide also a regime of keeping a physical distance from one another (so-called social distance) has been adopted; different models of testing people for infection with the virus, as well as a quarantine and tracing regime, have been applied to people suspected of carrying the virus (e.g. because of contact with sick people) or people who could spread the virus (hence, in the Democratic Republic of Congo, tracing and mandatory testing were applied to all travellers – also within the borders of the country).

It is worth noting that although the lockdown regime and other measures to limit the spread of the COVID-19 virus have been applied quite universally, a closer look at the measures reveals some variation (in terms of the territorial scope of application in a given country, in terms of measures applied to restrict contact, etc.). Even within the European Union there has been some variation, due to the policy adopted in Sweden, whereby very mild measures were used, in an effort to slowly acquire collective immunity. For posterity, it should be noted that the primary motive for these measures was to protect national health systems from overload – hence countries with sufficiently developed systems could afford more extensive and altogether less socio-economically disruptive protective measures. Such countries certainly include Sweden.

4.2 The economic consequences of the SARS-CoV-2 pandemic and the physical containment measures such as lockdown

Epidemic phenomena have a number of obvious economic consequences. They always result in a decrease in productivity due to the sheer loss of population and absenteeism of workers due to sickness; thus, they contribute to an increase in the under-utilisation of other factors of production; also in relation to modern societies, pandemics increase the total social costs of treating infected patients, as well as the secondary, often long-term, social costs of families affected by the pandemic.

Brahmbhatt and Dutta's studies (published as recently as 2008) suggest that the most important factor negatively affecting the economy, however, are the pandemic containment measures themselves, which can be called secondary consequences.(Brahmbhatt & Dutta, 2008). The literature notes that there are four channels of transmission of stimuli negative to the economy (Maliszewska, 2021):

(a) the channel of employment reduction;
(b) the channel of increased international transaction costs;
(c) the channel of reduced travel;
(d) the channel of decreasing demand for goods and services requiring direct contact between the parties to the transaction.

With regard to the consequences of secondary public policy measures used to contain the pandemic, the following should be mentioned in particular:

(a) reduction of economic activity resulting directly or indirectly from the lockdown regime;
(b) cost pressures resulting from the need for economic organisations to adapt to the new conditions – in particular to reorganise work in conditions of temporary or permanent absence of workers from their places of work;
(c) strong reduction in demand and its shift from the offer of enterprises of contact-based (physically) provided goods/services to the offer of goods/services that can be rendered.

In addition, it should be noted that these effects are captured statistically. In dynamic terms, it should also be taken into account that some industries experience a time-shift phenomenon as a result of any reduction in demand. This implies that, for a certain period of time, they bear the costs of storage, as regards both products needed for manufacture and end products, yet after some time, the deferred demand reappears and in an amount reflecting the current and deferred demand. Thus, in such cases what is referred to as friction costs emerges in the economy.

Ultimately, the pandemic caused – in all countries of the world – a fall in production and levels of trade, as well as the resulting secondary phenomena involving losses to enterprises in many economic sectors, as well as unemployment and underemployment.

The already mentioned analysis by Brahmbhatt and Dutta provisionally estimates (with emphasis on the conservative nature of this estimate) that, on a global scale, the COVID-19 pandemic caused (i.e. can be attributed to) a 10% decline in employment, a 25% increase in the cost to exporters and importers of goods, a 50% decline in tourism turnover, and a 15% decline in overall household demand for all goods and services, with most of the decline occurring in the direct-contact industries. It is only the conservatism of these calculations that allows them to be accepted, given the failure to take into account the frictional phenomena identified here. In any case, these phenomena did occur and must have had a negative impact on global economic growth.

However, due to the economic divisions of countries already existing before the pandemic, including in particular the division of labour resulting primarily from a specific map of comparative and competitive advantages, all the phenomena considered in this analysis had an asymmetric form. It is estimated, for example, that the direct impact of the pandemic resulted in a decline in global GDP of just over 2.1% per year, but distributed unevenly across countries. Economically weaker countries, especially those with strong economic integration with China, are more affected by the pandemic in this respect. A conservative estimate indicates the fall in GDP in China alone at 3.7%; the pandemic has also increased the trade costs (imports and exports) relating to Chinese products, worsening their competitiveness; however, it is not clear whether – given the widespread nature of the pandemic – this process is offset by the loss of competitiveness relating to other economies and how significantly it affects the terms of trade. Countries that are more economically integrated with China have also recorded declines higher than the world average: Cambodia and Thailand by around 6%, Vietnam by 2.7%. It should be noted, however, that to a significant extent this decline was the result of a significant slowdown in tourism. The different situation of these countries is also indicated by the dynamics of the value of their exports – in relation to Vietnam, where the drop was only 1% (evidently at the expense of China), to Laos – 3.6%, Cambodia – 3.9%, and Singapore by 4.4%.

By comparison, the EU has seen its GDP fall by 3.4%, Japan by 4.6%, and the United States by 3.4%. At the same time, relatively smaller negative consequences of the pandemic have been recorded in countries in North Africa, sub-Saharan Africa, and the Middle East. The less conservative estimates are more than double for each of the given values.

4.3 The policy mix applied

Assessing the policy mix applied by different countries of the world to combat the economic impact of the COVID-19 pandemic is difficult primarily because:

(a) the lockdown measures themselves adopted by individual countries show significant variation in terms of specific arrangements;
(b) the lockdown measures were adopted under different models of law enforcement, which implies that the assessment must take into account not only the formal intensity of the measures adopted, but also their actual intensity, as determined by the capacity of the competent state bodies to exercise authority over the entire national territory;

(c) even relatively identical lockdown measures have different (asymmetric) impact on the economies of different countries due to their structure; in large territorial states with complex regional economic structures, the impact of these measures may also be asymmetric.

In addition, it should be noted that an important determinant of the vulnerability of the economies to what we can generally term "pandemic impact" is their openness (regional and especially international) and their integration into international production and exchange networks. This is clearly shown by the example of Sweden (an important exporter of goods and services), where the applied policy mix was geared towards the least possible disruption to society (and therefore to the economy), but which did not avoid a negative (largely exogenous) demand shock due to the reduction of trade with Sweden by other countries.

The adopted lockdown measures also show significant dynamics of change. In the first phase, individual countries adopted a relatively unified policy mix. The variation in the intensity of its measures was mainly due to the scale of infections, the recorded number of deaths, and the observation by the authorities of the cross-border and interregional spread of the COVID-19 virus, as well as the assessment by the authorities of the efficiency of national healthcare. Thus, for example within the group of the EU Member States, Italy had the widest catalogue of lockdown measures with the highest relative intensity; whereas in Sweden the catalogue of measures was the least extensive and the measures themselves were of low intensity. Especially due to the efficiency of the health service, there were no major problems in Sweden – but with the important exception that the Swedish authorities failed to stop a significant number of deaths among the elderly. A significant feature of the policy mix of the first phase of the pandemic was also the lack of vaccination – for the simple and obvious reason that no suitable vaccines were available.

An important feature of the applied measures in the second and subsequent waves of the pandemic was the introduction of lockdown measures that were far less economically disruptive than those applied in the first wave. In this context, the most important was the opening of borders (with some of them being closed to passenger traffic from countries where the number of infections was above the accepted norm for the countries concerned). Vaccination was an important new measure in later waves of the pandemic. In the group of EU Member States, only France made it compulsory; nevertheless, it should be noted that various other countries (e.g. Germany) have adopted solutions that strongly enforce vaccination.

In terms of measures to stimulate the economy, individual countries worldwide have applied measures that significantly reflect their lockdown regimes – hence the basic regularity has been the introduction of business support measures proportional to the intensity of the impact of this regime on economic life. It is worth noting that individual countries used

Table 4.1 COVID-19 measures of the first wave of the pandemic

	A	*B*	*BL*	*CY*	*CZ*	*DK*	*EST*	*SF*	*F*	*GR*	*HR*	*ESP*	*IRL*	*LT*	*L*	*LV*	*MT*	*NL*	*D*	*PL*	*PT*	*RU*	*SL*	*Slo*	*S*	*H*	*I*
Lockdown																											
• ban on movement	X																			X	X	X	X	X		X	X
• ban on business activity	X	X	X		X	X	X	X	X	X	X	X	X	X	X	X	X	X	X	X	X	X	X	X		X	X
• closing of educational institutions	X	X	X	X	X	X	X	X	X	X	X	X	X	X	X	X	X	X	X	X	X	X	X	X		X	X
• ban on gatherings	X	X	X	X	X	X	X	X	X	X	X	X	X	X	X	X	X	X	X	X	X	S	X	X	X	X	X
Order of social distancing	X	X	X	X	X	X	X	X	X	X	X	X	X	X	X	X	X	x	X	X	X	X	X	X		X	X
Closing of borders	X									X	X	X															X
Quarantine and tracing	X	X	X	X	X	X	X	X	X	X	X	X	X	X	X	X	X	X	X	X	X	X	X	X	X	X	X
Testing and special treatment	X	X	X	X	X	X	X	X	X	X	X	X	X	X	X	X	X	X	X	X	X	X	X	X	X	X	X

Source: Author's own elaboration.
x – low invasiveness
X – high invasiveness

Table 4.2 Measures in the following waves

	A	*B*	*BL*	*CY*	*CZ*	*DK*	*EST*	*SF*	*F*	*GR*	*HR*	*ESP*	*IRL*	*LT*	*L*	*LV*	*MT*	*NL*	*D*	*PL*	*PT*	*RU*	*SL*	*Slo*	*S*	*H*	*I*
Lockdown																											
• ban on movement																											
• ban on business activity	X	x	x	x	X	X	x	X	X	X	X	X	x	x	X	X	x	x	x	x	x	x	x	x		X	x
• closing of educational institutions	X	X	X	X	X	X	X	X	X	X	X	X	X	X	X	X	X	X	X	X	X	X	X	X		X	X
• ban on gatherings	X	x	x	x	X	X	x	X	X	X	X	X	x	x	X	X	x	x	x	x	x	x	x	x		x	x
Order of social distancing	X	X	X	X	X	X	X	X	X	X	X	X	X	X	X	X	X	X	X	X	X	X	X	X	X	X	X
Closing of borders																											
Quarantine and tracing	X	X	X	X	X	X	X	X	X	X	X	X	X	X	X	X	X	X	X	X	X	X	X	X	X	X	X
Quarantine and tracing	x	x	x	x	X	X	x	x	X	X	x	x	x	x	X	x	x	x	x	x	x	x	x	x	x		
Vaccination	X	x	x	x	X	X	x	X	X	X	X	X	x	x	X	X	x	x	X	x	x	x	x	x	x	x	X

Source: Author's own elaboration.
x – low invasiveness
X – high invasiveness

two different stimulus channels: through direct assistance to enterprises or through stimulating household demand. In most countries both channels were used – but in different proportions. In the EU, the first system was dominant, while in the United States, much more than elsewhere, emphasis was placed on the measures of the second system. This was also justified by the expected – due to the level of regulatory job security – dynamics of rising unemployment. The measures of the second and subsequent waves of the pandemic differ even among the EU countries; this differentiation is based on a greater or lesser link between aid measures and the structure of social policy.

For example, in Austria, where the first cases of infection were identified in the first half of March 2020, a total lockdown and border closure (from 16 March to 16 April 2020) was applied for a short period. From mid-April 2020, the authorities started a gradual easing – small shops, building material shops, and garden shops were allowed to open. In May 2020, the cosmetics industry was allowed to operate. At the beginning of June of the same year, the borders with neighbouring countries (except Slovenia) and Switzerland were opened; by mid-June, traffic was allowed with almost all European countries and a significant number of third countries (except Brazil, India, Russia, and the United States). At the end of the first phase of the pandemic, businesses were already allowed to reopen – with the ban remaining for restaurants, bars, and shops. A second, milder lockdown was ordered in November 2020. In the second wave, a lockdown was ordered that lasted between 3 November and 6 December 2020 – this one, however, did not cover most "no-contact" or limited-contact industries. A third lockdown was ordered on 26 December 2020 until 18 January 2021 (extended to 25 January). Thereafter, the lockdown was already only regional in scope – hence "light" lockdowns were ordered in Vienna and Burgenland from 1 April to 17 May 2021.

With regard to the policy mix of the first and subsequent phases of lockdown, an example of a country that has incorporated policy measures into social policy is Bulgaria. This one, in order to limit the negative effects of the pandemic, put special emphasis precisely on social policy, which in this particular context can also be interpreted as choosing primarily household income as the essential channel for introducing additional liquidity into the economy. Hence, in Bulgaria, in order to combat the economic impact of the pandemic, tax reliefs were introduced for households with children in need of constant care, supplementary benefits for parents (due to children remaining at home, outside the institutional pre-school and school system; special supplementary benefits for pensioners were also provided). Bulgaria also reduced (with effect until the end of 2021) the VAT rate on restaurant services, books, baby food, wine, beer, tourism services, fitness services (to 9%), and applied a VAT and duty reduction mechanism on medical supplies. In addition, Bulgarians introduced a number of programmes for labour market support measures, including wage subsidies, financial support for professional activation and re-branding, as well as for those deactivated as a result of the pandemic. These took the form of the "Keep Me," "Work for You," and "Employed Parents" programmes, support for artists and agricultural producers. As far as wage subsidisation is concerned, the most important easing was the financing from the state budget of 60% of the wage costs (including social security contributions) of enterprises which would otherwise have had to lay off employees. Bulgaria has also introduced tourist vouchers for its citizens in the border regions. In addition, in Bulgaria – as in other EU countries – the deadlines for payment of certain taxes have been extended.

An example of a differently designed – but thus rather typical of the EU – business support programme is Croatia. Here, a deferral of the deadlines for payment of public levies was introduced (three months with the possibility of extension for a further three months), as well as the possibility to remit tax liabilities of enterprises affected by the pandemic (if they employed at least ten employees). Important, and by no means typical, support measures adopted to help those affected by the COVID-19 pandemic included: interest-free loan support for local authorities, increased advance payments to beneficiaries of the EU funds, the implementation of a programme of low-interest micro-loans and new credit lines, a loan guarantee programme, a programme of intervention purchases (of agricultural crops and processed food products, among others). In Croatia, a programme of support for the "leisure" industry (cultural, sports-related, and event sectors) has also been important.

A generally similar (in terms of logic) support system was adopted in the Czech Republic. This country decided to adopt a system ensuring that enterprises affected by lockdown measures continue their economic activity and maintain employment. Already at the beginning of the restrictions, a conditional remittance of social security contributions (for companies with up to 50 employees) or wage compensation (the companies' choice) was introduced. It also established – for the period from April to December 2020 – a system of covering 50% of rental costs (under the conditions of an official limitation of 30% – until June 2020, and then without such a limitation. Quarantined employees were paid, from March to June 2020, a compensation benefit, and pensioners were paid a one-time "Covid" benefit of CZK 5,000). The support system also covered companies in cultural services, sports, tourism, agriculture, restaurant services, bus transport, and others that would have to cease operations. Slightly later, a refund of 60% or 100% of wages was extended to employees of enterprises directly or indirectly affected by measures restricting economic activity. The Czech Republic also adopted a number of tax support instruments resulting in a reduction of the burdens on enterprises:

(a) accelerated depreciation of fixed assets acquired in 2020 and 2021;
(b) reduction of the effective personal income tax rate;

(c) reduction (by 25%) in vehicle tax;
(d) reduction in VAT on selected services provided by hotels, restaurants, cultural, and sports businesses.

In addition, the Czech Republic adopted solutions which generated fiscal transfers to enterprises. This group of solutions includes:

(a) allowing the loss for 2020 to be offset against the tax bases of 2018 and 2019 (i.e. in other words, introducing a carry-loss-back system in this respect);
(b) payment of a compensation benefit for self-employed persons and small companies (of CZK 1,000, and for construction companies – CZK 500);
(c) special support programme for companies whose turnover has fallen by 50% (year-on-year) – to cover fixed costs.

Some other EU Member States have introduced a system of differentiated (generally by type of tax) tax deferrals (e.g. Denmark, Poland, and Hungary) and established a public bank credit guarantee scheme (e.g. also in Denmark), a state-supported export credit guarantee scheme (e.g. Denmark and Sweden), an investment intervention scheme for companies that have lost financing as a result of the pandemic (e.g. Denmark).

It should be emphasised that the support system in the European Union was very generous as its Member States benefitted (and still benefit) from support from the EU budget and from a major relaxation of the rules on public aid to enterprises (in principle, prohibited under Article 107 of the Treaty on the Functioning of the EU). This support from the EU budget initially came from the Solidarity Fund and involved the reallocation of a number of budget sums to deal with the impact of the pandemic. The main channels for providing liquidity to countries were balance-of-payments assistance, the use of funds from the European Financial Stabilisation Mechanism (EFSM), and, in particular, from a new SURE instrument (Support to Mitigate Unemployment Risks in an Emergency). In 2021, the first funds were released from an instrument containing massive funds (just over EUR 2 trillion), coming partly from the EU budget and partly from the Union's issuance of debt – *NextGenerationEU* (NGEU). An important way of supporting the capacity of the EU Member States to deal with the impact of the pandemic was also providing the possibility to jointly negotiate with suppliers of medical supplies (especially vaccines) the terms of their delivery.

In the United States, a universal legal framework for helping economic entities to deal with the negative consequences of the pandemic was established in the form of the CARES (Coronavirus Aid, Relief, and Economic Security Act) (Public Law, 2020), which provided for programmes to allocate over USD 2.2 trillion for this purpose. The principal channels of impact of the US policy in dealing with the aftermath of the pandemic and its control measures were:

(a) households;
(b) the financial and credit system (Sahm, 2021).

Through the former channel, the US authorities sought to provide households with liquidity and thereby also stimulate their demand for goods and services. An important programme with the same effect was also one geared towards increasing the provision of publicly funded health services. In the latter channel – the financial and credit channel – solutions were adopted to facilitate the issuance of debt by enterprises and its placement on the market: the reduction of interest rates by the Federal Reserve Bank and the establishment of preferential credit lines partly financed by the federal budget were also important tools of support related to this channel.

An important component of actions of a fiscal nature was also an impact through monetary policy tools. These have typically involved lowering interest rates (also in an inflationary conditions – a relative novelty), as well as the use of various liquidity mechanisms (e.g. in the form of even new tools, such as the European Central Bank's PELTRO, based on a series of longer-term refinancing operations with interest rates below the average MRO (main refinancing operations) of a given day, as well as the expansion of the catalogue of assets that can be subject to open market operations, and the easing (or rather increasing flexibility) of capital requirements for credit institutions undertaking credit issuance actions.

Monetary policy was also a certain component of the policy mix in some countries. China has allowed the yuan (RMB) to fluctuate freely in the (largely fulfilled) hope that fluctuations in its exchange rate against leading international currencies will have a toning effect on trade with the world. In the EU and the United States, exchange rate policy did not matter much. In smaller countries without international currencies, the rule was to increase foreign exchange controls, the primary motive of which was to defend the balance of payments (but which – at the same time – acted as a substitute for devaluation to create a trade balance surplus).

4.4 Interpretation and conclusions

The pandemic caused by the SARS-CoV-2 virus came as a surprise to all the countries of the world, including China, where the first outbreaks were detected. Their response to the identified cases of infection with a previously unknown virus and their subsequent reactions correspond to a model of decision-making under high uncertainty, and therefore within a model of greatly reduced (but increasing) rationality. In terms that refer to the location of the locus of control, the implication is that at the very beginning of the pandemic, states were externally controlled (i.e. their locus of control was outside of them), i.e. they succumbed to the influence of their environment, but – as could be expected in the absence of a fundamental structural change in the pandemic – as time went on, the locus of control shifted inwards. This means that they have managed to regain some (albeit limited) ability to influence the situation. This differentiation is shown in Figure 4.1.

The efficient market hypothesis and population ecology theory are extreme concepts. The former assumes that all participants in a given social system have full knowledge about that system. This assumption is connected with the hypothetical assumption that the subject of a given system – its actor – has unlimited access to the information he needs to make all decisions (Burton, 2003). The population ecology theory, on the other hand, assumes the complete impossibility of obtaining relevant information about the system in which an intervention is being considered. Moreover, it assumes that no rational predictive model can be created at all, since there are significant and unpredictable turbulences in social systems, which are the result of the random dynamics of these systems and which human beings have no way of influencing. Hence, periods of stabilisation of systems (in equilibrium or near equilibrium) are merely the work of chance (Hannan & Freeman, 1977). They result from the accidental (and thus

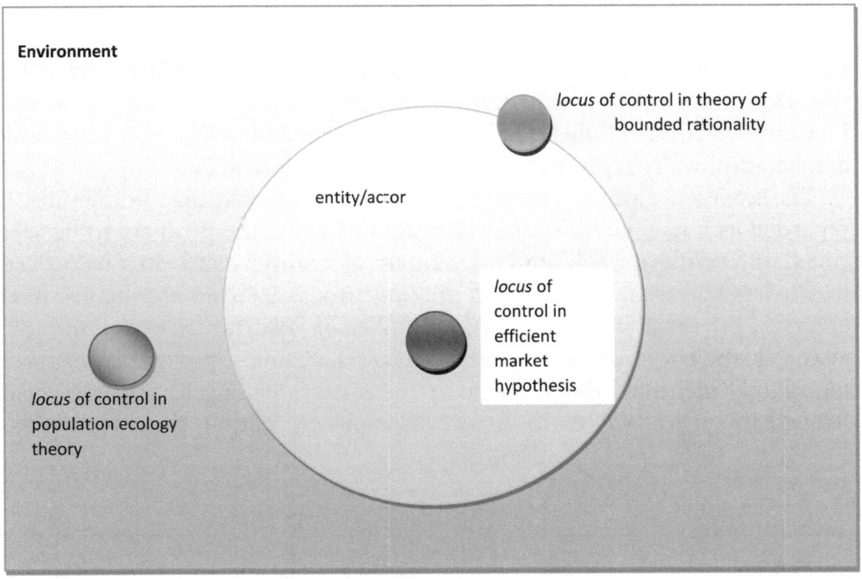

Figure 4.1 *Locus* of control in model behaviours of entities in efficient market hypothesis, theory of bounded rationality, and population ecology theory. Source: Author's own elaboration.

completely uncontrollable by the individual/actor) adjustment of his own environment to external conditions which, from his point of view, are in a state of chaos.

In this context, the theory of bounded rationality describes the transition between the population ecology theory to a system in which, as a result of the accumulation of information, the conditions of the efficient market hypothesis are not actually met, but which nevertheless reduces its chaotic nature and increases the rationality of its participants. The decision-making process in the model designed on the basis of the theory of bounded rationality is imperfect, as the lack of some information may significantly impair this process due to the fact that not all planning premises are known and verified as true here (Kahneman & Tversky, 2000). The rules of logical inference dictate that the outcome of a planning inference here cannot be certain as to its qualification in the dichotomous category of "true" and "not true." It is worth noting that a threat to such rationality of the decision-making process in this model is not only posed by areas where information was unavailable, but also those where reliance was placed on one's own or someone else's social experience. For in this case, it turns out that it may firstly, not be interpreted correctly, and secondly, that it relatively often leads to partial inferences that are carried out correctly. Hence, the assumptions for further inferences obtained in this way are not true (in the logical sense, they form incorrect syllogisms). This means that similar actions of the states around the world, based in many cases on imitation, carry a significant risk of sub-optimality.

In assessing the actions of states relating to the pandemic, it should also be noted that the decision-making model itself did not show any deviation from the model identified, for example, by Gerald Zaltman, Robert L. Duncan and Jonny Holbek (Zaltman, Duncan & Holbek, 1973) This model can be graphically represented as follows (see Figure 4.2):

The emergence of the pandemic of such a significant magnitude must be regarded as a new circumstance that did not allow the problem to be identified sufficiently quickly and adequately to reality – and thus to proceed to further stages of the decision-making process. Given the highly likely errors of inference in such a case, a number of governments (including, for example, the UK government and, it seems, the Chinese government as well) incorrectly identified the problem at the outset, leading to attitudes being formed in such a way as to distort decisions by leading them to favour a

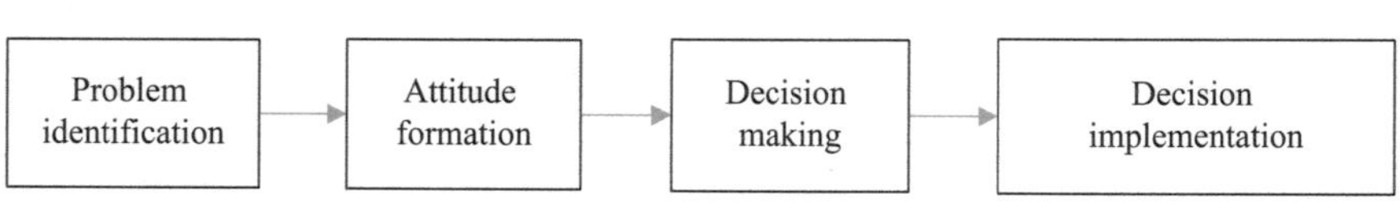

Figure 4.2 A model of decision-making. Source: based on (Zaltman et al., 1973).

decision to limit the response. Once the extent of the pandemic was recognised, such governments reiterated the process.

The pandemic demonstrated that the state has exclusive rights to many of the tools necessary to fight large-scale pandemics. At the same time, the pandemic revealed the strength of interrelationships among the states – the speed of its spread confirmed the significant degree of openness of economies and their integration: in this context, it also revealed that in their actions to combat the pandemic and its economic consequences, states create (positive and negative) external effects and are themselves subject to such effects generated in other states (a good example is Germany, which in the first phase of the pandemic did not have to close its border with Poland as Poland did it – with obvious, and at the time considered desirable, effects for Germany). This regularity revealed the incompatibility of the actions of states in this regard, which was compounded by the secondary asymmetric effect of both exogenous (i.e. originating in other states) and endogenous factors (for which the incentives were the actions of the state itself). At the normative level, this altogether complex cause–effect conditionality has revealed the necessity for all these states to apply policies that are compatible with each other, which means that they will create positive external consequences. At the same time, this interdependence has shown that the actions of states in their response to the COVID-19 pandemic can be interpreted as structures of reciprocity – i.e. in terms developed by Serg-Christophe Kolm. This researcher identifies these structures as *simple* (in which single-value benefits are exchanged at the same time) and *complex* (in which no such simple exchange occurs). Kolm further divides complex forms of reciprocity into specific types, which are characterised by the essence of the relationship between, on the one hand, facts (which are actions, feelings, attitudes and evaluations made by people in their mutual relations) directly related to motivations (which are equilibrium-seeking, affinity, desire to continue the relationship), and, on the other hand, people (individuals or groups of people) who may be affected by these facts. Based on the differences precisely in this respect, Kolm distinguishes the following reciprocal structures:

(a) *basic*, in which there are only two entities and two facts – and the reciprocation can be simple or complex; in the latter case, the reciprocation may not be one-off, nor be in a direct motivational relation to the action initiating it;
(b) *extended*, in which the number of non-initiating entities in the relation exceeds 2, which means that at least there is an entity I that initiates the action (I→),[1] an entity towards which I has directly taken an

1 Reciprocation (towards I) can therefore be designated as "I←." When we know that A is the reciprocator, the notation will be as follows: "I←A."

action (→A) and another entity (B…, n); extended structures may take the form of:

- *generalised one*, where, if I→A, then A→B or even A→(n-I),
- *general ones*, where, equally, I→A, then A→B or even A→(n-I), but on the condition that the initiating benefit is made to B or any other entity (n-I) due to the fact that they belong to a particular (specifically defined) group, or where the benefit is defined by I as being the benefit of the whole community of which B or (n-I) are merely members;
- *reverse one*, where if I→A, then I←B or I←(n-A), which in any case implies reciprocation of the action of I by a third party who is not the direct beneficiary of the original action of I;
- *chain one*, which occurs when the benefit of I causes any reaction that I→A→B→(…n), where "n" does not have to be an infinity or even a large number; thus, it is sufficient that the chain of benefits ends with an entity B, or may include any number of entities greater than 2 (Kolm, 2009).

Kolm's concept allows attention to be drawn to the nature of the system of benefits that – also under the specific conditions of the COVID-19 pandemic – relatively selfish states expect. This is because they are willing to accept not only benefits based on the model of simple reciprocity (which means that they are also ready for individual reciprocal benefits), but also benefits in more complex models, in which it is not so much the benefit that is valued (because others benefit from it), but e.g. the fact that it can be justifiably expected in an unspecified future in an appropriate situational configuration (i.e. in a situation of non-individualised benefit of the type A←(n-A) where "n" stands for any group of entities (except of course for country A itself, which is included in the notation).[2]

Under COVID-19 pandemic conditions, to the most typical extent, structures of reciprocity emerge that can be described as general in Kolm's typology. Here, however, the variation among countries in terms of the intensity (and therefore value) of mutual benefits that cannot be meaningfully captured in this typology is also revealed. Richer countries or those with greater capacity to generate unique health benefits (e.g. in the form of offering vaccinations unavailable to a certain group of countries) simply provide differently (more widely, more intensively) than countries that cannot afford to do so. In any case, however, due to the obvious biological nature of the virus causing the pandemic, the actions taken by states contribute to the production of externalities that can – within existing structures of interdependence – precisely be interpreted as benefits to other states. By the same token,

2 E.g. if one does not currently receive some sort of paid (private or public funding mechanism) medical care, one can expect to receive it when needed.

these positive externalities are offset by negative externalities resulting from a sharp reduction in the demand and supply of products and international trade. Precisely for this reason, countries that applied relatively mild lockdown measures (e.g. Sweden) had to secondarily adopt measures to support their own economy due to the mentioned externalities. This necessity was all the greater the more open their economy is.

The analysis also reveals the emergence of a subtype of complex reciprocity other than the one described, or the initiation of simple reciprocity – which occurs when richer countries or groups of such countries offer their partners assistance in the provision of pandemic-relevant health services such as vaccines/vaccination in particular.

Complex forms of reciprocity (also referred to as *extended reciprocities*) (Kolm, 2009) can therefore be seen when one recognises the diversity of relationships and motivations of states. The category of extended reciprocities can also include those in which we perceive a lack of simultaneous or near-simultaneous temporal correlation between one action and the response to it; also a complex type of relationship is one in which the reciprocal action for some reason is not even supposed to result in any concentrated reciprocity, but rather occurs in a diffuse formula.[3] Still another, very special type of mutual benefit is all that the present generation does for the benefit of future generations with whom it cannot have direct contact.

By interpreting the policies of different countries relating to the COVID-19 pandemic, taking into account externalities and interpreting them in terms of reciprocity structures, one can see an important procedural aspect of these structures. The essence of this is that sensible management of health and economic policies with respect to aspects arising from the pandemic in such a setting must prioritise procedures and seek to configure them in such a way that they form a compatible system with the relevant policies of other countries. International compatibility is in fact decisive for the success in achieving the expected effects of national policies. It is worth noting at this point that this procedural management can be adequately interpreted in terms of game theory – each country must take into account its resources and determine its strategy by estimating the likelihood of certain reactions from other countries – which are at the same time a strong determinant of the policy within which the strategy is formulated and implemented. This, in turn, indicates that strategies based on the cooperation of the players in the game may yield optimal results. In the context of a pandemic, however, the problem is that such cooperation must be designed by the leading players in the game (i.e. countries with the most resources) in such a way as to take into account the imbalance of countries in terms of available resources.

3 The reciprocator is then not the entity towards which the service initiating the relationship took place, but any other relevant entity or even a certain group of entities or even all of them.

In addition, they need to reflect in the strategy the time shifts in the impact of the pandemic and the public policy measures that relate to its course and impact. This is most evident in the relationship of the relatively rich countries of the northern hemisphere to the countries surrounding them (e.g. the countries of the European Union to its partners in North Africa and the Middle East).

It is worth noting that the pandemic has also become a test of the systemic resilience of states to external (exogenous) challenges of a large-scale and significant impact. Capacities in this regard are of mutual interest to states (which, after all, as mentioned, must formulate and implement sensible policies that take into account the need for relational procedural governance). Based on the analyses carried out, the assessment of the place of states in the world geopolitical hierarchy is verified. Most likely, it is this aspect that has given rise to many countries treating pandemic policy as a kind of demonstration of the potential for resource mobilisation.

As for the conclusions that can be drawn at all from a comparative analysis of the policy mix applied by different states, it should be noted that states had different resources at their disposal. Countries integrated in an economic bloc such as the European Union, for example, received a significant bonus of support from this organisation, which additionally managed to generate loan funds in the global credit market. It is also clear that countries with open economies have turned their attention to the need to support their exports; countries have used various channels and tools to increase liquidity. An important element of the policy mix has been the fiscal tools, which have interacted with monetary tools. In some countries, the monetary regime included the tightening of exchange controls; in others, the substitute was rather exchange rate controls.

As for the verification of the hypotheses, it should be concluded that:

(a) hypothesis 1, that the COVID-19 pandemic highlighted the important role of states and the apparatuses within them – was positively verified;
(b) hypothesis 2, that the response of states to the economic phenomena resulting from the COVID-19 pandemic consisted in the transition of states from an external controllability to an internal controllability model, in which the locus of control placed itself in a position characterising actors operating under conditions of greatly reduced rationality – was verified positively;
(c) hypothesis 3, that the initial response of countries to the COVID-19 pandemic was fairly homogenous, with a high level of imitativeness; yet, as time passed, regulatory intervention diverted considerably, representing the transition from an external controllability to a relatively internal controllability model of reaction, was tested positively;
(d) hypothesis 4, according to which the diversity of measures of regulatory intervention was strongly determined by the ability to activate internal and external resources of the state, and the intervention scenario with

respect to the economy was strongly determined by (a) what the state used as measures to combat the pandemic in the external controllability phase and (b) the influence of the external environment, the strength of the impact of which was determined by the strength of links of the states' economies with the world (i.e. the level of openness of these economies) – was verified positively;

(e) hypothesis 5, that countries with relatively open economies had to use tools of more intensive regulatory influence, not so much because of the adopted lockdown model, but because of the perceived external effects – cannot be – based on the presented, "shallow" comparative analysis – verified.

References

Brahmbhatt, M., & Dutta, A. (2008). On SARS Type Economic Effects During Infectious Disease Outbreaks. *World Bank Policy Research Paper, No. 4466*, World Bank, Washington, DC. Available from: http://documents.worldbank.org/curated/en/101511468028867410/On-SARS-type-economic-effects-during-infectious-disease-outbreaks

Burton, G.M. (2003). The Efficient Market Hypothesis and Its Critics. *CEPS Working Paper, No. 91.*

Carter, D.P., & May, P.J. (2020). Making Sense of the US COVID-19 Pandemic Response: A Policy Regime Perspective. *Administrative Theory and Praxis*, 42(2), pp. 265–277. https://doi.org/10.1080/10841806.2020.1758991

Goyal, N., & Hawlett, M. (2021). "Measuring the Mix" of Policy Responses to COVID-19: Comparative Policy Analysis Using Topic Modelling. *Journal of Comparative Policy Analysis, Research and Practice*, 23, pp. 250–261. https://doi.org/10.1080/13876988.2021.1880872

Hannan, M.T., & Freeman, J.H. (1977). The Population Ecology of Organisations. *American Journal of Sociology* 82, pp. 929–964. http://www.jstor.org/stable/2777807

Kahneman, D., & Tversky, A. (1973). On the Psychology of Prediction. *Psychological Review*, 80(4), pp. 237–251. https://doi.org/10.1037/h0034747. A broader picture of the science in this respect comes also from: Kahneman, D., & Tversky, A. (Eds) (2000). *Choices, Values and Frames*. Cambridge University Press.

Kolm, S.-Ch. (2009). *Reciprocity: An Economics of Social Relations*. Cambridge University Press, pp. 74–95.

Maliszewska, M., Mattoo, A., & van der Mensbrugghe, D. (2021). The Potential Impact of COVID-19 on GDP and Trade: Preliminary Assessment. *World Bank Policy Research Working Paper, No. 9211*, World Bank, Washington, DC.

Public Law (2020). Public Law 116-136-March 27, 134, Stat. 281.

Sahm, C. (2021). COVID-19 is Transforming Economic Policy in the United States. *Intereconomics – Review of European Economic Policy*, 56(4), pp. 185–190.

Zaltman, G., Duncan, R.L., & Holbek, J. (1973). *Innovations and Organisations*. John Wiley & Sons, New York.

5 State security and the pandemic

Tadeusz Klementewicz, Andrzej Misiuk, Kamil Mroczka, Grzegorz Rydlewski, and Jacek Wojnicki

5.1 Strategic dimension of the challenges of the pandemic for social and state security

The modern world is not free from tangible and real threats which have their origins in political and economic frictions, nationalism, and ethnic and religious antagonisms. Conflicting and varied interests generate a wide range of threats: from armed conflicts and terrorist attacks to common and organised crime, hooligan excesses, infecting IT systems and corruption. Apart from dangers caused by human attitude and activity, natural disasters and pandemics are also gaining a great importance for security. Due to the process of globalisation, also international threats quickly become a real danger, which upsets national or local security.

Security has always been an important element of people's individual needs, internal relations in particular countries, and international relations. Historically, the origins of security lie in man's feeling of being threatened in an unknown natural environment, and the resulting dangers. In this original meaning, security has an individual nature and is a person's mental state. The establishment of social relations such as family or tribe contributed to the perception of security as a social phenomenon. Assuming that the state is one of the most developed forms of social organisation, security has become an integral part of functions performed by the state. According to the traditional perception of the role of the state, it fulfils two basic functions: internal and external. The first one involves ensuring the security and order on the entire area of state jurisdiction. According to Leon Petrażycki's theory, the main task of the state is to fulfil mental needs, including those in the area of security. This view may be too radical, but if we look at state organisation in its original stage, a vast majority of institutions and legal regulations concerned the area of security. Let us remind that the classic function of state administration is law enforcement and regulation. The statement "security is not everything, but without security everything is nothing" proves that the main fabric of the institution of state as a compulsory organisation, equipped with attributes of superior power, is to protect against external and internal threats to the order, which provides the

DOI: 10.4324/9781003353805-6

society living in its territory and consisting of co-dependent groups with varied interests with favourable conditions for existence, corresponding to the power of their economic position and political influence (Gulczyński, 2007). The subject matter of security and its functions changed together with the state's political evolution.

The global COVID-19 crisis became an invisible threat for humanity and the main challenge for the security of particular societies and countries. As it was bluntly put, the pandemic shook up the world (Žižek, 2020) and created a great reset in many areas (Schwab & Malleret, 2020). Mitigating the financial and economic effects of the pandemic, which are deadly for people as well as social, financial and economic relations, has become a major challenge (Koley & Dhole, 2020).

The existing experience in combating the global COVID-19 pandemic caused by SARS-CoV-2 raises serious doubts as to whether the modern state is ready to ensure sanitary (health) security to its inhabitants. The traditional view still persists that the state should ensure personal security to its citizens by protecting them against threats to life and health resulting from crime, social pathologies, wars, and terrorism. However, the state becomes helpless when faced with the consequences of natural disasters and pandemics.

Specialised state institutions should be ready to prevent such threats, and, if they do occur, take preventive and combative actions. Law enforcement forces have undergone a long evolution, from entities with a very broad scope of functions to highly specialised ones. Modern states have extensive public administration, which is mainly responsible for protecting order and the citizens' safety, but also protects the legal and constitutional order as well as citizens from external threats. However, it has limited institutional possibilities in the area of diagnostics, risk analysis, and disease prevention when it comes to health security.

The understanding of the essence of security is strictly connected with threats. One may assume that there is coherence between them due to which the nature and scale of threats have an impact on the security of a given entity (person, social group, nation, state, etc.). The needs in this regard, in turn, influence the ways and methods of action (protection of security) which would lead to the state of lack of anxiety, peace, and confidence in development. Quoting Franz-Xaver Kaufmann as cited by Ryszard Zięba, danger is "the possibility of the occurrence of one of the negatively valued phenomena" (Zięba, 2004). Without going into details, one can state that a general theory of security should take into account these three main intrinsically connected problem areas.

The impact of coronavirus-related threats should be effectively mitigated as part of state systems of security. These systems include normative, programmatic, institutional, procedural, and HR solutions, which are to guarantee, under any circumstances, the performance of goals considered in a given state as important in the context of core values and interests. Each of these systems consists of numerous functional subsystems, includes numerous parts (segments), and is supposed to cater for the needs relevant to programming, prevention, emergency response, removing the impact of critical situations, determining responsibility, administration of justice, as well as evaluating and improving the solutions. Security systems vary from state to state and are closely related to the tradition and dynamic of the political system, the system of government, features of a given state (including geographical location, structure and territorial division) and society, the specifics of threats and crime, and the state's position in international and transnational structures. The systems of security are supposed to combat threats in a comprehensive and ordered manner.

The experience of the pandemic shows that this time the power of security threats has often proved greater than the capacity to mitigate them. It has been confirmed that the functioning of national security systems in each country is closely connected with the events and processes occurring in its social, normative, cultural, political, and economic environment. The challenges and threats in the international arena have proved to be of key importance in this context. The pandemic has become a factor which affects the balancing and direction of the activities of states, various international and transnational structures, and individuals. In most countries, especially in the first phase of the pandemic, the possibility of the functioning of healthcare and social care facilities was blocked. The crisis quickly became trans-sectoral. The area of necessary activities quickly covered most domains of human life and work and most spheres of the functioning of institutions (Hajder et al., 2020). It was necessary to systemically shift states into emergency mode and to additionally protect the nodes of critical infrastructure solutions. In particular countries, it also became necessary to launch, frequently radical and cumbersome, protection mechanisms and build reserve alternative solutions, e.g. remote communication with the use of the internet. Pandemic-related crime emerged, to name only cyberthreats and irregularities in the intervention purchase of equipment for fighting the effects of infections. The cross-border nature of the pandemic has created the need to launch special solutions and mechanisms for transnational and international cooperation. The course of the pandemic proved that in this case, the key role is played by the concentration of significant systemic risk related to limited programmability of events and significant volatility of the situation (Waliszewski & Solarz, 2020; Klimczuk, 2021). Response time and the ability to programme actions taking into account a number of options in the context of potential developments have become an asset of the greatest potential. The security systems of particular countries were faced with a multitude of competing expectations and needs. The development of COVID-19 vaccine was followed by the task of obtaining vaccines and distributing them in an optimum manner to vaccinate the biggest possible number of people, with preferential treatment of high-risk groups. It also became necessary to encourage people to get vaccinated. The blocking of professional activity and operation of many industries by administrative measures made it necessary to create a transparent system of financial compensation for the income lost.

At the moment, one may already talk about the first strategic conclusions related to the pandemic. There are more and more publications on this topic. On the COVID-19 website: Novel Coronavirus Content Free to Access, bringing together scientific, technological, medical and humanities research on COVID-19, there were over 4,900 publications as of the end of October 2021 (Taylor & Francis 2021).While the situation across countries varies, one can clearly see the directions of thinking in matters related to combating the threats and effects of the pandemic, which are of a universal nature and in the strategic perspective concern all countries. They are situated in the context of the future of conflict, competition, and cooperation in the world (Brands & Gavin, 2020).

The experience of the pandemic clearly confirms the strategic importance of the state's responsibility for security in its territory, and the need for an end-to-end approach to security. In spite of the processes of globalisation and institutionalisation of transnational and interstate integration (exemplified by the European Union and NATO), the responsibility for protecting the security of the society and the state in all its aspects, including prevention, intervention in the case of the occurrence of threats, and removing the effects of crises, will in future, as it does now, lie on public authorities of each country. The pandemic has shown that threats of key importance for societies and states may quickly migrate between particular sectors and, in a cascading manner, lead to the blocking of particular spheres of social, political, and economic life. Due to the nature of security threats which should be viewed as relevant in the strategic perspective, and such are the threats to public health, a broad definition of security should be adopted in particular countries' public policies. It was confirmed that traditional thinking about security, focused only on matters of national defence and crime, is faulty. Both in theory and in practice, it is necessary to shift from narrowly understood state security to the concept of the security of state and citizens, and to shift from isolated treatment of national defence and fight against crime to linking those matters with other public policies and including them in the system of development strategies of states and regions. Strategic reflection in particular countries should cover, as elements of the same system, the issues of protecting: international order, constitutional order, public security, life and health of citizens, and the country's resources. One should pay attention to the intermingling of particular types of security, including political, economic, information, health, ecological, energy, and ICT security. One should take into account interactive correlations between security phenomena and processes and their environment, as well as the growing importance of the relations between security policy and the shifting of technological boundaries and the related emergence of new opportunities and threats connected with the development of digital solutions and the growing power of information, communication, and technology.

In particular countries, the pandemic became a circumstance which forced people to a quick review, and often to a forced change, of the solutions in security matters (Biden, 2021). It has laid bare numerous weaknesses of security systems, particularly in the area of obtaining information on developing threats and the ability to respond in real time, coordinate actions, mobilise potentially available resources and use them in the optimum manner, build social awareness and support for the actions taken, and counteract the spread of various, often extensive, conspiracy theories related to the pandemic itself and the alleged harmfulness of vaccines, which were favourably received in the situation of trauma caused by the pandemic (Breggin & Breggin, 2021). It became urgent to identify the reasons for and draw conclusions from the failure of the global threat monitoring and warning system. It was also necessary to conduct an in-depth analysis of how a crisis situation transforms into a global crisis. This should be achieved by identifying the weakest links in the information and decision-making cycle and determining which part of that process – obtaining, selecting, transmitting, analysing information, using it for decision-making or implementing the taken decisions – included loopholes and errors (MacKenzie, 2020b; Horton, 2021). As subsequent coronavirus waves and variants are highly likely, the importance of that operation is a strategic challenge. It is necessary to identify and effectively mitigate the most important factors, which will influence the transmission of infections in future. In the next few years, [...] of disclosed deficiencies and imperfections related to the manner of thinking about potential security risks and frictions in the area of responding to a wave of illnesses and deaths caused by SARS-CoV-2 infections (Dowling & Kenney, 2020).

In each case, one should list and consider the strengths and weaknesses of a given country's COVID-19 response as well as the future opportunities and threats in the area of preventing pandemic threats. Defining a relevant programme vision should be preceded by an end-to-end assessment covering the criteria of: purposefulness, efficiency, effectiveness, usefulness, consistency, completeness, and durability of the outcome. This vision should govern the definition of: the main purpose and operational goals and directions of intervention, a system of performance and implementation, criteria and methods for assessment (evaluation) and rules for modification, financial framework for strategic actions, and rules of social communication in matters related to combating threats such as the pandemic. In particular countries, a balance of needs in the area of effective fight with the threats of global epidemics should be placed against a backdrop of the recognised system of values and interests, and coordinated with an end-to-end diagnosis of the functioning of society and state in the conditions of pandemic. One should notice that the assessments of the actions of states related to the pandemic show the intermingling of criteria which are heterogeneous in their dispositions regarding action: axiological, normative, social, political, economic, related to praxeological criteria, criteria resulting from social communication needs, criteria connected with the adopted obligations and agreements, as well as criteria connected with the need to take into account the civilisation challenges and the potential of new technologies. It prompts us to consider the heuristics adopted in decision-making related to the pandemic, and to evaluate the available variants of behaviour and build the standards of behaviour. Activity in the matters of security deserves a positive assessment only when it optimally responds to all of the following challenges: intellectual (related to identifying problems, choosing courses of action and creating programmes), organisational and logistics (related to securing the implementation), political (including ensuring leadership and support), financial (related to securing paths of financing), and challenges related to communication and mobilisation (in the area of assigning meaning to facts and giving direction to social behaviours).

The experience gathered during the fight against the pandemic makes it possible to build a universal catalogue of the state's abilities which are of particular importance during a pandemic crisis. A key role is here played by proper performance of detailed tasks and overcoming frictions which occur in state security systems in the area of: obtaining and managing information in real time; developing detailed programming and planning solutions; guaranteeing the system's integrity in the case of frictions; strengthening synergies and communication within the system; effective implementation of decisions taken; communication with the social and political environment (within the state and in interstate and transnational relations); effective evaluation of, and the ability to use, the obtained results, and seamless modification of ill-judged solutions. The activity of the entities of the state security system related to the pandemic includes many simultaneous, crossing decision processes adopted at various levels and in various segments of that system. The strengths and weaknesses of those processes must be subject to multi-criteria evaluation. This should cover, as part of follow-up evaluation, all stages of those processes, i.e.: generating particular decision initiatives, indexing and selecting available variants of decision behaviour and selecting the variant to be implemented, necessary consultation and arrangements, transforming initiatives into end-to-end projects, initial evaluation of the decision behaviour project selected for implementation, securing the decision under preparation in terms of communication, formal decision-making, and implementing the decision connected with follow-up evaluation and activities on the outcome combined with a possible correction and starting new loops of a decision process.

The experience of the fight against the pandemic confirmed the need for a cooperative security strategy to be taken by the state. The attempts to solve problems resulting from global or transnational threats by the actions of public bodies in particular countries, without cooperating with other entities, are doomed to fail. This is caused in particular by: the processes of globalisation; transnational integration; development of personalised mass communication via the internet; growing digitisation of the public domain and social and economic relations, and the development of artificial intelligence tools. In this context, an important role is played by intensive, mass, and quick cross-border movement of people and extensive international supply chains. The concept of cooperative security must be the basis for thinking about national security, particularly with regard to global and cross-border threats. It must also accompany the fight against crises resulting from the transmission of infections. The pandemic, especially its first phase, brought to light material shortcomings in the involvement of international and interstate entities in mutual activities limiting the spread of coronavirus. They resulted mostly from slow response as part of bureaucratic structures and complicated decision procedures (Czachór, 2020; Gjørv, 2020; Kiwerska, 2020). Some states attempted to act in a manner not agreed on an international level, e.g. in terms of the policy of closed borders and inconsistent rules of taking vaccine protection into account. The pandemic brought to light the lack of quick information flow between allies, particularly in a sudden and difficult situation, as well as the threats related to chaotic actions in interstate relations. In later months, the situation in that area significantly improved. However, the pandemic also laid bare the weaknesses of the current international order, while also becoming a subject of international political game and disinformation campaigns. Nation states should still put pressure on international organisations of which they are members to make them, to the maximum possible extent – within the boundaries of their statutory goals – take into account the cooperation-related content in the matters of broadly defined security. At the same time, they should give up country-specific actions which, as the examples have shown, bring – especially in the long term – more costs than benefits.

It was confirmed that the state's having a clear normative system and institutional solutions in place in case of crisis was of key importance. The pandemic demonstrated that those should be solutions under universal law, which clearly defines the circumstances justifying the introduction and content of special crisis management regulatory solutions, regulations related to combating infectious diseases, and states of emergency. Regulations regarding strengthening the authorities' capacity to act in situations of crisis, such as the pandemic crisis, must take into account the need to balance different factors in matters of guaranteeing equally important rights and freedoms of people and citizens which are enshrined in international law and the constitution, and which are often in conflict during a crisis. Even a cursory review of practice in this domain (Dobrzeniecki & Przywora, 2021) raises numerous doubts. One should respect the rule that protecting specific rights and freedoms must not prevent the exercise of other fundamental rights and freedoms, but may only – to a justified extent – limit the scope for their exercise. In these matters, it is necessary to try, to the maximum extent possible, to eliminate ad hoc solutions introduced by executive authorities. There is a need to strengthen the guarantees of rights and freedoms in situations of crises and to limit the use of solutions similar to states of emergency in which there are no guarantees of rights included in the legislation on states of emergency (Izdebski, 2020; Radajewski, 2020). These matters require particular attention in a situation in which many governments attempted to use the pandemic to strengthen their policy by administrative measures and to expand surveillance over the society on a great scale (Lyon, 2022). The pandemic reminded us of the key importance of an ordered and efficient crisis management system within the state. Such a system must include constant identification, monitoring, and evaluation of risks and threats, as well as a mechanism of seamless launch of predefined reserves with regard to powers and means which can be used in the case of escalation of crisis situations and crises, and a set of actions to be performed in the case of crisis situations and crises. It should be pointed out that in numerous countries, the pandemic revealed systemic and coordination frictions at the level of management and the level of operations, between crisis management solutions and the solutions of the state of epidemic.

Optimisation of the fight against security threats should be excluded from the political game as much as possible, should form part of a joint fight against crises, and be the area of using all available resources. Crises, such as the pandemic crisis discussed here, which in their various aspects concern many areas of people's lives and work, force states to launch, in order to protect common values and interests, restrictive solutions which are often controversial and give rise to disputes and a social and political resistance. Therefore, the optimum solution would be to expand the systems for the organisation of the public domain by adding constant and non-discretionary mechanisms for building common positions of significant political parties and non-government public authorities, particularly self-government authorities with general competence. Every other situation, as numerous examples from the previous two years showed, becomes a basis for a political game, which is particularly fierce in those countries in which the manner of treating the majoritarian democracy rules by the authorities makes the dispute between government and opposition a total dispute. In such conditions, we witness the politicisation of security threats (Rydlewski, 2021b). The government makes its anti-pandemic measures conditional on the opinion of its political environment and its political interests, while the opposition uses the coronavirus threat to strengthen its political position. Questions emerge about the democracy being prepared to meet the challenges of the pandemic (Allen, 2021). Restrictions on rights and freedoms, orders and prohibitions related to reducing the spread of infections, and bans on particular areas of the economy and social life for months need to be intensively and effectively secured by social communication, the authorities' ordered narrative, and a well-thought-out educational message (O'Hair & O'Hair, 2021). Wherever it was forgotten, we saw fierce social conflicts, civil disobedience, and signs of rebellion. They were particularly strong in the countries where public authorities do not enjoy public trust.

5.2 Government and self-government administration in the face of the pandemic crisis – searching for safe solutions

The pandemic crisis brought to light a basic question: Which of the administrations has more effective tools in the fight against COVID-19, which is a threat for both state and society. State structures usually consist of two complementary administrative models: government administration and self-government administration. Each of them fulfils other functions in the structure of public administration, which complement each other. Government administration fulfils mostly general state functions, which are of key importance for the functioning of the state, while self-government administration – depending on its organisational structure – usually has subsidiary functions, towards both the state and a specific self-government community (Hausner, 2009; Mazur, 2011; Osiński, 2011).

The pandemic is a new challenge for administrative structures, in terms of identifying threats, eliminating risk for inhabitants, and introducing solutions in the area of protecting public health. It is usually assumed that it is government administration (or even broader – state administration which covers whole structures of the state) that is responsible for identifying and limiting threats for the population (Hausner, 2009).

It should be borne in mind that the pandemic crisis means not only a serious threat to inhabitants' health, but also a significant restriction of the functioning of the social and economic domain, due to restrictions on movement, temporary lockdowns, and shutting down entire sectors of the economy (tourism, culture, sports, leisure, etc.). In this context, a fundamental question arises: Which of the administrations has more effective tools for defence and protection, for both the community and the weakened sectors of the social and economic life? Or maybe the cooperation of both administrative structures is needed, due to the scale of the pandemic crisis, unprecedented in the modern world? Let us look at the solutions used in particular countries and try to develop global responses to global threats.

Among numerous analyses on the health crisis caused by the COVID-19 pandemic, numerous researchers searched for those which will make it possible to assess institutional solutions (Górniak et al., 2020). A thesis has been put forward that the existence of good institutions (with appropriate regulations, resources and experts) is necessary to take quick, appropriate, and effective protection and treatment measures. A team of Polish researchers asked experts from other countries to answer, using the competences in the area of health protection, questions related to public governance in the first half-year of the pandemic (from January to June 2020), when lockdown was commonly used and gradually lifted. What is particularly important for the evaluation of management in a situation of a health crisis, the invited experts represented countries which greatly differed in terms of: state decentralisation, social structure, available resources, public health organisation, and the political traditions in the area of settling disputes (Italy, the

Netherlands, the United Kingdom, Germany, the Czech Republic, Ukraine, and Canada) (Golinowska & Zabdyr-Jamróz, 2020).

An important role in crisis management was played by cooperation within governments: between ministries and government agencies. Siloed government structures always make it difficult to combine matters which need to be approached in a comprehensive manner. In a crisis situation, domain (industry) divisions are a particularly troublesome feature of public governance. To prevent this, in the countries subject to the analysis, decision-making and coordination bodies were established within governments, usually headed by prime ministers themselves, as well as ministers for the interior and ministers for health. On the other hand, the emergence of the pandemic in countries with a decentralised structure of the state and the public health organisation (the case of the Netherlands and Canada) meant a serious restriction to central authorities' quick and effective decisions regarding the use of prevention measures. Italian experts admit that it was only during the first period of the pandemic that legal regulations and institutions were established in self-government administration, which enabled the intervention in the functioning of health and social care facilities, also the private ones (Golinowska & Zabdyr-Jamróz, 2020; Orłowska et al., 2021).

In this context, the example of Canada is worth looking at, which already in 2004 prepared an action plan related to the flu epidemic, updated in 2017, regulating the matters of the responsibility of public authorities on all administrative levels. At the same time – what is particularly important – there was no questioning of the decision autonomy of provincial authorities in conducting public policy related to health protection and the COVID-19 pandemic. A report on actions in the Ontario province exemplifies the scale of autonomy and problems related with the independence of regional measures in Canada. Regardless of the scope of autonomy of decentralised structures, central authorities transferred budget funds or health insurance funds to regional and local institutions for the necessary equipment and compensation for sanitary and medical personnel (Golinowska & Zabdyr-Jamróz, 2020). While calling for limiting social contacts and stay at home, the federal government of Canada refrained from announcing a state of emergency. Under local statutes, prime ministers of all Canadian provinces announced states of emergency, meaning restrictions of public liberties, including a ban on gatherings, shutting down of public venues (schools, restaurants except for takeaways, nightclubs, churches, cinemas) and increasing control over regional traffic. "Our efforts focus on helping Canadians, and not corporations as foggy entities," said the head of the federal government in parliament (Kanada: po epidemii pomoc..., 2020).

The Netherlands established the Team for Coordinating Regional Actions (National Operational Team-Corona; LOT-C), which enabled the operational cooperation of all rescue services, security services, health and social care activities, and administrative activities. All heads of regions (mayors) were its members.

In the presented analysis, Nordic countries are also worth looking at. It should be pointed out that the strategies of particular Nordic countries were not the same; they greatly differed. In the first phase (spring 2020), the countries generally limited themselves to monitoring the situation, and then tried to slow down the development of the pandemic as much as possible. To achieve it, they used a wide range of measures – Finland introduced a state of emergency, and Denmark and Norway introduced restrictions based on special statutory laws. The measures taken by Sweden were relatively least restrictive. In general terms, the strategies of Nordic countries in the first phase of the pandemic consisted in slowing down the spread of the disease as much as possible and in providing special protection to the most vulnerable persons (especially older and chronically ill persons). It was a stage which followed the failure to prevent the emergence of coronavirus in Scandinavia (Szacawa, 2020).

The fight against the COVID-19 pandemic – as the Polish researchers agree – requires a close monitoring of the current epidemic situation. It is vital that on both the central and local levels the epidemiological data should be comprehensive, updated on a current basis, and digitised. In particular, it is necessary to obtain data which make it possible to assess the intensity of the transmission, and not only the frequency of identified infections which depends on testing. It is also necessary to monitor the circumstances of infection. The indicators of the efficiency of sanitary services and healthcare are also vital (Duszyński et al., 2020)

The above strategy greatly aligns with multilevel governance processes, so it constitutes an example of network governance of public matters, and in particular refers to matters of global significance (such as the described pandemic case in the modern world) (Bache et al., 2016). The examples analysed above make it possible to formulate the thesis that no single strategy of fighting the pandemic crisis has been developed after 2020. The adopted solutions constituted a product of political, social, economic, and cultural factors. The example of the functioning of the administration of Canadian provinces (especially Ontario) points to the benefits of decentralised solutions. The same applies to the regulations adopted in the Netherlands. In countries which are unitary or have a more centralised public administration, it was government administration that bore the main responsibility for developing and implementing a health policy and then developing remedial and aid measures for the most affected areas of social and economic life (e.g. Taiwan). On the other hand, the case of Nordic countries points to a responsible role of trade union syndicates in the process of developing government and parliamentarian positions. In the case of EU states – referring to the theory of multilevel governance – one should pay attention to the decision factors at the community level, which, on the one hand, prolongs aid strategies, but, on the other hand, makes it possible to develop remedial programmes for the European societies and economies affected by the pandemic.

5.3 State security in cyberspace

The purpose of this subchapter is to characterise the topics related to the challenges faced by the state due to new phenomena which emerged in cyberspace during the pandemic. It has been rightly pointed out that owing to the growing digitisation of state and services, "cyberspace not only contributes to the development of state (non-state) entities or persons, but also causes serious threats to their security" (Zawisza, 2015). As we all know, cybercrime has become a major challenge of our times – operation of criminals directly affects not only the lives of ordinary citizens, whose sensitive data or funds are stolen, but also the business activities of smaller and bigger organisations, multinational corporations, entities, which are indispensable for the functioning of the economy. More and more often, actions in cyberspace also have an impact on the situation of particular countries. For several years, cyberspace-related matters have been addressed in strategic documents of many countries worldwide, which result from the weight of that matter and its potential impact on security.

Due to the main features of cyberspace – namely global reach, efficiency, universality and generally low costs of access – more and more domains of social life move to the virtual world (Hoffman, 2018). Cyberspace has become a natural environment for human activity, and at the dawn of the third decade of the 21st century it may be stated that its expansion, e.g. in the context of Internet of Things, was largely caused by the level of development of an information society. The literature on the subject rightly stresses that cyberspace has become "a new security environment," which requires the introduction of numerous and deep changes both to the pragmatics and to the legal and organisational dimension of the functioning of security systems throughout the world (Zawisza, 2015).

There is also no doubt that cyberspace has both a bright and a dark side. The former makes it possible to increase the effectiveness of the economy, public services, or healthcare, while the latter results from the fact that it has become dangerous and can be used by criminals. Thus, various phenomena have emerged in cyberspace which cause threats to external and internal security. The relevant literature points to the following negative developments in cyberspace: (1) cybercrime, (2) cybersurveillance, (3) cyberterrorism, (4) cyberespionage, (5) cyberwar (Sienkiewicz & Świeboda, 2010). However, a detailed analysis of those phenomena is outside the scope of adopted research assumptions.

During the pandemic, the cyberspace has played both a positive ("bright side") and a negative role ("dark side"). The "bright side" of cyberspace made it possible to computerise many processes and services which are of key importance for maintaining the continuity of states and economies. A range of public services have been digitised – from education, through issuing decisions (exercising public authority) and performing decision-making processes, to supporting the processes of forecasting, detecting and combating coronavirus in the public health sector.

The accelerated migration of business and social activity to cyberspace during the pandemic, mainly caused by the internet which enabled the traditional market of goods and services to be transformed into an electronic market, and in terms of public sphere enabled citizens' activity online, brought changes to the functioning of social, political, and economic life. It led to the emergence of "e-organisations" which "virtualise" their activities by using cyberspace to optimise interactions with stakeholders.

The "dark side" of cyberspace during the pandemic has been revealed in many areas of the functioning of state and economy. Since the outbreak of the pandemic, cybercrime figures have significantly increased. It is estimated that in 2020 the number of ransomware attacks increased by 150% compared to 2019 (CERT Polska, 2021). Cybercriminals significantly increased ransom amounts, while also improving the process of victim support. For example, they put guides and tutorials on the internet which show how to anonymously transfer ransom to the criminals' account. Due to the spread and rapid development of technology, it is also an area of pathological and criminal activities. A low entry threshold, broad availability of attack vectors, and a low risk of detection combined with relatively high profits gave rise to the activity of organised – very often international – cybercrime groups which have an extensive structure and are characterised by hierarchy and distribution of tasks. The activities of cybercriminals are aimed at achieving financial profit by carrying out criminal activities targeted at individuals, businesses, and financial institutions alike (Maderak et al., 2021). Virtually every day, we come across information on cyberattacks aimed at disrupting the functioning of selected IT systems, breaking into systems, causing data leaks, or other "negative phenomena which not only undermine trust in the processes of digitisation, but first of all cause tangible losses to network users" (Banasiński & Rojszczak, 2020).

The media hype caused by uncertainty and the mass of information, financial troubles of many entrepreneurs, and thus also of citizens, and the fear of infection all contributed to increased activity of cybercriminals, who became "particularly active" during the pandemic (Bartosiewicz & Borkowski, 2020). Moreover, companies which quickly switched to remote work appeared to be very vulnerable to attacks. Two types of attacks proved to be most effective: distribution of malware as an e-mail attachment, and the failure to protect, or insufficient protection of, the company's network infrastructure (CERT Polska, 2021). In addition, the pandemic significantly increased the number of attacks on healthcare facilities around the world. This was mainly due to the bad condition of hospitals' network infrastructure and its huge workloads. What is more, it is estimated that due to the pandemic and the fight for their patients' life, healthcare facilities were more likely to pay ransom in order to recover data or the functionality of IT systems. Ransom amounts ranged from 50,000 to even 10 million dollars (Ransomware Threat Report, 2021). There were also cases where cybercriminals, upon learning that they had attacked a hospital, provided decrypting data keys for free (BBC, 2020; POLITICO, 2021).

The pandemic enables organised crime groups to cheat, among others, the users of sales platforms and courier companies on a massive scale. During the pandemic, repeated attacks on customers of online shops and courier companies were reported in many countries. Cybercriminals create fake websites of those organisations and then send text messages to random users on a massive scale with links to those websites, encouraging them to go to a given website. The customer, unaware of the fraud, is redirected to a false payment website used to obtain online banking credentials or other sensitive data.

In our view, the professionalisation of cybercrime, which we have been witnessing for over a dozen months, cybercriminals' acting in the CaaS model (cybercrime as a service, i.e. the development and sale of cybercrime tools, components or services by some groups which are then purchased and used by other groups), has significantly contributed to the development of cybercrime – criminals no longer have to be proficient IT specialists to conduct cybercrime activities.

Appropriate tools or entire processes may be purchased on the Dark Web or on hidden websites, unavailable to the general public. Depending on the service, one can purchase single malware or an entire platform including technical support. However, some groups operate in the subscription model – a "commission" for a crime group is deducted from the money stolen by a criminal. Many groups recruit not only money mules, who are used for money laundering, but also criminals of the lowest order, whose task e.g. only consists in conducting a conversation in such a manner as to encourage the victim to click on the link they were sent.

An analysis of the negative aspects of cyberspace may not ignore the net being used for creating and spreading fake news (Mroczka, 2020). This phenomenon gained particular importance especially in the context of the role of the authorities of the People's Republic of China in covering up information on the pandemic and its sources, and also in connection with the vaccination process. Many countries see the spread of untrue information about the quality of vaccines, their production process, and their potential effects. There are also fake news which question the existence of the pandemic itself, or its scale and scope. There are no reliable statistics on the impact of fake news on mortality, but we may venture that fake news regarding the pandemic have contributed to the death of thousands. Many countries made more or less effective attempts at eliminating that phenomenon, but according to the authors, the fight against fake news requires a systemic approach which involves international organisations, states, and key Big Tech companies. Piecemeal and uncoordinated activities will not solve the problem.

During the pandemic, countries were forced to increase the scope of obtaining and processing various types of data, including medical and geolocation data. Particular countries developed special tools for conducting detection and prevention activities. They very often involved the need to obtain detailed data on citizens. Governments are tempted to constantly expand those activities, which may lead to threats in the context of human rights, as it can be assumed that governments "get used to" the current standard and scope of data and apply them also after the pandemic.

There is no doubt that the pandemic has revealed the scale of potential and actual threats related to cyberspace (Maderak et al., 2021). Many countries have experienced acute negative effects of cybercriminals' activities. In this context – according to the authors – it is necessary to take joint actions to increase security in cyberspace and educate the public in that area. The level of hardware and software security solutions is constantly growing. However, this progress does not go hand in hand with increased awareness of internet users, and it is humans that are the weakest links in that system. The lack of relevant knowledge about the risks which accompany the benefits of cyberspace, and the ways of mitigating them, causes a real threat to the state and its citizens. In this context, it is necessary to develop a global model of educating the society from a very young age. These activities must be coordinated and standardised, so as to ensure an appropriate security level on a global scale. Without such activities, a situation may occur whose negative effects will be irreversible.

5.4 Human impact on the environment. Black swans are certain, the time is uncertain

The history of humanity is an area of competition between macro-parasitism of humanity towards nature and its reaction – the micro-parasitism of pathogens. Humanity has not subdued the Earth. It only became dependent on nature in a different manner – on its climate, arable land, raw materials, and pathogens. The nature's revenge takes the form of pandemics, lifestyle diseases, climate disruptions, desertification, increased energy prices, and currently – a deep recession. Black swans are lurking everywhere; only the time of their arrival is unknown. Let us not delude ourselves. Limiting wildlife trade is only an ad hoc measure. In the long run, humanity must repair its relationship with nature.

Until recently, it seemed that human beings had cast off the yoke of nature forever. However, the human population, growing by a billion every dozen years, has found itself in a new trap – Meadows's trap (named after a co-author of the report *The Limits to Growth*, published in 1972). As opposed to the Malthusian trap, which concerned agrarian societies, it has three new features. Firstly, modern economy exploits the global ecosystem, while pre-industrial economy exploited local ecosystems, and within them mainly land and wood. Modern economy leaves its trace on all biosphere components – atmosphere, hydrosphere, and lithosphere. Secondly, an industrial economy in the form of free-market capitalism has a different nature. Its efficient functioning requires constant accumulation. New areas of accumulation and increasing consumer demand increase the ecological footprint. Thirdly, escaping this trap requires the cooperation of the entire international community to define boundary conditions of the functioning of the economy: hours of work, energy mix, taxes. Escaping this new trap will require funds to finance the solutions to global problems – the energy, raw material, and food problem, and the problem of protecting rainforests or freshwater resources. The progress of bioengineering and the shift from energy provided by hydrocarbons, e.g. through the use of nucleosynthesis, offer a chance to overcome the energy barrier. The market mechanism will not solve these problems, e.g. a prototype ITAR nucleosynthesis device will cost c. 25 billion dollars. At the dawn of a market-based society, this tendency was noticed by Karl Polanyi, an English sociologist with Hungarian roots. He noticed the "double movement" of intertwined tendencies: on the one hand, constant expansion of socially eradicated markets, and on the other hand – regulatory efforts to limit the destructive effects of the free-market mechanism. To date, that task has been performed by the state, through changing the regulatory order. It is not only about minimising cyclical instability and mitigating a recession such as that which occurs as a result of a pandemic.

Black swan is a domesticated species in the civilisation established by *Homo sapiens* on various continents. For the biological exchange between continents, the turning point was the coupling of continents by new sailing routes in the 16th century. It was the time of the movement of genes, crops, and weeds, as well as wild animals and farm animals. People and animals, by exchanging bacteria and viruses and combining their variants, bred many dangerous diseases.

Humanity has always helped its perennial enemies – pathogens – by transporting germs from one city, port, region, and continent to another. According to the book *Black Death. Epidemics in Europe from Antiquity to Modern Times*, by epidemiologists and historians Ch. Duncan and S. Scott, as many as 400 diseases passed from animals to humans have already been identified. Currently, it is China that has become a reservoir of new viral diseases. In Chinese society, tradition and prestige uphold the legal and illegal trade in wild animals; it offers the meat of wild animals for culinary purposes. That market is worth 73 billion dollars and employs 1 million people (Cedro, 2020).

Currently, we see the emergence of superbacteria, also those artificially created thanks to the progress of bioengineering. Especially dangerous are antibiotic-resistant organisms which emerge in hospitals (methicillin-resistant bacteria (MRSA)), microbes which destroy trees, and microbes which attack farm animals and domestic animals (foot-and-mouth disease, African swine fever, infection with bluetongue virus). Using antibiotics in industrial breeding of poultry and porcine animals is also dangerous. Globalisation has only increased the ease with which pathogens cross the borders of states and continents. Today, the difference consists in the possibility of using two previously unavailable methods of preventing epidemics: the science and the state. The first one significantly accelerates the development of vaccines. In former times, populations had to develop resistance through spontaneous mutation of a gene (for the black plague, it was the CCR5-delta 32 receptor, which blocked the entry gate for the virus). The second one was the Enlightenment state and its biopolicy. The care about public hygiene, building sewage systems in cities, and providing access to clean water blocked the main highway for microbes. Also the current fight with the coronavirus epidemic led by the state shows that the state is the only efficient and functional mechanism in a situation of threat. The Chinese state is a model here. Its central government, in cooperation with local government units and voluntary organisations, has implemented a secure system for providing citizens with necessities, thus ensuring isolation necessary to stop the virus spread. It was also necessary to use the internet, Big Data, and Artificial Intelligence to identify potentially infected persons. Chinese e-commerce corporations as well as the contactless delivery system were a great help. All this was accompanied by discipline and respect for the authority of the state, characteristic for a post-Confucianism society.

However, neither "knowledge-based economy" nor digital capitalism will change the fact that any functioning economic system is doomed to a functioning ecological system. That is why humanity can develop only such an economic system which will maintain the balance of the global ecosystem. According to the book *Climate Change: Biological and Human Aspects* by climatologist Jonathan Cowie, "we are biological creatures that are involved in, and dependent on, many biological systems, which in turn are affected by climate." Humanity uses natural resources whose exploitation brings changes to local ecosystems – by deforestation, overexploitation of arable land, meadows, tropical rainforests, and currently also oceans, and also by expanding the settlement network. Currently, concrete covers a surface of the Earth which is the size of France, or even, according to pessimists, of India. Each year, 12 million hectares of arable land are lost. Forests are shrinking, especially rainforests in Indonesia and the Amazon. Nature reserves free from human intervention are disappearing. Humanity is already using 20% more resources than nature is able to regenerate (WWF, 2012). Human economic activity has already led to the fragmentation of natural environment, chemical pollution, and the presence in new habitats of species which are foreign to a given ecosystem. Species of fauna and flora, which live in various ecosystems, lose their habitats, biodiversity decreases, and there is human intervention into biogeochemical cycles – the circulation of coal or oxygen, or the hydrological cycle. A kind of free market has emerged which can be used by various species, especially pathogens.

It is easy to find a vehicle for increasing expansion between species (SARS-CoV-2 probably travelled the following way: bat=>civet=>man).

In a world without pandemics, the dogma about the primacy of the economy, driven by the need to overcome the barrier of demand, must not apply. The GDP criterion is fallible. The effects of economic processes reach further than market exchange, especially monetary exchange: those are mainly environmental costs, which are not taken into account in the price of products. The social value of a profession may significantly differ from its market valuation. One thing is certain: nowadays, no society is able to carry on its own the burden of external effects of the great civilisation success of industrialisation and capitalism. The coronavirus and the pandemic remind us of this truth.

The pandemic has made us aware of great opportunities and threats to security connected with the development of personalised mass communication on the internet and the solutions of the digital civilisation (Rydlewski, 2021a). It has become a time of alert for e-government and e-administration solutions. This also concerns the functioning of the security systems themselves. The experience gathered during the fight against the pandemic has brought to light the strategic importance of: internet access, the ability to use interactive online communication by the society, and guaranteeing electronic commerce security. In this context, the state is facing strategic challenges related to cybersecurity and information security. Valuable new opportunities are accompanied by frictions and dysfunctions that need to be addressed by particular states, which go beyond technology and concern fundamental values and rights and freedoms. Areas of friction include relations between freedom and privacy on the one hand and security on the other; online information war; pathological links between politics and technology; technological war disrupting international order, the security of data, and online contacts; and individuals' and states' dependence on digital tools.

In a strategic perspective, there is a chance that in particular states the pandemic crisis has been won for the future (MacKenzie, 2020a) and has become an opportunity to free the security systems of ineffective solutions with shortcomings and limitations. However, in order to achieve it, the phase of intervention should be followed by the phase of thoughtful modernisation of security systems. In this case, the key role will be played by the ability to treat policies such as health policy or scientific policy not as competitive to economic policy, but as a prerequisite for stability and development. The pandemic may be treated as a test of usability of scientific research and the implementations of development projects. Without vaccines, the world would now be in an entirely different place. However, this concerns not only research on the tools which are important directly in the context of combating the pandemic and its effects, but also social science research regarding matters related to identifying the principles governing the actions of individuals, entire social groups and countries in conditions of crisis.

References

Allen, D. (2021). *Democracy in the Time of Coronavirus*. The University of Chicago Press.

Bache, I., Bartle, I., & Flinders, M. (2016). Multi-level Governance. In Ch. Ansell, & J. Torfing (Eds), *Handbook on Theories of Governance*. Edward Elgar Publishing.

Banasiński, C., & Rojszczak, M. (2020). *Cyberbezpieczeństwo*. Wolters Kluwer.

Bartosiewicz, M., & Borkowski, P. (2020). *Jak COVID-19 zmienia podejście do bezpieczeństwa w cyberprzestrzeni*. Rzeczpospolita. Available from: https://www.rp.pl/dane-osobowe/art716601-jak-covid-19-zmienia-podejscie-do-bezpieczenstwa-w-cyberprzestrzeni

BBC (2020). *Police Launch Homicide Inquiry after German Hospital Hack*. BBC News. Available from: https://www.bbc.com/news/technology-54204356

Biden, J.R., Jr (2021). *National Strategy for the COVID-19 Response and Pandemic Preparedness*. The White House.

Brands, H., & Gavin, F.J. (2020). *COVID-19 and World Order: The Future of Conflict, Competition, and Cooperation*. Johns Hopkins University Press.

Breggin, P., & Breggin, G. (2021). *COVID-19 and the Global Predators: We Are the Prey*. Lake Edge Press.

Cedro, M. (2020), *Skąd się wziął koronawirus? Wszystko się zaczęło od jedzenia dziczyzny*. Dziennik Gazeta Prawna. Available from: https://www.gazetaprawna.pl/wiadomosci/artykuly/1463091,koronawirus-z-chin-targ-dzika-przyroda.html

CERT Polska (2021). *Krajobraz bezpieczeństwa polskiego internetu – raport roczny z działalności CERT Polska 2020*, NASK CERT.pl. Available from: https://cert.pl/posts/2021/09/krajobraz-bezpieczenstwa-polskiego-internetu-w-2020-roku/

Czachór, Z. (2020). Unia Europejska a pandemia koronawirusa SARS-CoV-2. Ujęcie deterministyczne i indeterministyczne. In K. Hajder, M. Kacperska, & Ł. Donaj (Eds), *Konsekwencje pandemii COVID-19. Świat i gospodarka*. Wydawnictwo Naukowe Wydziału Nauk Politycznych i Dziennikarstwa.

Dobrzeniecki, K., & Przywora, B. (2021). *Ograniczenia praw i wolności w okresie pandemii COVID-19 na tle porównawczym. Pierwsze doświadczenia*. Wydawnictwo Instytutu Wymiaru Sprawiedliwości.

Dowling, M.J., & Kenney, Ch. (2020). *Leading Through a Pandemic: The Inside Story of Humanity, Innovation, and Lessons Learned During the COVID-19 Crisis*. Skyhorse.

Duszyński i in. (2020), *Zrozumieć COVID-19. Opracowanie zespołu ds. COVID-19 przy Prezesie Polskiej Akademii Nauk*. Polska Akademia Nauk.

Gjørv, G.H. (2020). *Coronavirus, invisible threats and preparing for resilience*. NATO Review.Available from: https://www.nato.int/docu/review/articles/2020/05/20/coronavirus-invisible-threats-and-preparing-for-resilience/index.html

Golinowska, S., & Zabdyr-Jamróz, M. (2020). Zarządzanie kryzysem zdrowotnym w pierwszym półroczu pandemii COVID-19. Analiza porównawcza na podstawie opinii ekspertów z wybranych krajów. *Zdrowie Publiczne i Zarządzanie*, 18(1), pp. 1–31. http://dx.doi.org/10.4467/20842627OZ.20.001.12655

Gulczyński, M. (2007). *Nauka o polityce*. Wyższa Szkoła Ekonomiczna. Wydawnictwa, DRUKTUR.

Górniak, J., Krupnik, S., & Koniewski, M. (2020), *Państwa wobec pandemii; perspektywa porównawcza [in:] M. Kossowska i in., Człowiek w obliczu*

pandemii: psychologiczne i społeczne uwarunkowania zachowań w warunkach kryzysu zdrowotnego. Smak Słowa.
Hajder, K., & Musiał-Karg, M., & Górny, M. (Eds) (2020), *Konsekwencje Pandemii COVID-19. Państwo i społeczeństwo*. Wydawnictwo Naukowe Wydziału Nauk Politycznych i Dziennikarstwa Uniwersytetu Adama Mickiewicza.
Hausner, J. (Ed.) (2009). *Administracja publiczna*. Wydawnictwo Naukowe PWN.
Hoffman, T. (2018). *Wybrane aspekty cyberbezpieczeństwa w Polsce*. FNCE.
Horton, R. (2021). *The COVID-19 Catastrophe: What's Gone Wrong and How to Stop It Happening Again*. Wiley.
Izdebski, H. (2020). Legislacja dotycząca COVID-19 i ustawowy nihilizm prawny. In T. Gardocka, & D. Jagiełło (Eds), *Pandemia COVID-19 a prawa i wolności obywatela* (pp. 29–58). C.H.Beck.
Kanada: po epidemii pomoc (2020). *Kanada: po epidemii pomoc dla małych i średnich firm, nie dla korporacji*. Dziennik Gazeta Prawna. Available from: https://www.gazetaprawna.pl/wiadomosci/artykuly/1468839,kanada-po-epidemii-pomoc-dla-malych-i-srednich-firm-nie-dla-korporacji.html
Kaufmann, F.-X. (1970). *Sicherheit als soziologisches und sozialpolitisches Problem. Untersuchungen zu einer Wertidee hochdifferenzierter Gesellschaften (Soziologische Gegenwartsfragen, N.F., 31)*. Stuttgart: Enke.
Kiwerska, J. (2020). Stosunki transatlantyckie w kryzysie nie tylko „pandemicznym". In K. Hajder, M. Kacperska, & Ł. Donaj (Eds), *Konsekwencje pandemii COVID-19. Świat i gospodarka*. Wydawnictwo Naukowe Wydziału Nauk Politycznych i Dziennikarstwa.
Klimczuk, A. (2021). Pandemia COVID-19 z perspektywy teorii ryzyka. In K. Księżopolski, A. Bartoszewicz, & A. Zybała (Eds), *Polska...Unia Europejska... Świat... w pandemii COVID-19 – wybrane zagadnienia. Wnioski dla kształtowania i prowadzenia polityki publicznej* (pp. 35–57). Dom Wydawniczy ELIPSA.
Koley, T.K., & Dhole, M. (2020). *The COVID-19 Pandemic: The Deadly Coronavirus Outbreak*. Taylor & Francis Ltd.
Lyon, D. (2022). *Pandemic Surveillance*. Polity.
MacKenzie, D. (2020a). *COVID-19: The Pandemic That Never Should Have Happened and How to Stop the Next One*. Hachette Books.
MacKenzie, D. (2020b). *Stopping the Next Pandemic: How Covid-19 Can Help Us Save Humanity*. Hachette Books.
Maderak, K., Mroczka, K., & Zieliński, K. (2021). Nadzór nad cyberbezpieczeństwem rynku finansowego w Polsce: perspektywa nadzorcza. In L. Gąsiorkiewicz, & J. Monkiewicz (Eds), *Finanse cyfrowe: informatyzacja, cyfryzacja i datafikacja* (pp. 255–277). Oficyna Wydawnicza Politechniki Warszawskiej.
Mazur, S. (Ed.) (2011). *Państwo integrujące zasoby – potencjał rozwojowy a jakość regulacji publicznych*. Małopolska Szkoła Administracji Publicznej Uniwersytetu Ekonomicznego w Krakowie.
Mroczka, K. (2020). *Fake newsy w czasach pandemii koronawirusa – analiza wyzwań i problemów sektora bankowego w Polsce*. Ośrodek Analiz Politologicznych i Studiów nad Bezpieczeństwem. Available from: http://oapuw.pl/fake-newsy-w-czasach-pandemii-koronawirusa-analiza-wyzwan-i-problemow-sektora-bankowego-w-polsce-analiza-dr-kamila-mroczka/
O'Hair, D., & O'Hair, M.J. (2021). *Communicating Science in Times of Crisis: COVID-19 Pandemic*. Wiley-Blackwell.

Orłowska, J., Pawłowska, Z., & Rösler, J. (2021). Europejska współpraca i rywalizacja w zakresie polityk zdrowotnych w dobie pandemii COVID-19. In P. Baranowski, J. Kardaś, & A. Pohl (Eds), *Unilateralny i multilateralny wymiar polityk zdrowotnych w warunkach globalnej pandemii SARS-COV 2*. FNCE.

Osiński, J. (Ed.) (2011). *Administracja publiczna u progu XXI wieku: wyzwania a oczekiwania*. Oficyna Wydawnicza SGH.

POLITICO (2021). Hackers Who Stole Ireland's Hospital Records Offer Decryption Key. *POLITICO Europe*, Available from: https://www.politico.eu/article/ireland-hospital-hack-records-donnelly-cybersecurity/

Radajewski, M. (2020). Prawa i wolności człowieka i obywatela w dobie pandemii. In T. Gardocka, & D. Jagiełło (Eds), *Pandemia COVID-19 a prawa i wolności obywatela* (pp. 77–92). C.H.Beck.

Ransomware Threat Report (2021). *Ransomware Threat Report 2021*. Palo Alto Networks.

Rydlewski, G. (2021a). *Rządzenie w epoce informacji, cyfryzacji i sztucznej inteligencji*. Dom Wydawniczy ELIPSA. Available from: https://www.researchgate.net/publication/349405248_Rzadzenie_w_epoce_informacji_cyfryzacji_i_sztucznej_inteligencji

Rydlewski, G. (2021b). Political Context of the Fight Against the COVID-19 Pandemic in Poland. *European Research Studies*, 24(3), pp. 1011–1019. http://dx.doi.org/10.35808/ersj/2398

Schwab, K., & Malleret, T. (2020). *COVID-19: The Great Reset*. Forum Publishing.

Sienkiewicz, P., & Świeboda, H. (2010). Analiza systemowa bezpieczeństwa cyberprzestrzeni państwa. *Studia i Materiały Polskiego Stowarzyszenia Zarządzania Wiedzą*, 33, pp. 27–36

Szacawa, D. (2020). Państwa nordyckie wobec pandemii COVID-19. *Komentarze Instytutu Europy Środkowej*, No. 153 (56/2020). Available from: https://ies.lublin.pl/komentarze/panstwa-nordyckie-wobec-pandemii-covid-19/

Taylor & Francis (2021), *COVID-19: Novel Coronavirus Content Free to Access*. Available from: https://taylorandfrancis.com/coronavirus/

Waliszewski, K., & Solarz, J.K. (2020). *Całościowe zarządzanie ryzkiem systemowym. Pandemia COVID-19*. Edu-Libri.

WWF (2012). *Living Planet 2012. Biodiversity, Biocapacity and Better Choices*, WWF International.

Zawisza, J. (2015). Cyberprzestrzeń jako zagrożenie bezpieczeństwa państwa. *Journal of Modern Science*, 27(4), pp. 403–416.

Zięba, R. (2004). *Instytucjonalizacja bezpieczeństwa europejskiego. Koncepcje – struktury – funkcjonowanie*. Wydawnictwo Naukowe SCHOLAR

Žižek, S. (2020). *Pandemic!: Covid-19 Shakes the World*. Wiley.

6 The impact of the pandemic on the development of international relations

Marcin Górnikiewicz, Katarzyna Kołodziejczyk, Wiesław Lizak, and Marzena Walkowiak

6.1 The impact of the SARS-CoV-2 pandemic on international cooperation

International relations play a key role in addressing global issues. The world entered the third decade of the 21st century in the shadow of the COVID-19 pandemic, which has noticeably affected the shape of international relations. The consequences of the pandemic relate to all aspects of human activity and to most areas of the functioning of the state. Blockades, quarantines, and border closures led to many negative consequences and disrupted the proper functioning of societies. In addition to repercussions on the health system, the economy, and public security, the consequences of the pandemic also include disruption of international cooperation among states and non-state actors. There is a slowdown in joint international efforts for sustainable development in the world, and in interactions among countries in many regions. International research cooperation, on the other hand, is accelerating. In addition, one should take into account an increase in national egoism, a slowdown in European integration processes, and an increase in internal disputes. The international response to the crisis has revealed weaknesses resulting from too little international cooperation.

International cooperation has for many years been a prerequisite for maintaining global security and for the effective implementation of sustainable development goals. This cooperation is carried out at many levels: state, local government, and non-state actors. Progressive globalisation processes gradually influencing the formation of the so-called information societies have significantly contributed to the strengthening of interstate relations in all aspects. However, the created interstate relations and dependencies have been tested by the outbreak of the SARS-CoV-2 virus pandemic. People around the world have suffered, in terms of both health and disruption of social norms and behaviours. At the intergovernmental level, this affected the ability and willingness to cooperate. Assumed international policy objectives had to temporarily give way to implemented tasks arising from the fight against the pandemic. Representatives of individual countries were fully focused on the ongoing mitigation of the negative effects of the epidemic

DOI: 10.4324/9781003353805-7

emergency at the national level. Moreover, the varied (diversified) policies of individual government administrations in introducing and limiting social and economic restrictions incited international public opinion to criticism of one another. It should be noted, however, that efforts to develop an effective drug or vaccine for COVID-19 have been made both at the level of individual countries and through international cooperation. The very invention of an effective vaccine has proved to be a challenge to interstate relations. Limited quantities of vaccine and the emerging dilemma between the need to effectively solicit as large a supply of vaccine as possible for one's own nation (in line with public expectations) and the need to fulfil standards of interstate solidarity became a major challenge and test for international cooperation. International research cooperation is an important part of modern science. The trend of internationalisation of research is becoming a prominent feature of the new global geography of science (Olechnicka et al., 2019). As Mukhisa Kituyi, Secretary-General of the United Nations Conference on Trade and Development (UNCTAD), points out, we learn more and faster together – and the pandemic highlights the key role of international collaboration at the intersection of science and technology.[1] In recent months, doctors, researchers, epidemiologists, and scientists representing almost every field of knowledge around the world have worked tirelessly together to tackle the COVID-19 pandemic outbreak. Mukhisa Kituyi also recalls that a team of Chinese and Australian scientists published the first genome of the new virus, and the genetic map was made freely available to scientists worldwide.

The blueprint for joint international efforts for "people, planet and prosperity" are the Sustainable Development Goals (SDGs) adopted by resolution of the UN General Assembly on 25 September 2015 in New York (Resolution adopted by, 2015). A recent UN report, *The Sustainable Development Goals Report 2020*, confirmed concerns about the threats to the achievement of the above goals in the wake of the COVID-19 pandemic. As indicated in this document, the COVID-19 pandemic caused an unprecedented crisis, causing major disruptions to the SDGs, with the world's poorest and most vulnerable being most affected (Sustainable Development Goals Report, 2020). Furthermore, the report indicated that the COVID-19 pandemic contributed to growing food insecurity, environmental deterioration, and increased inequality. It was estimated that over 71 million people would be pushed into extreme poverty according to data from the year 2020. The severe increase in unemployment caused by the epidemic crisis has been highlighted. The UN predicts that as a result of the COVID-19 crisis, global human development, as expressed by the Human Development Index (HDI), which measures education, health, and living standards in

1 https://unctad.org/system/files/non-official-document/ecn162020_s02_opening_SG_UNCTAD_MKituyi_en.pdf

countries, will decline for the first time since it was first measured in 1990 (UNDP, 2020). It highlighted the problem of more than one billion slum dwellers worldwide who are more vulnerable to COVID-19, suffering from lack of adequate housing, lack of running water at home, shared toilets, and limited or non-existent waste management systems. Moreover, the results of a global study dedicated to the impacts of COVID-19, published by UNRISD with participation from 82 countries, "confirm the narrative that – as a result of lockdowns – many people around the world have faced a terrible choice between lives and livelihoods" (Ladd & Bortolotti, 2020).

Meanwhile, at the European Union level, sharing information with Chinese researchers has become a new priority. The European Centre for Disease Prevention and Control (ECDC) has been cooperating (under a memorandum of understanding) with the Chinese Center for Disease Control and Prevention for years, so the experts defined a legal framework for cooperation and were in regular contact (Orłowska et al., 2021). In the face of the COVID-19 pandemic, individual countries adopted their own independent policies to combat the negative effects of the crisis. Often the governments of one region did not establish cooperation and did not unify their actions in this regard. This was the attitude adopted by the Nordic countries. Their actions were not coordinated. While Denmark, Finland, Iceland, and Norway pursued a strict policy of implementing restrictions, Sweden adopted the opposite model of combating the pandemic. Sweden limited its response to recommendations and information policy. The lack of a coordinated response between neighbouring societies was important because cooperation would have helped minimise the damage to economic activity. If all Scandinavian countries managed to keep the rate of new infections low, with little strain on hospitals, common borders could be maintained (Hedlund, 2021).

The different and uncoordinated policies of the Nordic countries have had serious consequences. In the social media, nationalist resentment began to surface, resulting, for example, in demands to close the borders with Sweden, which had a very liberal policy towards a rapidly developing pandemic. Relations among the Nordic societies deteriorated, which had a huge impact on mutual cooperation at all levels. As a result, the four remaining Nordic countries eventually went so far as to close their borders. The effect of imposing quarantine on travellers from Sweden was the deepening of the economic downturn. The lack of a common Nordic response to the pandemic has also caused serious disruption to cross-border integration, which is so important for cooperation among the countries in the region.

The situation of the Nordic countries is just one example of the deepening divisions among some countries following the outbreak of the COVID-19 pandemic. The resulting global epidemic crisis has highlighted and exacerbated many weaknesses in international relations, including within other forums for bilateral and multilateral cooperation such as the Visegrad Group, the Weimar Group, but also much wider within ASEAN and the

European Union. In conclusion, the COVID-19 pandemic is one of the greatest challenges to the global community and world security since the harrowing experience of the outbreak of two world wars. In their aftermath, world leaders decided to work together through multilateral international cooperation and to ensure peace, prosperity, and security for the global community. Currently struggling with the COVID-19 pandemic, all actors in international relations hope to develop a supranational system to prevent similar epidemics. The crisis caused by the COVID-19 pandemic is a watershed moment for the world, with many implications in all areas of the functioning of states. Its consequences also relate to international cooperation and interstate relations. The global response to the epidemic has revealed and exacerbated new problems and hitherto unknown issues. International work on sustainable development in the world has come to a halt. The ambitious goals of minimising the development gap among societies, combating poverty, hunger, and climate change had to be postponed. Relations between states in many regions have also deteriorated. The different, inconsistent ways in which many governments implemented (socially unpopular) restrictions exacerbated the differences among societies. A positive effect of the outbreak of the pandemic was the acceleration of international research cooperation. The COVID-19 pandemic has changed the life of the international community in many areas. It has also exposed many weaknesses in individual countries and governments that had not been recognised before the emergence of the SARS-CoV-2 coronavirus. Both experts and governments have begun to pay special attention to global health security, which until now has not been given the attention it deserves, giving way, for example, to military and economic security and even environmental security. Global cooperation on health security, which was initiated during the COVID-19 pandemic, will undoubtedly continue, and it is to be hoped that this will make it possible to protect against the effects of epidemics and pandemics predicted in the future. At the same time, however, it is worth bearing in mind that it has happened, not infrequently, that the most noble expectations have fallen short of the brutal pragmatics of interpersonal relations at the level of dynamically changing circumstances affecting the actual shape of international relations.

6.2 The global pandemic and transatlantic relations

Transatlantic relations during the most difficult period of the global pandemic (as of August 2021) were determined by the presidencies of Donald Trump and Joe Biden, whose visions for international cooperation and the form of combating the virus differed radically. The beginning and the peak of the global pandemic occurred when the Trump administration was in power in the United States, which was of fundamental importance for transatlantic relations. Already during the election campaign, D. Trump became known as a politician undermining the existing principles of international cooperation and striving for political and economic nationalism understood as the implementation and defence of American interests. In a speech delivered on 27 April 2016, he clearly stated that "No country has ever prospered that failed to put its own interests first. (...) The nation-state remains the true foundation for happiness and harmony" (Transcript of Donald Trump's, 2016). American nationalism understood in this way was best reflected by the slogan "America First," which at the same time suggested changes in existing international cooperation and a retreat of the United States from the processes of globalisation.

The views and conduct of foreign policy by President Trump and his administration directly influenced transatlantic relations. Close to the European Union, multilateral cooperation contradicted the new US administration's vision of international relations. D. Trump repeatedly criticised multilateral institutions; threatened to cut funding to the UN; withdrew the United States from, among others, the climate agreement, the UN Human Rights Council, the Trans-Pacific Agreement, and the Iran nuclear deal; suspended negotiations on multilateral trade agreements with the EU; and paralysed the World Trade Organisation's (WTO) dispute settlement system by blocking the appointment of new members to the Appellate Body.

Trump has openly supported Brexit by calling it a "great victory," questioned the legitimacy of alliances such as NATO, announced the withdrawal of US troops from Germany, devalued Germany and Chancellor Angela Merkel's leadership position, and treated the European Union itself as a trade enemy that has exploited the United States in trade. The Trump administration's trade protectionism triumphed when the US introduced tariffs on steel and aluminium exports to the United States from 8 March 2018. The decision was felt not only by the EU, Canada, or Mexico (subject to tariffs since 1 June 2018) accounting for around 40% of steel and aluminium exports to the United States, but also by South Korea, Russia, China, Brazil, and the United Arab Emirates. In response, the European Union imposed retaliatory tariffs on selected US goods (including clothing, leather and sports shoes, cigars, peanut butter, corn, alcohols) worth a total of EUR 2.8 billion. Both sides have also filed complaints with the World Trade Organization. Canada and Mexico took an analogous position on the tariffs. The following year, the Americans, in retaliation for unauthorised financial aid to European aircraft manufacturer Airbus, increased tariffs on EU goods worth a total of USD 7.5 billion (including wine, civil aircrafts, selected types of cheese, olive oil, oranges, seafood, clothing, whisky). The Trump administration decided to take this step after receiving WTO approval, despite the fact that back in 2018 the US president and European Commission president Jean Claude Juncker agreed that the United States would not introduce new tariffs for the time being, and instead the EU agreed to increase imports from the United States of, among other things, soybeans and liquefied natural gas (Werner, 2018). Nevertheless, the threat of US tariffs on cars from the EU hung over transatlantic trade relations, which could ignite a trade war.

US policy under President D. Trump has led to a deterioration in transatlantic relations not seen since the end of World War II. Until the outbreak of the global pandemic, in just the first three years of Trump's presidency, transatlantic relations, which since their establishment have always supported and implemented the values of the liberal international order such as freedom, democracy, the rule of law, human rights and free trade, were severely undermined.

The announcement of a new coronavirus pandemic by the World Health Organisation on 11 March 2020 did not contribute to changing the transatlantic relationship. On the contrary, D. Trump ruthlessly blamed Europe for the spread of the virus in the United States and imposed a 30-day entry ban on people coming to the United States from 26 Schengen countries. Despite the global threat of a COVID-19 pandemic requiring the cooperation of states and international organisations, relations between the United States and the EU have not changed. Moreover, there was no US-EU cooperation contributing to a more effective fight against the pandemic. States reacted selfishly by introducing, as the EU did, export restrictions on selected medical supplies, including masks and hazmat suits, or, as the United States did, by buying up available stocks of the drug Remdesivir, which helps severely ill COVID-19 patients. The vaccine arms race also failed to bring together forces from both sides of the Atlantic, and the so-called vaccine nationalism became a tool of diplomacy.

The pandemic did not change D. Trump's approach to multilateral cooperation, in contrast to the European Union, which took a number of actions at the international level. While D. Trump adopted unilateral actions during the pandemic and openly criticised the World Health Organisation for inadequately responding to the pandemic outbreak and serving Chinese interests, the European Union sought to play a leadership role in the global fight against the pandemic. It was the first to respond to WHO's call for joint global action on 6 April 2020, first by formulating a global response to the pandemic, then by creating Team Europe with EUR 36 billion in funding to fight the pandemic, co-organising the Global Response Summit with countries such as Canada, the UK, Japan, Norway, and Saudi Arabia, and partner organisations such as the Bill and Melinda Gates Foundation, the Wellcome Trust, and the World Bank Group, among others. The Summit has so far been the most important global event bringing together many countries and international and non-governmental organisations to work together to fight the pandemic. The event (4 May 2020) was attended by China, but lacked countries such as the United States, Russia, Brazil, and India. Furthermore, as one of the largest humanitarian donors, the EU actively supported the United Nations Global Humanitarian Response Plan, promoted vaccine research and global equitable access through the COVAX programme, and, as a leading player in the international trade system, the EU took action to support the continuity of supply of goods. The United States and the EU during the pandemic and the presidency of D. Trump participated jointly in only three international initiatives. The first two were undertaken in the framework of the G20 and concerned supporting the poorest countries, in turn, on the issues of debt service suspension in the middle of the pandemic (15 April 2020) and food security (23 April 2020). The third initiative, launched in response to an appeal by WTO, WHO, and FAO (Food and Agriculture Organisation), concerned supporting open and predictable trade in agricultural and food products during the pandemic (22 April 2020) (Schmucker, 2020).

In contrast to D. Trump, the new US president, Joe Biden, noted that a global pandemic requires global cooperation. In his first US foreign policy speech, J. Biden spoke of "restoring American engagement internationally and earn back our leadership position, to catalyze global action on shared challenges" (Remarks by President Biden, 2021). A very strong emphasis on the role of diplomacy, international alliances together with a declaration on regaining US credibility and the "return of America" conditions a real chance for the normalisation of transatlantic relations. In his first days in office, the new president proved his commitment to international cooperation by signing, among other things, a document initiating the process of re-accession of the US to the climate agreement and a regulation suspending US exit from WHO. At the same time, the US administration announced its renewed commitment to the work of the UN Commission on Human Rights and decided to join the international COVAX programme of production and distribution of vaccines, pledging to support the programme with the sum of USD 4 billion, of which the first half was to be delivered immediately, and the second – in 2021 and 2022 – depending on the implementation of the promises of suppliers and the vaccine distribution programme (Biden Administration Reengages, 2021).

The EU–US summit of 15 June 2021, held after a seven-year hiatus, proved that the US-EU dialogue has returned to a level familiar in the world of diplomacy; however, the most important interests of both sides remain unchanged, and it is too early to speculate about a historic turn in mutual relations. On two very important issues, for both the European Union and the United States, no progress has been made. These are, above all, the settlement of trade disputes and the fight against the pandemic. While a five-year truce was reached in the Boeing–Airbus dispute, in the case of aluminium and steel tariffs and retaliatory measures it was only possible to reach a conclusion committing the parties to do their utmost to find a comprehensive solution to trade disputes and to rebuild transatlantic trade relations by the end of the year (2021) (EU–US Summit Statement, 2021).[2] The launch of

2 On the occasion of the G20 summit in Rome on 30–31 October 2021, the United States and the EU agreed to remove tariffs on aluminium and steel, ending the trade dispute that determines transatlantic relations.

the Trade and Technology Council is certainly a good start for the renewed transatlantic partnership in the economic dimension; however, the following years will verify to what extent it is to be a tool for expanding bilateral trade, investments, and technologies and strengthening the position of the United States and the EU in the global economy, and to what extent it is to be an instrument used to fight the growing position of China in the technological dimension (e.g. 5G network). Similarly, on the issue of combating the pandemic, both the EU and the United States pledged cooperation to promote equitable access to vaccines and vaccinate at least two-thirds of the world's population by the end of 2022, but transatlantic relations on this issue were determined by a "patent dispute." President J. Biden called on pharmaceutical companies to revoke vaccine patents against COVID-19, while the European Commission called on President Biden to abolish the US vaccine export ban and defended vaccine patents. Leaving aside which option is more appropriate for the global fight against the pandemic, one thing is certain. In addition to revoking vaccine patents, additional measures are needed, including countries such as the United States and the UK lifting their export bans on vaccines and on ingredients for their manufacturing. The US administration's global vaccine sharing strategy, presented on 3 June 2021, is certainly a new deal in the vaccine diplomatic game. However, it will not strengthen the renewed transatlantic partnership; on the contrary, the United States, which is supposed to be "the vaccine arsenal for the world," is weakening the European Union's position as a leader in the global fight against the pandemic and is competing with China in the vaccine race.

The joint statement of the EU-US Summit also includes issues on which both sides have convergent positions. These include climate issues; strengthening cooperation for reform of WHO and WTO; pursuit of a sustainable and balanced global recovery in accordance with the UN Agenda; support for developing countries; strengthening of democracy, peace, and security; and the need for a firm stance against Russia's actions. The pandemic can be a reason to strengthen transatlantic cooperation on security and defence. The United States has already accepted the EU's invitation to join the European PESCO "Military Mobility" project, and both sides have expressed unwavering support for solid NATO–EU cooperation. In the context of threats such as the pandemic, the United States and the EU should increase the capacity of NATO in the future, which should include the spread of viruses in its security strategy and provide assistance by building up stocks of medical equipment (Donfried & Ischinger, 2020).

The topic that will determine transatlantic relations to the greatest extent in the near future, however, is the rising position of China. According to a US intelligence report of 13 April 2021, China seeks global power and is increasingly becoming an equal competitor challenging the United States in many fields. The COVID-19 pandemic has intensified the US-China global rivalry, so now the Americans are seeking to create a coalition of democratic states to balance the rising China, economically, militarily, and technologically. However, the idea of an alliance of democracies is sold in a "different package," with the message that only liberal democracies acting together are able to meet global challenges, and that the rules of trade and technology that govern the 21st-century world should be set by free market democracies, not by China or other autocracies (Press Briefing, 2021). Whether the European Union will remain neutral in the US-China rivalry is difficult to estimate. The pandemic and D. Trump's inept response to COVID-19 made the EU stop believing in the US leadership role and start looking for its own way in the face of new challenges. The return of the European Union to the idea of strategic autonomy understood as the ability to respond independently to crises and threats may mean that the Union, as Josep Borell stated, in order to "avoid becoming entrenched between the US and China, the EU should deal with them in its own way: it should look at the world from its own point of view, defending its values and interests, and using the instruments of power available to it" (European Parliament, 2020). This will mean that the EU will have to redefine its values and interests on the international stage. However, every EU decision in the context of the US-China rivalry will have an impact on the state of transatlantic relations, including even a scenario in which the price for US support of NATO will be the EU's alignment with the US strategy towards China (Walt, 2019).

President D. Trump had led to a huge breach in transatlantic relations. The pandemic did not contribute to mutual cooperation to combat it, and today one can only speculate what the fight against the virus would have looked like if the United States and the EU had jointly initiated mechanisms to combat COVID-19 and worked to strengthen WHO and the international vaccination programme. Paradoxically, this has strengthened the EU, which has realised that, regardless of who is in power in America, it must identify its own interests and defend them. However, the problem may be the divergent interests of individual EU Member States, which will undoubtedly weaken the EU's response to global challenges such as China, Russia, Iran, North Korea, disinformation, or climate change. President Biden, despite assurances of his commitment to the role of international cooperation, has concentrated in the first 100 days of his presidency on the US vaccination programme. He has not led to a dramatic change in transatlantic relations, and the unresolved trade disputes initiated under President Trump cast a shadow over the EU–US relations. It is also difficult to find joint EU–US initiatives to combat the pandemic and to influence a fairer distribution of vaccines worldwide.

However, the effects of the pandemic will be felt in the near future. Saving states' own economies, struggling for the survival of national health systems, mounting states' debt, humanitarian and migration crises, and climate change are just some of the challenges that could spark social and political unrest in many countries around the world and lead to global instability. In the face of these challenges, a strong transatlantic alliance based on a more symmetrical relationship needs a new start, as it is the only fair and rational solution not only for mutual benefit but also to guarantee a more stable post-pandemic world.

6.3 The impact of the SARS-CoV-2 pandemic on the development of the New Silk Road in Eurasia and Africa

The New Silk Road, i.e. the flagship project of the People's Republic of China, is a specific formula for exporting economic and social solutions developed in the Middle Kingdom to other countries in Central Asia, Europe, and Africa. The question arises, therefore, whether the global pandemic caused by the unrestricted spread of the new SARS-CoV-2 virus (and its subsequent variants) has also hit one of the fundamental projects of Red China. Referring to the Chinese cultural codes determining the perception and way of thinking about international reality, one can safely assume that this kind of "minor" (a few years) problems are included in the process of project implementation even without specifying their exact causes and consequent effects. For example, in the European Union there are countries whose authorities contributed to blocking some elements of investments related to the construction of the New Silk Road. Beijing's response has, for the most part, been very parsimonious and even politically and economically restrained. In many other cultures, blocking the realisation of a strategic project would be considered a reason to exacerbate mutual relations or even apply various pressures and eventually even sanctions. From the Chinese perspective, this is a temporary problem, at worst as long as a given political option is in power in the country (after all, it may also happen that a different faction takes power or simply new people coming from the ruling option, but with a completely different approach to the Chinese project). The Chinese are well aware of this and prefer to wait these few years calmly, rather than provoke a crisis that could lead to an almost open conflict in mutual relations, which could adversely affect the success of the project even in the long term (Gornikiewicz & Zelkowski, 2020). Similarly, the effects of the COVID-19 pandemic were treated as a temporary problem only delaying the hitherto planned pace of the New Silk Road implementation. On the other hand, policymakers in Beijing would not be themselves if they did not try to gain every possible advantage from the crisis, following the principle that wise people get rich in times of prosperity, but fortunes are built only during crises.

Following the initial shock of the outbreak of the pandemic and the introduction of a global "lockdown," together with numerous difficulties in air and, even more so, sea transport, the transport of goods by rail gradually began to increase. From January to May 2021 alone, for example, container traffic between China and the European Union almost doubled. Only a slightly smaller increase was recorded for goods sent on the same route from the European Union to China. In the whole of 2020, the increase in rail freight capacity reached 546.9 thousand TEU, which was largely due to reaching the maximum of the infrastructure and logistics capacity at the time (according to ULTC ERA with 90% of the rail container traffic between the PRC and the EU). Accordingly, the Russian railways, which are a fundamental component of the New Silk Road architecture, began to develop their own capabilities in the area in question this year, including opening alternative rail links, with the aim of being able to secure a carriage of one million TEUs (TEU) by 2025.

In total, despite the restrictions resulting from the pandemic, the EU's trade volume with China increased by two percentage points and, consequently, there was a deficit in the availability of free containers on the market. As a result, container rental prices to the whole of Europe have started to rise. The price can even fluctuate by up to 10% of its previous value within a week. The choice of rail transport was influenced not only by the much faster delivery time and price (as an alternative to the hitherto widespread transfer by sea), but also by the restrictions on ocean trade due to the prevailing pandemic situation. While the world held its breath, preoccupied by the global pandemic, Beijing's flagship project found an ideal application, which had a very positive impact on the rapid development in the area of rail transport. It is hard to imagine a better exemplification of the New Silk Road idea in the economic pragmatics of international markets during the global crisis (Czubiński, 2021; Przybylski, 2021).

It is therefore worth looking at how the pandemic has affected international relations in this area as well. Moving from China towards Europe, it is worth starting with Central Asia. This area now encompasses Kazakhstan, Turkmenistan, Uzbekistan, Kyrgyzstan, and Tajikistan, and almost since the dawn of the Chinese empire has always enjoyed the understandable interest of the rulers of the Middle Kingdom. Dominion over this area ensured China not only peace on its borders, but also control over the flow of goods, services, and people. The inability to even partially control this area would have been just as troublesome as the inability to ensure complete security from the East and South China Seas. In other words, Central Asia was and is strategically important for the pursuit of China's vital interests. In recent years, another, no less important reason has been added, namely the deeper possibility of controlling the situation in Xinjiang, where separatist tendencies are still very much alive (Rogers, 2018). Thus, controlling the province's international surroundings makes it much easier to secure Chinese interests in the area. Afghanistan will soon be overrun again by Taliban forces, which means that it may, after a short period of stability, be interested in supporting centrifugal forces in Xinjiang, among others, which support would necessarily have to be provided precisely by Central Asia (Tariq et al., 2020).

An important building block in the vision of mutual benefits among Beijing and the capitals of particular states is the possibility of mutual benefits arising from the disposal of energy resources and the development of infrastructure for this purpose. In return, the countries of Central Asia gain access to the most lucrative trade route with the opportunity to develop not only their own supply but also their own demand. In other words, along with the growing importance of the New Silk Road, the level of affluence of the inhabitants of these developing countries is also expected to grow, in exchange for raw materials supplied to China in the form of oil and natural gas (the supply of energy obtained from these two sources is expected to double in the Middle Kingdom in the next two decades). The result is a coherence of political and economic vision, which explains why, despite pandemic constraints, the New Silk Road cooperation across Central Asia has been gaining unabated momentum since 2019 (Toktogulova & Zhuang, 2020; Dudkiewicz, 2021).

Moving on to Europe, here, the demand, but also the supply, for goods transported bi-directionally along the New Silk Road is also increasing by leaps and bounds. This is due to the COVID-19 pandemic-induced reduction in air and sea transport traffic. At the same time, the pre-pandemic market of consumer needs has by no means slowed down, but has moved from public and office spaces to private homes. However, the river of goods still has to flow in both directions, which also positively influenced the economic rationale for the development of the New Silk Road in Europe. On the other hand, due to the enormous emphasis placed on the need to combat the epidemic in public spaces, much less has been said about the possible dangers of strengthening the Chinese flagship project in Europe – probably also because, among other things, the project has managed to maintain a relatively decent balance of supply and demand in individual EU countries. China has ceased to be just a supplier of raw materials or cheap parts (including sub-assemblies), and is becoming a leading supplier of complex equipment, machinery, and the most advanced technologies. This means that developing European countries, in contrast to developed countries, increasingly understand the need to participate in the great project of the Middle Kingdom, regardless of internal fears and political animosities. Exclusion from this project at one's own request means lack of access to many benefits accelerating the development of individual countries – for example, Poland alone may gain nearly USD 48 billion if it participates in the construction of the New Silk Road (Woźniak, 2021; Ignatowicz, 2020).

The economic benefits of becoming involved in China's strategic project seem obvious, but on the other hand they are indirectly linked to the need for political restraint in the so-called "internal Chinese affairs," such as the issue of Xinjiang, Hong Kong, Tibet, and Taiwan. Moreover, there is concern that China, even against its own economic interests, could in the future use its growing economic ties to exert political pressure on the EU states (as it happened in the past, for example, in the case of Sino-Vietnamese relations in the last century). The COVID-19 pandemic had a negative impact on the economies of all European countries, making investment offers from the Middle Kingdom take on added significance. The Italian government initially succumbed to their spell in 2019, but soon, under pressure from the rest of the EU, it changed its front and began successively blocking Chinese investment in its own country. In this front of scepticism towards Chinese investments that are part of the great New Silk Road initiative, Germany, France, and, of course, the aforementioned Italy play the most important role in the European Union. Apart from considerations of a political and pro-humanitarian nature, there are mainly very pragmatic reasons behind this stance, such as the desire to ensure protection for one's own economy against too close an integration with that of the Middle Kingdom. These countries are also exerting pressure on other EU Member States in this respect to also be very cautious in accepting Chinese investments and the development of the New Silk Road on their own territory (Wagener et al., 2020).

Even Belarus could not resist Chinese influence, and now Ukraine is increasingly falling into the spiral of economic interdependence (Samakhavets & Hrechyshkina, 2020). This is reminiscent of a situation in which the hard core of the European Union is very slowly but methodically being surrounded by Chinese investments clustering and supporting the New Silk Road increasingly tied to Beijing's political and economic interests. The pandemic has actually accelerated this process on the economic side, and the Chinese, being diplomatic by nature, are so far not linking political motives to this process. Meanwhile, it is to be expected that at the right moment they may play this card, which, it must be said, only excites the admiration of experts who study the complexity of the matter of international relations.

Finally, it is worth looking at the last part of the world to which the New Silk Road leads, namely North Africa. Here, as on the entire continent, a permanent and almost unlimited investment process is under way, with the end of the Belt and Road merely being the proverbial "icing on the cake." The ruling elites of the African states are indebting their own countries in exchange for the development of infrastructure serving, on the one hand, the development of raw material exploitation, the creation of a new market, and the slow rise in the standard of living of the inhabitants (buyers of Chinese goods must, as consumers, be able to purchase them). On the other hand, most Chinese companies (mainly various manufacturing and mining enterprises) employ Chinese people to a limited extent, using workers drawn from the local population. In the opinion of Chinese managers, the local population is not capable of working to Chinese standards. At the same time, the Chinese run numerous schools in Africa, where they educate the young generation according to their own expectations (including learning Chinese), which is likely to reverse the proportion of employees on the labour market in the future and, at the same time, really contribute to increasing the wealth of these societies (School Construction, 2013) – in line with the Chinese vision of growth and prosperity announced in the last century by Deng Xiaoping. Whether this process ultimately turns out to be positive or negative for African societies should be judged by the people of this vast continent themselves and by history. In conclusion, in the case of African countries involved in the New Silk Road, there can be no question of any slowdown in Chinese investment potentially triggered by a global pandemic. Currently, the New Silk Road has covered Senegal, Morocco, Egypt, Nigeria, Angola, South Africa, Mozambique, Tanzania, Kenya, and Ethiopia.

The New Silk Road is a massive project, the outline of which is slowly emerging from the mists of conjecture. The enormity of this undertaking may thrill or terrify, but it is rather difficult to imagine it stopping. When completed, it will encompass not only China, Central Asia, Europe, and South Africa, but also South Asia, North Asia, West Asia, the Arabian Peninsula (the nucleus of the future infrastructure is already in place in Saudi Arabia), and all of Africa. Goods will circulate over the largest land area on the planet and their movement will be directly managed from Beijing. In the final phase, it will probably no longer matter whether the route passes through a particular country or not, as the economy of each country will already be directly and indirectly linked to the route. According to the principle – even if someone else controls international finance, it is equally important who controls the tracks on which all the goods move. Thus, as has been shown, the COVID-19 pandemic outside the western part of the European Union has not only not slowed down the pace of development of the New Silk Road, but has even contributed to its accelerated development. The global crisis arrived, which the decision-makers of the Middle Kingdom were able to exploit perfectly for their own purposes, proving that probably already their flagship project, according to the American saying dedicated to the largest banks and corporations operating in times of crisis, "is too big to fall down." However, it would be more correct to say that the Chinese Silk Road is already too big and too fast to come to a sudden halt.

COVID-19 has left its mark on the Chinese economy, which can be clearly seen in the fact that the Middle Kingdom's GDP fell by 6.8% in 2020 compared to the previous year. It is worth noting that this is the worst result since 1992. In China, the threat posed by the risk of the spread of the pandemic has been taken very seriously, so the successive restrictions which have been introduced have had a negative impact on economic indicators in almost all areas of the country's economic activity. In the first quarter of 2020, declines were recorded: consumption by 19%, industrial production by 8.4%, exports by 11.4%, imports by 0.7%, and investments by 16.1%. A gentle rebound from the downward trend was observed at the end of the quarter in April 2020. The authorities of the People's Republic of China have taken a number of measures to support the observed and more acutely noticeable economic progress by investing in infrastructure, financially stimulating the market for new technologies (including 5G and AI), increasing the liquidity of the banking sector, and stimulating dying consumption. A much larger stream of financing is to be diverted from foreign markets, to the domestic market, which constraints are also to affect the New Silk Road (Wnukowski & Przychodniak, 2020). Since September

2020, there has been economic growth as a result of the indicated stimulation of the economy and the post-epidemic gradual lifting of restrictions. As a result, in 2021 the Chinese economy recorded single-digit growth comparing with 2019 and double-digit if we refer to the period of sudden decline in the first quarter of 2020 (Czego nie mówi, 2021). During the 2019–2020 transition period, when the Middle Kingdom deliberately froze its own economy, this approach did not negatively affect the further development of the New Silk Road. It can therefore be assumed that the implementation and development phase of the flagship project of the People's Republic of China is already so advanced that not only has it not been harmed by the global recession resulting from COVID-19, but even that Beijing is not forced to over-invest in the project to ensure its further development. The New Silk Road has survived the global COVID-19 pandemic and the severe economic consequences it caused in the Middle Kingdom. It has become independent of external support, gaining self-sufficiency for further development, and in this context it is a special project. It may therefore be assumed that in the future rapid economic growth of the Middle Kingdom will depend only in part on its own potential, and in part on the comprehensive potential of several dozen countries around the world, successively accumulated thanks to the Road. At the same time, all economic crises (caused, for example, by successive generations of epidemics) will weaken the economies of individual countries, but strengthen the potential of large international projects. These projects will be able to serve as a kind of stabiliser of the global economy, which will be exposed to increasing difficulties caused by future crises resulting from progressing climatic, economic, political, and even sociocultural changes. COVID-19 is arguably only a prelude to what is yet to come. As a result, the amazing functionality of global projects such as the New Silk Road in the face of crises may prove to be one of the few global forms of protection of the existing international order.

6.4 SARS-CoV-2 pandemic and the situation in Africa and Latin America (Global South)

The intensive communication, transport, and economic links of African countries with China or Europe meant that the SARS-CoV-2 virus appeared very quickly in Africa – the first case of the disease was reported in Egypt as early as February/March 2020. On 5 March, the pathogenic virus was detected in a man returning to South Africa from Milan. The country soon became the one most affected by COVID-19 on the African continent and one of the global centres of infections.[3] The countries most affected by the

3 At the end of July 2021, the number of infected people in South Africa was approximately 2.37 million out of a population of 57 million.

pandemic – apart from South Africa – included North African countries and Ethiopia, Kenya, Zambia, and Nigeria.[4]

For several months of the pandemic, however, its course in Africa was milder than in other regions of the world – at least according to official data. The slower rate of spread of the virus in Africa was due to several reasons. First, the age structure of the population in most countries in the region indicates a predominance of young people in those societies. Long-term underinvestment in healthcare infrastructure and high population growth rates mean that the proportion of older people in societies in the region is low (60% of the population in Africa is under 25 years of age), and it is this age group that is most at risk of high mortality. Second, it is important to point to the lower mobility of the population in many parts of Africa, which has entailed a slower spread of the virus, although at the same time, accelerated urbanisation during the post-colonial period has led to the emergence of huge agglomerations with poor infrastructure securing basic human needs, a factor that favours the expansion of epidemiological risks. Finally, the official results of infections were probably also influenced by the lack of medical equipment to test the population, which underestimated the official figures. At the same time, there was a pattern indicating that successive phases of the pandemic showed an increase in the number of infections and deaths – underinvestment in health systems meant that over time mortality rates in Africa exceeded the global average.[5] Awareness of the magnitude of the resulting threat underpinned policymakers' decisions to create new and improve existing regional cooperation mechanisms to increase access to healthcare resources and to develop prevention and rapid response mechanisms in situations of increased epidemiological threats.

It is worth remembering that similar situations are not new in Africa. For many African countries, the emergence of epidemiological threats related to COVID-19 represented a further step in the long-term process of eliminating pathogens in the region. For many years, Africa has been faced with a succession of threats of a similar nature. Diseases such as malaria, tuberculosis, and AIDS are constantly present in Africa, and in some regions of the continent so-called haemorrhagic fevers appear periodically (e.g. Lassa haemorrhagic fever, Ebola haemorrhagic fever, Rift Valley haemorrhagic fever, Dengue fever, yellow fever), where the mortality rate is usually much higher than in the case of COVID-19. The persistent nature of these threats provided the rationale for the creation of appropriate regional institutions for both prevention and the establishment of cooperative mechanisms for rapid response in the event of a new outbreak. The impetus for the creation of these institutions was created in particular by the 2013–2015 Ebola

4 The number of infections in Africa at the end of July 2021 was about 6.5 million, and the number of deaths was about 164,000.

5 By mid-2021, the ratio for Africa was 2.6 against a global average of 2.2.

haemorrhagic fever epidemic in West Africa – it was then possible to limit the spread of the disease to Guinea, Sierra Leone, and Liberia, while single cases in Mali, Nigeria, and Senegal remained isolated thanks to appropriate medical and administrative action. The lessons learned from this have been firmly embedded in the emergency response system of many countries in the region (e.g. at the airports), ensuring that African countries were not completely helpless when another pathogen emerged. It has also stimulated the creation of platforms for international cooperation, both among countries in the region and with non-African actors. Precisely because of the persistent nature of epidemiological threats on the continent, international institutions have been present there for a long time, supporting countries and societies in the development of local healthcare systems and widely understood activities to raise the level of hygiene (including institutions of the United Nations system, such as WHO or UNICEF, the European Union, as well as NGOs involved in humanitarian and development aid).

As a result of these processes, in January 2016, during the 26th Assembly (the AU Summit with Heads of State and Government) of the African Union, an organisation bringing together all African countries, a decision was made (at the initiative of Guinea's president Alpha Conde) to create the Africa Centres for Disease Control and Prevention (Africa CDC). This decision was preceded by a preparatory meeting with African health ministers in Malabo (Equatorial Guinea) in July 2015. In January 2017, the centres became operational. In essence, it is a cooperation mechanism consisting of a central unit based in Addis Ababa (Emergency Operations Centre), to which five sub-regional centres report: in Egypt (for 7 Northern African countries, including Western Sahara), Nigeria (15 Western African countries), Gabon (9 Central African countries), Kenya (14 Eastern African countries), and Zambia (10 Southern African countries). The Africa CDC is primarily tasked with strengthening the capacity of African public health institutions and assisting countries affected by crisis, establishing an early warning system, harmonising health policies, and promoting partnerships for effective responses to epidemiological threats. The emergence of the pandemic in early 2020 therefore came at a time when institutions already existed in Africa that could make efforts to coordinate international cooperation for prevention and containment of the spread of the pandemic. The African Union and its functioning institutions became the main interface of the regional collective of states for pandemic prevention; thus, the importance of the Africa CDC increased significantly (Africa CDC: Centres; Research and Development Priorities, 2021).

This cooperation was multidirectional. Among other things, in response to the outbreak of the pandemic, informational activities were undertaken in an attempt to reach people on the continent with appropriate hygiene recommendations. An example of such an operation, undertaken in mid-2021 in conjunction with the South African–based telecommunications company MTN Group, is the "One More Push" outreach campaign to encourage people in the region to practise preventive measures for as long as possible (Africa CDC and MTN, 2021). On the initiative of South African president Cyril Ramaphosa, the AU's president in 2020, the African Union's COVID-19 Vaccine Acquisition Task Team (AVATT) was established on 6 November, tasked with ensuring equitable access to vaccines across African countries and adequate funding for these activities. As a result, an agreement to deliver 400 million Johnson & Johnson vaccines to the continent was negotiated on 28 March 2021, with financial support for the effort from the African Export-Import Bank (Afreximbank) and backing from the World Bank (The World Bank, 2021).

The scale of the coronavirus threat and infrastructural deficiencies in Africa prompted representatives of the political and medical communities to initiate a programme to increase vaccine manufacturing capacity in the region. The Partnerships for African Vaccine Manufacturing (PAVM) was inaugurated at a virtual summit (under the theme "Expanding Africa's Vaccine Manufacturing for Health Security: Building back better, bolder and bigger"), organised by the AU Commission and Africa CDC on 12–13 April 2021 under the chairmanship of President Felix Tshisekedi of DR Congo, who has been leading the AU in 2021. It worked out a plan to develop by 2040 an African vaccine manufacturing infrastructure providing 60% coverage. The meeting was attended in various forms by over 40,000 participants representing countries, international organisations, academic and research centres, aid institutions, medical communities, and other stakeholders from around the world. Such a great response to this initiative and the participation of major international institutions (such as the UN and major humanitarian organisations) raise hopes for the success of the project (Statement, 2021).

The above examples demonstrate the scale and scope of the cooperation mechanisms that were initiated in the context of the threats posed by the coronavirus. The cooperation mechanisms that were developed during the pandemic were obviously not able to prevent it from fully unfolding in individual African countries, nor were they able to secure the resulting hygiene or health needs. However, they do show that the political will exists to solve African problems both within a regional framework and through cooperation with extra-regional actors. It would appear that the intensity of international cooperation in Africa undertaken in relation to the development of the COVID-19 pandemic does not differ in scale and scope from similar activities in other regions of the world, and probably exceeds the global average. Unfortunately, this is not enough to quickly overcome the infrastructural deficiencies in healthcare systems or the lack of material resources that determine the still high risk of further expansion of the disease.

In the economic dimension, the COVID-19 pandemic has had a number of negative consequences for countries in the region. According to experts, in 2020, for the first time in 25 years, there was a decline in GDP for Africa (by about 3.2%), as a result of disruptions in international trade, a decrease in demand for African raw materials (slowdown in economic growth in China and OECD countries), or a reduction in tourism. The pandemic contributed to a six-month delay in the implementation of the provisions for the creation of the African Continental Free Trade Area (AfCFTA), established by the agreement of 21 March 2018. The provisions finally entered into force on 1 January 2021. However, the enthusiastic assessments of this step on the part of African leaders and the hopes that it will become a strong impetus for the development of the continent allow us to conclude that, in this case, the pandemic-induced disruption will have little impact on the process of economic integration in Africa, considered as one of the important means of overcoming deficits in the structure of the economies of the countries of the region.

The decline in Africa's GDP has contributed to lower living standards for many groups, disruptions in the functioning of and access to the labour market have emerged, the decline in the number of people living in extreme poverty has been reversed, pauperisation threatens to increase labour migration, including outside the African continent. The enormous socio-economic challenges that Africa faced before the pandemic have intensified. This will probably require modification of existing strategies and development of new strategies to recover from the crisis in which African countries found themselves. It is to be expected that the new challenges facing Africa will further strengthen the role and international position of African Union as a coordinator in the search for solutions to the continent's emerging challenges, both regionally and in its dealings with actors outside Africa.

Pandemic threats also create space for political risks to emerge. Deterioration of the socio-economic situation increases the mood of social discontent. Of course, the social costs of the pandemic are not the only source of threats here; nevertheless, they reinforce problems resulting from already existing negative phenomena, such as unemployment, lack of social security systems, or instability generated by the broadly defined dysfunctionality of countries in the region (Kłosowicz, 2017). The increase in COVID-19 infections, among others, became the reason for postponing by one year the general elections in Ethiopia in 2020, consequently leading to accusations of authoritarian tendencies by the authorities and reinforcing the contradictions underlying the conflict in Tigray province. Also, the attempt to extend the term of office of the Somali authorities in relation to the COVID-19 pandemic led to a political crisis and the eventual withdrawal of decision-makers from such steps. In Burundi and Tanzania, restrictions justified by the need for epidemiological protection of the population have been used, according to independent observers, as a means of restricting the freedom of action of the political opposition. The evolution of the political systems of many African countries towards authoritarianism is a process that has been observed for at least a decade, but the above examples show that the development of the pandemic has made the resulting threats in many countries a powerful means of limiting the ability of opposition forces to act freely and strengthening the existing political regime.

Latin America has proved to be the region where the course of the coronavirus pandemic has been particularly dramatic. Brazil became the symbol of the irresponsible approach to the risks posed by the uncontrolled development of the pandemic.[6] The reason for this was, above all, the cavalier attitude of the country's president, Jair Bolsonaro, to the risks posed by the spread of infections. His reluctance to acknowledge the true scale of the threat and his unwillingness to take measures that might limit the spread of the virus have become the subject of controversy, both in Brazil and around the world. Other countries in the region, such as Mexico, Peru, Ecuador, and Colombia, have also experienced an above-average scale of infections. Mexico, Ecuador, and Bolivia are also among the countries with the highest mortality rates among those infected, according to official statistics.[7]

The reasons for such a violent course of the coronavirus pandemic in Latin America are mainly to be found in socio-economic conditions. A characteristic feature of countries in this region are huge disparities in the incomes of their populations, leading to great social stratification. This factor is one of the main barriers to development for the region, and during the expansion of the pandemic it has become a premise determining the ability to act effectively in terms of prevention and healthcare within particular social groups. High official unemployment rates and an expanded informal sector of the economy meant that attempts to introduce restrictions on population movement were not effective in a situation where the state was unable to provide the poorer classes of society with the necessary means of existence – aid targeted at excluded social groups proved to be far too small to ensure the survival of this population group in lockdown conditions, forcing them to take up gainful employment despite epidemic restrictions. Other barriers hindering the fight against the pandemic include underinvestment in healthcare systems and the relatively high level of privatisation of healthcare services, which for people with low incomes means, in fact, very often no access to medical care. A characteristic feature of this group of countries is also the lack of effective social security systems, which condemns marginalised social groups to vegetation on the margins of society. A significant role is also played by corruption, which disturbs the rationality of decision-making mechanisms in the use of public funds, and political instability in countries such as Venezuela, Bolivia, and Peru. In countries where the pandemic was particularly severe, negative phenomena such as

6 At the end of July 2021, the number of infections in Brazil approached 20 million. Globally, the figure was 194 million, representing a share of more than 10% (Brazil's population represents about 2.78% of the world's population).

7 The figures are: Mexico – 9.08% (only civil war–ravaged Yemen has a higher mortality rate globally), Ecuador – 5.04%, and Bolivia – 4.47%.

the erosion of the system of power or an increase in the level of contestation of the political system and ruling elites by various social groups have deepened. This was the case in Brazil, where the level of public approval of the incumbent president, who had ostentatiously denied the existence of epidemiological risks for many months, had significantly decreased. In Chile, the costs of the pandemic became one of the sources of social unrest in 2020 – they led to the initiation of a process of reform of the political system (COVID-19 in Latin America, 2020). Similarly, mass demonstrations erupted in April 2021 in Colombia due to the deteriorating living conditions of poorer sections of society. Crisis phenomena in the economy have also made themselves known, and with great intensity – according to the assessments of some experts, the decline in GDP for the Latin American and Caribbean region in 2020 was as high as 9.1% (COVID-19 Special Report No. 5, 2020). In practice, this means – combined with the scarcity of material and institutional social security resources, the closure of borders and the rupture of existing supply chains – an increase in the number of people living in extreme poverty (Regional Human Development Report 2021, pp. 65–78), and previous trends of improving living conditions for marginalised groups will be halted in the coming years.[8] This requires a redefinition of the assumptions of the implemented socio-economic development strategies in the following years.

The awareness of the existence of structural barriers affecting the ability to cope with epidemiological threats has given rise to reflection on ways out of the crisis. Among others, at the level of heads of diplomacy, a discussion on this issue was undertaken at the UN Economic Commission for Latin America and the Caribbean (ECLAC) in the framework of the so-called dialogue of ministers of foreign affairs and high-level authorities of Latin America and the Caribbean on the post-pandemic economic recovery. As a result, a Political Declaration for a Sustainable, Inclusive and Resilient Recovery in the Region was adopted by representatives of 28 countries at the 38th session of ECLAC on 26 October 2020.

The content of the Declaration indicated the main principles on which the cooperation of states should be based in the phase of recovery from the epidemiological and economic crisis. Such principles as financial solidarity of states, renewed multilateralism, deepening regional integration and sustainable development were cited. Reference was also made to the principle of solidarity in North–South relations and a call was made for the deepening of partnerships between the state and the private sector. At the same time, it was declared that within the framework of the developed strategies, efforts should focus on basic human needs, referring to the need to protect human rights and fundamental freedoms in their various dimensions (including

8 ECLAC estimates that the number of people living in extreme poverty in the region increased by 22 million in 2020.

women's rights). It was pointed out that the success of the efforts to eliminate epidemiological threats depends on the need to activate comprehensive global cooperation mechanisms and at the same time to refrain from unilateral actions that could disrupt such cooperation. The Declaration clearly emphasises the conviction that the fight against the pandemic and responses to crisis phenomena caused by it should be part of long-term strategies for eliminating negative phenomena and processes that prevent the region from achieving sustainable and balanced development (Foreign Ministers, 2020). The Declaration clearly refers to the common destiny of the countries and inhabitants of the region, announcing the deepening of mutual cooperation for the implementation of their goals. At the same time, one should bear in mind the enormous differences among the states of the region in formulating their visions for the future of the continent (economic potential, ethnic and ideological differences), which means that the implementation of the goals contained in the Declaration will require a readiness to make compromises and a deepening of the awareness of the common destiny of the region.

The Pan-American cooperation system (Organisation of American States) also has a regional health agency, the Pan American Health Oganization (PAHO), which dates back to 1902. It was within the framework of this agency that efforts were made to ensure the supply of vaccines to the various countries in the region in a manner designed to ensure equal and non-discriminatory access. To achieve this goal, PAHO joined the COVAX initiative, established in April 2020 and managed by four entities: the WHO; the Coalition for Epidemic Preparedness Innovations (CEPI), which has been pursuing its objectives since 2017; Gavi (Global Alliance for Vaccines and Immunization), whose mission is to support the vaccination of children against threatening diseases worldwide; and the United Nations Children's Fund (UNICEF). Many countries, international organisations, and non-governmental entities have joined the COVAX initiative with the task of coordinating efforts in accessing COVID-19 vaccines for all inhabitants of the planet. Thanks to PAHO's commitment, from 1 March 2021, supplies have been launched for almost all countries in the region, both in Latin America and for island states in the Caribbean region (Arrival of COVID-19 vaccines, 2021). However, this indubitable success is overshadowed by the fact that the Pan-American agency has had to face financial difficulties in recent months due to a lack of sufficient commitment from certain countries (COVID-19 in Latin America, 2020).

The examples described above show that, in the face of the epidemiological threats posed by coronavirus, countries in the global South are able to work together to minimise the negative effects of this phenomenon, both regionally and globally. The benefits arising from this create hope for the inclusion of countries and societies from less developed regions in global mechanisms of cooperation to raise health standards, which is particularly important given the cross-border nature of epidemiological threats. At the same time, for this mechanism to be effective, many barriers that have so far hindered the effective functioning of such cooperation platforms must be eliminated. This includes factors such as counteracting social exclusion, basing development strategies on the principle of sustainable development, or multilateralism and cooperation based on common interests.

References

Africa CDC and MTN (2021). *Africa CDC and MTN Accelerate Fight Against COVID-19 with "One More Push" Campaign.* 08.07.2021. Available from: https://africacdc.org/news-item/africa-cdc-and-mtn-accelerate-fight-against-covid-19-with-one-more-push-campaign/

Africa CDC: Centres for Disease Control and Prevention. Available from: https://africacdc.org/

Arrival of COVID-19 Vaccines (2021). *Arrival of COVID-19 Vaccines to the Americas through COVAX*, Pan American Health Organisation. Available from: https://www.paho.org/en/covax-americas

Biden Administration Reengages (2021). Biden Administration Reengages with International Institutions and Agreements. *American Journal of International Law*, 11(2), pp. 323–329. Available from: https://www.cambridge.org/core/journals/american-journal-of-international-law/article/biden-administration-reengages-with-international-institutions-and-agreements, accessed: 21.06.2021.

COVID-19 in Latin America (2020). COVID-19 in Latin America: A Humanitarian Crisis. *The Lancet*, 396, November 7. Available from: https://www.thelancet.com/action/showPdf?pii=S0140-6736%2820%2932328-

COVID-19 Special Report No. 5 (2020). *COVID-19 Special Report No. 5: Addressing the Growing Impact of COVID-19 with a View to Reactivation with Equality: New Projections.* Economic Commission for Latin America and Caribbean (ECLAC), 15 July. Available from: https://repositorio.cepal.org/bitstream/handle/11362/45784/4/S2000470_en.pdf

Czego nie mówi (2021). *Czego nie mówi o gospodarce gwałtowny wzrost PKB Chin.* Forsal. Available from: https://forsal.pl/swiat/chiny/artykuly/8143239,czego-nie-mowi-o-gospodarce-gwaltowny-wzrost-pkb-chin.html, accessed: 16.04.2021

Czubiński, R. (2021). *Nowy Jedwabny Szlak: Ruch do Chin mniejszy niż do Europy, ale rośnie szybciej.* Available from: https://www.rynek-kolejowy.pl/wiadomosci/nowy-jedwabny-szlak-ruch-kolejowy-do-chin-mniejszy-ale-rosnie-szybciej-103116.html, accessed: 24.06.2021

Donfriend, K., & Ischinger, W. (2020). *The Pandemic and the Toll of Transatlantic Discord.* Foreign Affairs. Available from: https://www.foreignaffairs.com/articles/united-states/2020-04-18/pandemic-and-toll-transatlantic-discord, accessed: 29.06.2021

Dudkiewicz, P. (2021). *Obszar Azji Centralnej w chińskim projekcie Nowego Jedwabnego Szlaku.* Available from: https://ine.org.pl/obszar-azji-centralnej-w-chinskim-projekcie-nowego-jedwabnego-szlaku/, accessed: 05.02.2021.

European Parliament (2020). *No Way Back: Why the Transatlantic Future Needs a Stronger EU*, p. 9. Available from: https://www.europarl.europa.eu/thinktank/en/document.html?reference=EXPO_IDA

EU-US Summit Statement (2021). *Towards a Renewed Transatlantic Partnership*, 15.06.2021. Available from: https://www.whitehouse.gov/briefing-room/statements-releases/2021/06/15/u-s-eu-summit-statement/, accessed: 28.06.2021.

Foreign Ministers (2020). *Foreign Ministers and High-level Authorities from Latin America and the Caribbean Sign a Political Declaration for a Sustainable, Inclusive and Resilient Recovery in the Region*. Economic Commission for Latin America and Caribbean (ECLAC), 26 October. Available from: https://www.cepal.org/en/news/foreign-ministers-and-high-level-authorities-latin-america-and-caribbean-sign-political

Górnikiewicz, M., & Zelkowski, J. (2020). Belt and Road Initiative in the Age of COVID-19 Pandemic: Implications for the Development of the Strategic Project of the People's Republic of China. *European Research Studies Journal*, XXIII(Special Issue 3), pp. 302–310, DOI: 10.35808/ersj/1884

Hedlund, S. (2021). *Covid-19 deepens Nordic disharmony, Geopolitical Intelligence Services*. Available from: https://www.gisreportsonline.com/opinion-covid-19-deepens-nordic-disharmony,politics,3536.html, accessed: 25.06.2021.

Ignatowicz, A. (2020). *Nowy Jedwabny Szlak – kiedy warto wziąć go pod uwagę?* Available from: https://www.namiary.pl/2020/07/16/nowy-jedwabny-szlak-kiedy-warto-wziac-go-pod-uwage/, 16.07.2020

Kłosowicz, R. (2017). *Konteksty dysfunkcyjności państw Afryki Subsaharyjskiej*. Wydawnictwo Uniwersytetu Jagiellońskiego.

Ladd, P., & Bortolotti, E. (2020). *Protecting and Supporting Vulnerable Groups Through the Covid-19 Crisis*. United Nations Research Institute for Social Development (UNRISD).

Olechnicka, A., Płoszaj, A., & Celińska-Janowicz, D. (2019). *The Geography of Scientific Collaboration*. Routledge.

Orłowska, J., Pawłowska, Z., & Rösler, J. (2021). *Europejska współpraca i rywalizacja w zakresie polityk zdrowotnych w dobie pandemii COVID-19*. Uniwersytet im. Adama Mickiewicza w Poznaniu.

Press Briefing (2021). *Press Briefing by Press Secretary Jen Psaki and National Security Advisor Jake Sullivan*. Available from: https://www.whitehouse.gov/briefing-room/press-briefings/2021/06/07/press-briefing-by-press-secretary-jen-psaki-and-national-security-advisor-jake-sullivan-june-7-2021/, accessed: 28.06.2021.

Przybylski, R. (2021). *Spedytorzy przesiadają się ze statków na pociągi*. Available from: https://logistyka.rp.pl/koronawirus/15939-spedytorzy-przesiadaja-sie-ze-statkow-na-pociagi, accessed: 27.05.2021.

Regional Human Development Report (2021). *Trapped: High Inequality and Low Growth in Latin America and the Caribbean*. UNDP. Available from: https://www.latinamerica.undp.org/content/rblac/en/home/library/human_development/regional-human-development-report-2021.html

Remarks by President Biden (2021). *Remarks by President Biden on America's Place in the World*. Available from: https://www.whitehouse.gov/briefing-room/speeches-remarks/2021/02/04/remarks-by-president-biden-on-americas-place-in-the-world/, accessed: 21.06.2021.

Research and Development Priorities (2021). *Research and Development Priorities for COVID-19 in Africa*. Available from: https://africacdc.org/download/policy-paper-research-and-development-priorities-for-covid-19-in-africa/

Resolution Adopted By (2015). *Resolution Adopted by the General Assembly, Transforming Our World: The 2030 Agenda for Sustainable Development A/RES/70/1 of 25 September 2015*. Available from: http://www.unic.un.org.pl/files/164/Agenda%202030_pl_2016_ostateczna.pdf, accessed: 25.06.2020.

Rogers, R.A. (2018). The Radicalisation of Xinjiang: Its Roots and Impact on Human Rights. *Contemporary Chinese Political Economy and Strategic Relations: An International Journal*, 4(2), pp. 487–512.

Samakhavets, M., & Hrechyshkina, O. (2020). Main Characteristics of the Foreign Investment Development of Belarus. *Bulletin of Geography. Socio-Economic Series*, 48, pp. 129–139. DOI: 10.1515/28349

Schmucker, C. (2020). The Effects on the Covid-19 Pandemic on US and European Commitment to the Multilateral Economic Order. *IAI Papers*, 20/39, pp. 6, 11. Available from: https://www.iai.it/en/pubblicazioni/effects-covid-19-pandemic-us-and-european-commitment-multilateral-economic-order, accessed: 20.06.2021.

School Construction (2013). *School Construction: World Bank versus China*. Available from: http://www.chinaafricarealstory.com/2013/01/school-construction-world-bank-versus.html, accessed: 29.01.2013.

Statement (2021). *Statement on the Remarkable Progress Made by Several African Countries as Part of the Partnerships for African Vaccine Manufacturing (PAVM)*. Available from: https://africacdc.org/news-item/statement-on-the-remarkable-progress-made-by-several-african-countries-as-part-of-the-partnerships-for-african-vaccine-manufacturing-pavm/

Sustainable Development Goals Report 2020. New York, 2020. Available from: https://www.un.org/development/desa/publications/publication/sustainable-development-goals-report-2020

Tariq, M., Rizwan, M., & Ahmad, M. (2020). US Withdrawal from Afghanistan: Latest Development and Security Situation. *Sir Syed Journal of Education & Social Research (SJESR)*, 3(2).

TEU (2002). A Unit of Volume Equivalent to a 20-Foot Container: OECD, Glossary for Statistical Terms. Available from: https://stats.oecd.org/glossary/detail.asp?ID=4313, accessed: 19.06.2002.

The World Bank (2021). *The World Bank and the African Union's COVID-19 Africa Vaccine Acquisition Task Team (AVATT) Agree to Work Together to Deploy Vaccines for 400million Africans*. Available from: https://africacdc.org/news-item/the-world-bank-and-the-african-unions-covid-19-africa-vaccine-acquisition-task-team-avatt-agree-to-work-together-to-deploy-vaccines-for-400million-africans/

Toktogulova, D., & Zhuang, W. (2020). A Critical Analysis of the Belt and Road Initiative in Central Asia. *International Journal of Managerial Studies and Research*, 8(8, August).

Transcript of Donald Trump's (2016). *Transcript of Donald Trump's Foreign Policy Speech*. Available from: https://www.nytimes.com/2016/04/28/us/politics/transcript-trump-foreign-policy.html, accessed: 21.05.2021.

UNDP (2020). *COVID-19 and Human Development: Assessing the Crisis, Envisioning the Recovery, Human Development Perspectives*. Available from: http://hdr.undp.org/sites/default/files/covid-19_and_human_development_0.pdf

Wagener, N., Aritua, B., & Zhu, T. (2020). The New Silk Road: Opportunities for Global Supply Chains and Challenges for Further Development. *LogForum*, 16(2).

Walt, S. (2019). *Europe's Future is as China's Enemy*. Foreign Policy. Available from: https://foreignpolicy.com/2019/01/22/europes-future-is-as-chinas-enemy/, accessed: 29.06.2021

Werner, D. (2018). *Was the Trump-Junker Meeting Really a Success?* Available from: https://www.atlanticcouncil.org/blogs/new-atlanticist/was-the-trump-juncker-meeting-really-a-success/, accessed: 21.05.2021

Wnukowski, D., & Przychodniak, M. (2020). Wpływ pandemii COVID-19 na gospodarkę Chin. *Biuletyn PISM*, No. 106 (2038). Available from: file:///C:/Users/GORNIK~1/AppData/Local/Temp/1/Biuletyn%20PISM%20nr%20106%20(2038)%2015%20maja%202020%20r.pdf, accessed: 15.05.2020.

Woźniak, A. (2021). *Polska może zgarnąć z Jedwabnego Szlaku 48 mld dolarów*. Available from: https://www.rp.pl/Gospodarka/301169978-Polska-moze-zgarnac-z-Jedwabnego-Szlaku-48-mld-dolarow.html, accessed: 17.01.2021.

7 The role of international institutions during a pandemic

Joanna Starzyk-Sulejewska

In the face of the COVID-19 crisis, not only states but also international institutions faced one of the most serious tests of the effectiveness of their actions. The aim of this chapter is to analyse the main instruments and forms of action used so far by selected international institutions in the fight against the COVID-19 pandemic in the context of their powers in this dimension. The choice of the UN, WHO, the EU, and the Visegrad Group is not accidental, as these are the institutions that play the most important role in the fight against COVID-19 and represent the activity in question at three basic levels, i.e. at the global, regional, and sub-regional one.

The chapter adopts a main hypothesis and an auxiliary hypothesis. The main hypothesis assumes that the pandemic period is an important test of the effectiveness of the functioning of international organisations and their relations with member states and other international organisations, which indicates potential opportunities and problems of their operation during similar crises in the future. As a subsidiary hypothesis, it has been assumed that during the current pandemic crisis, international organisations have only partially fulfilled their role as crisis managers and supporters of member states in this regard. Several research questions are used to verify the indicated assumptions, such as: Do the selected international institutions have sufficient powers to protect health and fight the pandemic effectively? What forms of action are used by international institutions to fight the pandemic – are they already in place or is this a period of shaping new practices that are more suited to unusual realities? During the pandemic, to what extent are international organisations and other cooperative structures using their capacities and are able to play an effective role as crisis managers on a global, regional, or sub-regional scale (the UN, WHO, the EU, the Visegrad Group)?

7.1 The United Nations and the pandemic

The primary international organisations of an intergovernmental nature that have general powers in the sphere of healthcare include the United Nations and selected specialised agencies, as well as certain programmes and funds

DOI: 10.4324/9781003353805-8

within the United Nations system. Within the UN, the main bodies with competences in the health dimension that are listed in the Charter of the United Nations are primarily the General Assembly and the Economic and Social Council. In this field, the General Assembly can mainly initiate studies and make recommendations, as well as enact conventions (UN Charter, Art. 13(1)). The Council, on the other hand, has the competence to study health and related issues, to make recommendations to the UNGA, the UN members and specialised agencies, as well as submitting draft conventions in this field and convening international conferences (UN Charter, Art. 62). The UN Charter also adopts an extremely broad interpretation of the conditions necessary for the maintenance of peace and friendly relations among the states, including the resolution of international health and related issues (UN Charter, Art. 55).

From the perspective of the experience of the past several months, it is important to note that the outbreak of the COVID-19 pandemic in early 2020 involved to a large extent almost the entire UN system, i.e. the designated principal bodies, as well as most of its component specialised agencies, programmes and funds.

The importance that the UN attaches to the fight against the COVID-19 pandemic is evidenced by the fact that the General Assembly, which has only once in its history to date adopted a convention on a health issue affecting persons with disabilities, drafted several resolutions on the issue, and held a special session on 3–4 December 2020 (A/RES/75/4). The Assembly adopted its first resolution on global solidarity in the fight against coronavirus disease on 2 April 2020 (A/RES74/270). It called on the international community to show solidarity and to work together, inter alia, in areas such as exchange of information, scientific knowledge, and best practices, and the development of common guidelines under the auspices of WHO. It was also pointed out, among other things, that the entire UN system should be involved in the fight against the pandemic, under the leadership of the Secretary-General of the organisation, cooperating with all interested parties in order to develop a coordinated response to the pandemic and its social, economic, and financial consequences. As a consequence of the adoption of the aforementioned resolution, further documents of this type were adopted on 20 April 2020 and 11 September of the same year. The resolution of 20 April 2020 called for international cooperation, under the leadership of the UN Secretary-General and WHO, to ensure global access to medicines, vaccines and medical supplies needed to combat the pandemic (A/RES/74/274). In its resolution of 11 September 2020, entitled *United Response against Global Health Threats: Combating COVID-19*, in addition to pointing out important short-term objectives, the member states and key organisations of the UN system were called not only to fight the pandemic from the point of view of its health aspects, but also to build an increasingly coordinated response in overcoming its social, economic, and financial consequences. In this context, in addition to WHO, particular attention was focused on the International Monetary Fund, the World Bank Group, and their necessary cooperation with other international organisations and regional banks. The role of coordinating efforts and all initiatives in this regard was again entrusted to the UN Secretary-General, who was required to report on activities in this regard to the General Assembly (A/RES/74/307). Pandemic issues were also addressed in other resolutions, such as another resolution of 11 September 2020 on a comprehensive and coordinated response to the coronavirus disease (COVID-19) pandemic (A/RES/74/306) and two resolutions of 16 December 2020 on strengthening national and international rapid response to the impact of the coronavirus disease (COVID-19) on women and girls from the perspective of protecting their rights and recognising the essential role which they play in overcoming its effects (A/RES/75/156; A/RES/75/157).

As a demonstration of the General Assembly's commitment to promoting international cooperation in the fight against the pandemic and guiding the international community's efforts in this dimension, the 31st Special Session of this body at the level of Heads of State and Government dedicated solely to COVID-19 (A/RES/75/4) was also held on 3–4 December 2020. During the general debate, interactive panel discussions and speeches by Heads of State and Government, the Secretary-General, the Presidents of the GA, the Economic and Social Council, the Security Council, the Secretary-General of WHO, representatives of selected specialised agencies and programmes and funds of the UN system, as well as other international organisations, in addition to BioNTech and the University of Oxford, took stock of the results of the UN organisation's and the UN system's efforts to date in combating the pandemic, reviewed work on vaccine development and preparedness for a global vaccination programme, and addressed the issue of the necessary overcoming of the socio-economic consequences of the pandemic using the resources and capacities of the UN system and other actors (GA: 31 Special Session: Summary). It should be stressed that this was an unprecedented event in the history of the UN, as only four special sessions on health issues had been held so far (Joanna Starzyk-Sulejewska a, 2021).[1]

As a symbolic confirmation of the UN's commitment to combating the pandemic, on 1 July 2020 the Security Council, established to maintain international peace and security, adopted Resolution 2532 (2020) on COVID-19, which called for the release of hostages worldwide and for all parties involved in armed conflicts to implement a ceasefire of at least 90 days to allow the delivery of humanitarian assistance to all parties in need, excluding groups and organisations designated by the Security Council as terrorist (S/RES/2532 (2020): (1–3). The resolution also urged the UN Secretary-General to develop and provide information and necessary training on integrating peacekeeping operations into efforts to prevent

1 They concerned drug issues three times and once HIV/AIDS.

further spread of the pandemic and provide assistance to groups particularly vulnerable to the humanitarian impact of the pandemic, including mainly displaced persons, refugees, and in carrying out medical evacuation operations (S/RES/2532(2020): (5–6). The Council also paid particular attention to the need to minimise the socio-economic impact of the pandemic on particularly vulnerable groups, which, in addition to those mentioned above, included women, children, the elderly and persons with disabilities (S/RES/2532(2020): (6). What is also significant is that the president of the Security Council, during his concluding remarks at the 31st Special Session of the UNGA on the COVID-19 pandemic, acknowledged that due to its multiple social, economic, and political consequences, it has serious implications for the maintenance of international peace and security (S/RES/2532(2020): (7).

The Economic and Social Council, at its level, is the main coordinator of the global effort to overcome the social and economic consequences of the pandemic, which is primarily due to the scope of its mandate (UN Charter, Art. 62), as well as to the fact that most of the specialised agencies of the UN system involved in the fight against the pandemic are linked to the UN on the basis of agreements made precisely with the Council (UN Charter, Art. 57, 63). The functional and regional commissions of the body also have a special role in coordinating activities related to COVID-19. In addition to the Sustainable Development Commission, the Council is also the coordinator for the implementation of the Agenda 2030 Sustainable Development Goals, which, under the auspices of the UN system, has been identified as the basis for long-term socio-economic recovery during and after the end of the COVID-19 pandemic (A UN Framework for the immediate socio-economic response to COVID-19: 2021).

However, the specific specialised tasks of combating and overcoming COVID-19 within the UN system are primarily carried out by the specialised agencies, programmes, and funds, being its elements. Currently, 23 entities are included in this group, primarily including: the World Health Organisation (WHO), as well as the institutions of the World Bank Group (the International Monetary Fund, the World Bank, the International Finance Corporation, the International Development Association), the UN Development Programme (UNDP), the World Food Programme (WFP), the UN Children's Aid Programme (UNICEF), and the UN High Commissioner for Refugees (UNHCR UN Report, 2020, p. 8), (Joanna Starzyk-Sulejewska b, 2021).

Similarly to the main bodies of the UN, they carry out, depending on the specificity of their competences, tasks in three priority areas in the context of the COVID-19 pandemic control, i.e. building a response to the pandemic, protecting life and quality of life during the pandemic and building the foundations for socio-economic development after the pandemic (UN Report, 2020, p. 6). It should be emphasised that in the framework of the current pandemic, the entity with the main role in coordinating and organising the activities of the UN system is the World Health Organisation (WHO).

In conclusion, the main UN bodies involved in the fight against the COVID-19 pandemic and in overcoming its consequences are the General Assembly and the Economic and Social Council. It is also noteworthy that a position on the pandemic has been expressed by the Security Council, which in its history to date has only spoken once on epidemic issues in 2014, in connection with the Ebola epidemic. It is clear that the actions of the principal bodies are important, but their main importance lies primarily in guiding the commitment of the entire organisation and the international community and its constituent entities in the fight against the pandemic, and in publicising the need for coordination and unification of actions in the various scopes identified by the principal bodies as particularly relevant. Hence, for example, in the resolutions of the UNGA, issues such as the need for solidarity and the preservation of unity in the actions of the international community in this field appear, pointing out the need to mobilise the resources and capacities of all units of the UN system and to coordinate their actions under the auspices of the UN Secretary-General, or the need to strengthen and respect the fundamental rights of social groups regarded as particularly vulnerable to the consequences of the pandemic. It is important that global conferences related to the assessment of the effects of the different stages of the fight against the COVID-19 pandemic and the identification of the most important deficits and needs in this area are also organised under the auspices of the UN (e.g. the 31st Special Session of the UNGA). The role of coordinators and organisers of such activities is played at the UN level primarily by the Secretary-General and the Economic and Social Council and its functional and regional commissions. However, the main operational tasks related to the fight against the pandemic in individual scopes can be and are performed primarily by individual units of the UN system, which carry them out according to the scope of their competence.

In this context, it is a source of great dissatisfaction that the UN Security Council, in relation to the COVID-19 pandemic, has not yet recognised it, despite its unprecedented scale and impact, as a situation posing a threat to international peace and security within the meaning of Chapter VII of the UN Charter, but only as one with serious consequences for international peace and security. The main reason for this situation is that a resolution of this content would not be accepted by China, and the other members of the Security Council do not want to complicate the already very tense international situation caused by the pandemic. However, it should be noted that paradoxically, the Security Council in 2014 recognised the Ebola pandemic as a threat to international peace and security, despite its far lesser scope and impact.

7.2 WHO and its role in fighting the pandemic

The World Health Organization (WHO) is a specialised agency within the UN system for international health, with 194 member states. Within the UN system, it currently plays the leading role in the fight against the COVID-19 pandemic. It is a classic intergovernmental international organisation with a coordinating role without any powers over its members, which in this case, according to the WHO Constitution, can only be states. The general objective of the organisation is to strive to ensure the highest possible level of health protection in all member states (WHO Constitution: Art. 1, 1948), through the implementation of a number of specific tasks, several of which are directly or indirectly related to the fight against epidemics (WHO Constitution, Art. 2, 1948). The principal instruments for implementing WHO policy include legally binding conventions that enter into force in accordance with the constitutional provisions of states who are parties to the International Health Regulations (IHR), and legislation that enters into force automatically regarding states that fail to notify the WHO Director-General of their rejection or objection to it within a reasonable period of time (WHO Constitution, Articles 19 and 20, 1948). In addition, the organisation may enact non-legally binding measures in the form of recommendations (WHO Constitution, Art. 23, 1948).

In its history to date, WHO has not enacted any international convention regarding combating infectious diseases and epidemics such as COVID-19. From an epidemiological perspective, however, the adoption of the International Health Regulations by the organisation in 2005, which replaced the International Sanitary Conventions and previous generations of International Health Regulations adopted since the establishment of WHO was of fundamental importance. Importantly, the IHR is now the only global legally binding instrument for the control of infectious and epidemic diseases.

The International Health Regulations (IHR), in force since 2005, are a comprehensive set of provisions adopted on the basis of Article 21 of the Constitution of the World Health Organisation, and their main purpose is to prevent the international spread of diseases and epidemics, protect against, combat and ensure a proportionate public health response to international outbreaks of disease and epidemics. The manner of response in such cases is to ensure that, in addition to eliminating public health threats, unnecessary disruption to international traffic and trade is prevented (IHR, Art. 2, 2005). As emphasised, however, the WHO member states who are parties to the IHR have the sovereign right to legislate and implement it, in the light of their own health policies (IHR, Art. 3(4), 2005).

Based on the IHR, the WHO member states that are also parties to the IHR and the organisation have established a network of authorities necessary for its international implementation and enforcement. At national level, these are the National IHR Focal Points and designated or specially established authorities, and, at the WHO level, the WHO IHR Focal Points (IHR, Art. 4, 2005). Obligations are placed on the WHO member states and parties to the IHR to report incidents occurring on their territory that may pose significant threats to the maintenance of public health of international concern. Such reporting should, where required, take place within 24 hours of an assessment being made in this regard. Importantly, also after such notification, the State Party is obliged to continue to provide WHO with timely, accurate and sufficiently detailed public health information available to it in relation to the notified event (IHR, Art. 6(1-2), 2005). WHO also retains the ability to seek information from other IHR State Parties as to events occurring on the territory of other IHR States Parties. However, verification in such cases is always carried out in consultation with the State Party on whose territory the event of international health significance is suspected to have occurred (IHR, Art. 9(1), 2005).

A system for responding to public health emergencies of international concern has also been established under the IHR. The WHO Director-General plays an important role under this system, determining whether an event is a public health emergency of international concern on the basis of information received, and consulting the state where the emergency occurs (IHR, Art. 12, 2005). If both parties agree on the nature of the event, the Director-General shall seek the advice of the Emergency Committee with a view to formulating recommendations. These may be temporary recommendations (adopted for up to three months with the possibility of extension for further three months) or permanent recommendations (to be applied routinely or periodically). In both cases, they may concern the implementation of specific public health measures of international concern, within the territory of the State Party where the public health emergency occurs, as well as other State Parties (IHR, Art. 15 and 16, 2005). They may apply to persons as well as to baggage, cargo, containers, means of transport, goods, and/or postal consignments.

At the request of the State Party, WHO cooperates with the State Party in its response activities by providing technical guidance, assessment of the effectiveness of measures taken and necessary assistance, and by mobilising international teams of experts to assist on-site. Cooperation with WHO may also involve mobilising international assistance to conduct and coordinate on-site assessments to support the authorities of the country concerned (IHR, Art. 13(3-4), 2005). WHO also provides appropriate guidance and support to other states if a public health emergency of international concern also exists in their territories and they formulate such a request (IHR, Art. 13(5-6), 20050. It should be noted that currently 194 WHO member states are parties to the IHR.

Complementary to WHO's response system to epidemiological emergencies is the Global Outbreak Alert and Response Network (GOARN), which was established by WHO in 1996. It is now a network of more than 250 specialised agencies whose activities focus on monitoring the epidemiological situation in specific regions and countries and, in the event of an emergency, providing assistance. Among other things, the activities consist in assisting countries, at their request, in identifying the threat and risk of a given disease or an epidemic spreading in individual countries or regions, and dispatching response teams equipped with the necessary resources. The GOARN Operational Assistance Team (OAST) is based at the WHO Headquarters in Geneva, with representatives also based at the WHO Regional Offices, in order to organise and contribute, as quickly as possible, to the response to specific epidemiological threats notified by countries (GOARN, 2021).

In carrying out its tasks related to preventing and combating the COVID-19 pandemic, WHO is taking action in several complementary dimensions, building on the existing and above-mentioned legal frameworks and mechanisms, as well as creating partially new or completely new solutions in this dimension.

Since the beginning of the COVID-19 outbreak, WHO, as a global health organisation, has taken steps to develop the basis for strategic planning in the fight against the pandemic. The first and, as it turned out, most comprehensive initiative in this case was the announcement of the WHO Strategic Preparedness and Response Plan (SPRP) on 4 February 2020, i.e. four days after WHO officially recognised COVID-19 as a public health emergency of international concern. In view of the rapid dynamics of the pandemic, as well as problems and needs revealed in the organisation's member states during its first months, it was supplemented as early as April of the same year. The plan, established in view of the need to develop the preparedness of the international community's response in the first year of the pandemic, had three main objectives: to control the transmission of the virus, to protect human health and life, and to protect the most vulnerable social groups (SPRP: Drafts as of 3 February 2020, pp. 5–6). WHO's 2020 Strategic Preparedness and Response Plan, according to its assumptions, was also intended to be used to define national response plans to COVID-19 using the assistance of the organisation's 6 Regional Offices and 150 National Focal Points. It should be noted that on 24 February 2021, WHO adopted, based on the experience of the first year, a revised second SPRP assuming the development of WHO's activities in nine areas. Within its framework, greater emphasis was placed on, inter alia, the need to build preparedness for a coordinated response to new variants of the virus, a strategy for the development and use of vaccines for COVID-19, the need to ensure equal and more equitable access to vaccines, medicines and diagnostics in this area, the fight against misinformation on COVID-19-related issues, and the reduction of coronavirus-related morbidity and mortality (SPRP: 1 February 2021 to 31 January 2022, p. 1).

An area closely related to strategic action planning is the coordination of activities undertaken at different levels to combat COVID-19. It should be noted that in this regard WHO, due to its area of competence, has a central role from the point of view of coordinating activities undertaken within the entire UN system.

At the global level, the unit of primary importance in this regard is the UN Crisis Management Team (UNCMT), launched on 4 February 2020, which operates under the leadership of WHO. It is the highest-level unit for crisis coordination across the UN system, and its activation in the case of the COVID-19 pandemic is the first example of this mechanism being used for a public health crisis. The Team during the current pandemic serves as a platform for coordinating activities and ways to leverage the capacities of 23 specialised agencies and UN programmes and funds for fighting COVID-19. It was activated more than 25 times over the course of 2020 to identify and revise global-level strategic objectives as the pandemic unfolded, and to formulate ways to respond to crises signalled by a network of 130 UN country teams in individual countries and resident coordinators of various UN entities (e.g., UNDP) around the world (SPRP: 22 January 2021, p. 11). One of the outcomes of the Team's activities was the establishment, under the auspices of WHO, of the COVID-19 Supply Chain System (COVID-19 Supply Chain System, 2021).

As a major global health organisation, WHO is also taking a leading role within its mandate in the implementation of the *Global Humanitarian Response Plan* (GHRP) for COVID-19, announced on 25 March 2020 and supplemented on 7 May of the same year. Here, WHO is responsible for coordinating and providing assistance in collaboration with more than 900 national and international partners consisting in supporting the essential health services in 30 countries with the greatest health needs. GHRP activities address 63 countries with the greatest humanitarian concerns in relation to the COVID-19 pandemic (SPRP: 22 January 2021, p. 12).

WHO also co-chairs the Global Information Management, Assessment & Analysis Cell (GIMAC), which analyses information on the COVID-19 pandemic to support global decision-making (SPRP: 22 January 2021, p. 13).

As part of the UN Crisis Management Team (UNCMT), WHO also plays an important role in coordinating national responses to COVID-19, primarily through its network of 150 country offices and 6 WHO Regional Offices. The most tangible result of this activity is the support provided to countries through country offices and technical missions organised by the WHO Regional Offices for the development and revision of national response plans to COVID-19. The results of these activities consist, inter alia, in the fact that while only 47% of countries and territories had such plans in March 2020, as many as 91% of countries and territories did so on 31 December 2020 (SPRP: 22 January 2021, p. 14). Plans of this type are then the basis for organising the necessary support and ensuring access to the missing resources for countries making such demands. One of the instruments used by WHO in this regard is the COVID-19 Partners Platform. The Platform assesses the implementation of activities in the nine priority areas identified in the WHO SPRPs, identifies the necessary scope of assistance to the public health sector of individual countries, and establishes a database of assistance offered by donors for COVID-19 purposes. Currently, the Platform brings together a group of 120 countries benefiting from the assistance offered by 80 donors under the WHO COVID-19 Supply Chain System (SPRP: 22 January 2021, p. 14).

A very important scope of the WHO activities aiming to combat the current pandemic is the provision of advice and the development of technical data on the pandemic. On this basis, guidelines are produced on how to deal with very specific COVID-19-related issues.

The broadly understood advisory activity applies to populations worldwide, but also relates to the public health sector as a whole and to decision-makers and governments in individual countries involved in decision-making in this area (Coronavirus disease (COVID-19) advice for the public, WHO, 2021). Compared to advice given to the general public, the provision of technical data and the formulation of guidelines based on this data are much more specialised and detailed. The data and technical guidance collected and made available under the auspices of WHO currently cover 16 categories of cases and are continuously updated and revised. They relate to, e.g.: degree of preparedness, readiness and response to emergencies, including management options depending on the evolution of the epidemiological situation; national coordination, planning and monitoring; serology and investigation protocols; clinical care; planning for access to essential resources; reduction of animal-to-human transmission; humanitarian operations, migrant and refugee camps; national laboratories; infection prevention and control; epidemiological safety rules in schools, institutions and workplaces; travel and border posts; medical workforce; maintenance of critical health services and systems. No less important is the continuously updated epidemiological data relating to countries, regions and overall trends on the pandemic, which serve to build the basis for the response and subsequent response to the crisis caused by COVID-19 at global, regional, and national levels (Country & Technical Guidance, WHO, 2021). These are published, inter alia, within the WHO COVID-19 Dashboard and in numerous WHO reports and publications. They refer primarily to identified daily and weekly infections and deaths in individual countries and WHO regions caused by SARS-CoV-2 virus and overall trends in these areas.

An important element of the WHO's activity during the current pandemic is the operational support offered to the member states of the organisation in the fight against the pandemic. One of the basic forms of its implementation is the activity of the Technical Support Missions (TSM) and the activity of the Emergency Medical Teams (EMT). Technical support missions are composed of WHO experts and representatives of WHO regional partners who provide assistance in requesting countries in the form of training, courses and technical guidance on how to organise and use critical medical infrastructure, equipment and systems. In 2020, WHO sent such missions to 130 countries and, where particularly difficult epidemiological situations prevented this, organised webinars and provided remote support to institutions in member states interested in this form of assistance (SPRP: 22 January 2021, p. 19). The activities of medical teams (EMTs) deployed at the request of countries in emergency situations, and especially in situations of inefficiency or overload of their health systems, were also promoted during the pandemic. In 2020, 30 such teams consisting of certified and highly trained specialists provided assistance to 60 countries (SPRP: 22 January 2021, p. 20). In an even greater number of cases, such teams were formed and organised within WHO regions from among specialists of neighbouring countries willing to assist each other in situations of serious and urgent emergency. The Secretariat of EMTs located at the WHO Headquarters is assessing the challenges and opportunities for deploying such teams and is developing a classification process in this regard. It should be noted that during the COVID-19 pandemic, WHO EMTs largely adapted their activities to the needs reported by Member States by organising, e.g. support and training for Ministries of Health on procedures to be followed in hospitals, strengthening infection prevention and control measures, including, for example, procedures to control the flow of patients in medical facilities.

The GOARN network is also extensively used to support the WHO's operational activities during the COVID-19 pandemic. In 2020 the Network's experts, working with more than 30 regional partners and other UN system entities such as UNICEF and OCHA, organised 400 technical support missions to countries making such requests mainly on various aspects of adapting their health systems to fight the pandemic (SPRP: 22 January 2021, p. 21).

It should be noted that WHO operational support is also provided in a number of other forms. Under the auspices of the organisation, from the outset of the pandemic, a global investigation system to identify cases of disease, track transmission and spread routes, and identify cases of disease at global, regional, and national levels has been created and developed. Importantly, during the current pandemic, the organisation has used for this purpose, among others, already existing investigative systems and platforms that have been established for the identification of cases of other diseases, including influenza, such as the already proven WHO Global Influenza Surveillance and Response System – GISRS (SPRP: 22 January 2021, p. 25).

WHO is also committed to assisting in the setting-up and development of laboratory activities for the diagnosis of SARS-CoV-2 cases through the establishment of a network of reference laboratories in each WHO region. They provide assistance in building capacity in this area in WHO member states. As a result of such activities, for example, Africa, by the end of 2020, had 750 laboratories with capacity to diagnose COVID-19 cases compared to only two such facilities in February of the same year (SPRP: 22 January 2021, pp. 26–28).

Undoubtedly, one of the most visible and measurable areas of WHO activity in the fight against the pandemic is its commitment to the development and promotion of vaccination campaigns on a global scale. It should be stressed that, in this dimension, the organisation has, from the outset, demonstrated a strong commitment to promoting and developing research leading to the development of vaccines, their production, as well as supply and the dissemination of the relevant expertise. In this context, it is particularly significant that WHO has been involved since April 2020 in the activities and development of the COVID-19 Tools ACT-Accelerator, which brings together the efforts of governments, scientists, business, philanthropists, and public health organisations to develop capacity in COVID-19 testing, treatment, and vaccination. The work undertaken under this formula has allowed an unprecedented acceleration and coordination of efforts in the area of accelerating research leading to the development of vaccines for COVID-19 (ACT-Accelerator & COVAX, WHO, 2021). WHO has a fundamental role in their approval process, and within WHO, established in 1999, the Strategic Advisory Group of Experts on Immunisation (SAGE), made up of 15 experts from all over the world, which assesses the conduct of clinical trials, risk elements for specific population groups, strategy for use, etc. The positive opinion of the group is the basis for the WHO recommendation on the authorisation to release a given vaccine on the market, the final decision being made by the individual countries.

In conclusion, despite the measures taken and indicated above, WHO is currently the international organisation where the undoubted limitations of the actions of global organisations in the fight against the current pandemic have been most strongly exposed. In fact, the COVID-19 pandemic has demonstrated obvious weaknesses of WHO and its cooperation mechanisms and procedures, as well as deficits in communication and interaction with Member States.

From a structural point of view, one of the most serious mistakes was that the organisation reacted, without any doubts, too late to the outbreak of the pandemic. Indeed, it was only on 30 January 2020 that the WHO Director-General, despite his broad powers in this area, identified the COVID-19 pandemic as a public health emergency of international concern. This delayed the possibility of using the organisation's activities during the first and also most difficult period of the pandemic, including in particular the activation of the basic procedures existing under the International Health Regulations. Second, the outbreak of the pandemic demonstrated the obvious limitations of the IHR, including in particular the inadequacy of the WHO's mechanisms for scrutinising the conduct of states, and the lack of adequate instruments for enforcing states' compliance with their obligations to report public health emergencies and subsequent cooperation with the organisation in this dimension. This has enabled, among other things, essentially entirely unilateral action by the Chinese authorities, which was not coordinated and agreed with WHO at the start of the pandemic and still is not to a large extent today, as well as very selective reporting by the Chinese authorities to WHO on the effectiveness of the procedures and instruments used, without the possibility of an objective assessment of the situation on-site by the WHO expert mission, acting on the basis of a very limited mandate defined by this country. In the case of the IHR, the inadequacy of its regulatory framework in the face of such a large-scale threat also proved to be a major problem, exemplified by the lack of sufficient coordination among the WHO member states, particularly in the first 3–4 months after the pandemic broke out, as regards the scope of restrictions on international trade and transport, even though the IHR had also been set up to minimise precisely the potential burdens in this area in the event of a pandemic outbreak. The COVID-19 pandemic also demonstrated the inadequacy of the scope of the organisation's assistance procedures provided for in the IHR in the event of such global threats in the future.

Undoubtedly, in addition to significant structural and procedural problems, a very serious constraint has also proved to be the repeated, even ostentatious unwillingness of some member states to cooperate with the organisation, the most striking example of which was the announcement of the decision of 29 May 2020 by the then president of the United States, Donald Trump, of the withdrawal of the United States from WHO, together with the initiation of the related procedure in accordance with the provisions of the WHO Constitution, which was stopped only by the next team of Joe Biden, or the denial, especially during the first wave of the pandemic, of almost all activities of the organisation by Brazil, including the denial of the existence of the virus and the legitimacy of the fight against it by WHO. The current pandemic has also revealed serious difficulties in funding WHO's efforts to combat the current pandemic. In this context, it is very important that the COVID-19 Solidarity Response Fund (WHO, 2021) was created under the auspices of the organisation, but, objectively speaking, it has to be said that the assumed amount of USD 1.96 billion of contribution for 2021 and the continuation of activities started in 2020 under its framework are far too small in relation to the needs of a global organisation dealing with international health. This is also confirmed by the fact that, as of 27 July 2021, receipts to the fund had only reached 46.7% of the projected amount and amounted only to USD 968.8 million. Generally speaking, the WHO's problems have revealed the general shortcomings and inadequacies of the international health system to combat pandemics of the magnitude revealed during COVID-19 (COVID-19 Solidarity Response Fund, WHO, 2021).

In this context, one of the most high-profile initiatives supported by WHO is indisputably the proposal for an international treaty on pandemic prevention and preparedness of 30 March 2021. This project, motioned for the time being in general form by the president of the European Council Charles Michel, the WHO Director-General Tedros Adhanom Ghebreyesus, and the leaders of 26 mainly European countries, envisages, among other things, strengthening international cooperation to improve epidemic warning systems at different levels, increasing and diversifying alert levels of threats relevant to the protection of public health, and enhancing data sharing and developing research and international cooperation in the production and distribution of resources such as vaccines or medicines. The option of an integrated approach within the treaty to combat diseases in humans and animals is also one of the legitimate, albeit bold, proposals in relation to current regulations. The initiative also calls for greater transparency and responsibility on the part of states for their actions in connection with epidemics, including stronger monitoring of their compliance with the adopted regulations by WHO.

Certainly, the potential negotiation of this treaty will be an enormous challenge for WHO and its member states, due to the need for compromise arrangements on the most sensitive issues identified above. It will also be a long process, since the adoption of a convention in the WHO legal order requires the approval of two-thirds of the members present and voting in the World Health Assembly. The need to reach the necessary compromise on this issue among the different groups of WHO member states, including those most important for epidemiological research and for the production and distribution of medicines and vaccines internationally, such as China, the United States, Russia, India, Germany, and the UK, may also prove to be a very difficult issue.

7.3 The European Union and the pandemic

The European Union is another international organisation whose competence in the area of public health protection, including in terms of preventing and combating epidemics, is gradually developing. Within the European Communities, regulations in this scope were very limited until the Maastricht Treaty came into force. For the first time, a separate Title X on "Public Health" appeared only in this very version of the Treaty and was further developed in the Treaty of Amsterdam. Currently, the basis of the EU's competence in the field of health is formed by Articles 4, 6, and 9 in Title I and the expanded Article 168 in Title XIV of the Treaty of Lisbon on the Functioning of the European Union. Some of these are directly related to measures to combat epidemics.

Under the dispositions of the Lisbon Treaty, health protection issues fall mainly under two types of competences. In the area of common safety concerns in public health with reference to the aspects set out in the Treaty (TFEU, Art. 168(1)) these are shared competences, whereas in other areas concerning the protection and improvement of human health they are competences intended to support, coordinate and supplement the actions of the Member States. However, and crucially, because of the relationship between health issues and other areas of the Union's functioning, the European Union, in defining and implementing its policies in other areas, is obliged to take into account, inter alia, requirements for the promotion of a high level of health protection (TFEU, Art. 168(1)). These provisions clearly reaffirm that states have the primary role within the EU in public health matters, and that the Union shall primarily engage in those areas where the results of coordinated action can be better than at the national level. As emphasised in the provisions of Article 168(7) of the Treaty of Lisbon, the Union's actions in this field shall fully respect the responsibilities of the Member States for the definition of their health policy and for the organisation and delivery of health services and medical care (TFEU, Art. 168(7)).

The instruments that the EU uses in the field of public health protection, including the prevention of epidemics and pandemics, are in particular: encouraging cooperation among Member States in these fields and supporting their action; supporting coordination by the European Commission of policies and programmes implemented by the Member States; and supporting cooperation of the Union and the Member States with third countries and international organisations (TFEU, Art. 168(2)). The Treaty of Lisbon also extended the EU's legislative powers in this regard by giving it the possibility to adopt, through the ordinary legislative procedure, legally binding measures encouraging the protection and improvement of human health, including in particular the fight against cross-border epidemics, as well as monitoring, early warning of and combating serious cross-border threats to health. Importantly, however, such measures may be adopted, excluding any harmonisation of the laws and regulations of the Member States (TFEU, Art. 168(5)). The Council of the EU, on a proposal from the European Commission, may also adopt recommendations to achieve objectives relevant to the protection of public health (TFEU, Art. 168(6)).

The implementation of the EU's epidemic prevention objectives has also been reflected in the development of secondary legislation and the EU's institutional development.

Of the secondary legislation most relevant to responding to threats from infectious diseases and epidemics such as COVID-19, the Decision of 22 October 2013 on serious cross-border threats to health (Decision No. 1082/2013/EU of the European Parliament and of the Council), which replaced the earlier Decision No. 2119/98/EC in this regard, is of primary importance.

Serious cross-border threats to public health under the Decision include, e.g.: threats of a biological nature, such as communicable diseases. Importantly, the decision also refers to events which may constitute a public health emergency of international concern in accordance with the International Health Regulations (IHR) of WHO (EP and Council Decision No. 1082/2013/EU, Art. 2). On the basis of the indicated regulation, the grounds for several types of relevant solutions at the EU level have been introduced:

- Member States and the European Commission committed to developing capacities for joint planning and response to health threats of a cross-border nature through, inter alia, consultation, exchange of information and joint assessments of the nature of the threat concerned (EP and Council Decision No. 1082/2013/EU, Art. 4(1));

- establishment of a joint procurement procedure common to the institutions of the Union and to the countries concerned for the advance purchase of medical countermeasures to combat serious cross-border threats to health, including epidemics (EP and Council Decision No. 1082/2013/EU, Art. 5);
- a network for the epidemiological surveillance of communicable diseases and related special health issues was established, providing a permanent link between the European Commission, the European Centre for Disease Prevention and Control (ECDC) established in 2004 and the national authorities responsible at the national level for epidemiological surveillance (EP and Council Decision No. 1082/2013/EU, Art. 6);
- the Early Warning and Response System (EWRS) for serious cross-border health threats was established. It enables a communication system between the Commission and national competent authorities in charge of early warning, and allows to coordinate the way threats are assessed and how to respond to them (EP and Council Decision No. 1082/2013/EU, Art. 8 and 9);
- a Health Security Committee was established to support the implementation of the objectives of the Decision, composed of representatives of the Member States and chaired by a representative of the EC (EP and Council Decision No. 1082/2013/EU, Art. 17).

The action taken at the EU level to combat epidemics and other cross-border public health threats is also supported by several institutions and bodies. These are primarily: the European Commission, and within it the Directorate-General for Health and Food Safety with the Commissioner at its head (DG SANTE) interacting in this respect with the Committee on serious cross-border health threats, the European Centre for Disease Prevention and Control (ECDC) (EP and Council Regulation (EC) No. 851/2004) and the European Medicines Agency (European Medicines Agency, 2021).

Based on this primary and secondary law, and drawing on the powers of the above-mentioned institutions and bodies, the European Union has taken a number of measures to coordinate and develop a common approach to the most important aspects of preventing the spread of and combating the pandemic and overcoming its health and socio-economic consequences. These include many complementary forms of response to the pandemic.

One of the most important forms of the EU's action in this context is the commitment to prevent the spread of the virus by promoting and building a common approach to the performance of diagnostic tests. In creating the formal framework in this area, the EU institutions adopted several framework recommendations. At the level of the European Commission, these were primarily: Recommendation on COVID-19 testing strategies, including the use of rapid antigen tests (European Commission: C(2020) 7502 final) of 28 October 2020, Recommendation on the use of rapid antigen tests for the diagnosis of SARS-CoV-2 infection (European Commission: C(2020) 8037) of 18 November 2020. In turn, the Council of the EU adopted, inter alia: Recommendation on a common framework for the use of rapid antigen tests and the mutual recognition of COVID-19 test results across the EU (EU Council: 5451/21) of 21 January 2021 and EU Health Security Committee: A common list of COVID-19 rapid antigen tests and a common standardised set of data to be included in COVID-19 test result certificates (European Commission: 17 February 2021) of 17 February 2021.

Pursuant to the indicated acts, the EU Member States should, inter alia, use rapid antigen tests to strengthen overall testing capacity, mutually recognise the results of such tests, create the conditions for them to be carried out by trained medical personnel under appropriate conditions, and, as before, mutually recognise the results of RT-PCR tests carried out by certified national health facilities. From March 2021, self-administered testing for COVID-19 began to be disseminated across the EU. On 17 March 2021, the European Centre for Disease Prevention and Control published technical guidance in this regard (Considerations on the use of self-tests for COVID-19 in the EU/EEA: European Commission, 2021). The EC's guidance on the methodology for coronavirus testing also complemented the strategy to disseminate the use of the tests.

Complementary to the coordination of activities in the area of testing since the beginning of the pandemic outbreak is the involvement of the EU in the research and development, as well as release on the EU's market and subsequent distribution, of COVID-19 vaccines. In this regard, since its launch in April 2020, the Union has been involved in the efforts of the international community under the auspices of WHO for the development of a COVID-19 vaccine, drugs and treatments under the COVID-19 ACT-Accelerator, and at the EU level in the development and implementation of the EU Vaccine Strategy (European Commission: COM (2020) 245 final). The Commission Communication on the EU Vaccine Strategy against COVID-19 was announced on 17 June 2020 indicating among the three main EU objectives in this scope to ensure: high quality, safety and efficacy of vaccines, rapid access to them for Member States and globally, and guaranteeing equitable access at an affordable price (European Commission: COM (2020) 245 final, p. 2). The Strategy envisages, e.g.: the support for vaccine development and production in the EU using the expertise of Member States, the European Centre for Disease Prevention and Control and WHO; the conclusion of advance purchase agreements for vaccines through the EU Emergency Support Instrument in the framework of a procurement procedure carried out by the Commission on behalf of all Member States while retaining the responsibility for release on the market and use of vaccines by the Member States making the final purchase; the development and application of common criteria for the qualification of potential vaccines at the Union level; the use of a flexible regulatory process within the EU based, inter alia, on early contact between vaccine manufacturing companies and the European Medicines Agency (EMA); speeding up the authorisation procedure for releasing a given vaccine on the Union market; adopting the necessary modifications to the GMO legislation introducing temporary derogations to accelerate the research on COVID-19 vaccines (European Commission: COM(2020) 245 final, pp. 2–10).

As a result of the adoption of the indicated strategy and supporting actions including the allocation of EUR 1.4 billion for vaccine research conducted through the COVID-19 ACT-Accelerator, the EU developed transparent procedures to allow for an accelerated process of evaluation of vaccines by the European Medicines Agency and, after a positive assessment at its level, for their release on the EU market. As a result, the European Commission has so far issued conditional authorisations for four vaccines to be released for use in the EU. These are vaccines from the companies: BioNTech (Pfizer) – since 21 December 2020, Moderna – since 6 January 2021, AstraZeneca – since 29 January 2021, Janssen (Johnson&Johnson) – since 1 March 2021. Efforts are also underway to accelerate the process of approval of other potential vaccines (Sanofi-GSK, CureVac, Novavax, Valneva) for the EU market. It should be noted that, in accordance with the adopted rules, the EU concludes advance purchase agreements with individual vaccine manufacturing companies to guarantee the supply of specific quantities of a given product to the common market. To date, such agreements have been concluded with BioNTech, Moderna, AstraZeneca, Johnson&Johnson as well as Sanofi-GSK and CureVac. In this way, to date the Union has managed to secure 2.6 billion total doses for the organisation's Member States (Council of the EU: COVID-19: Public Health, 2021). Once a product is authorised within the EU, all Member States gain access to it at the same time, with distribution in proportion to their population. However, it should be noted that the final authorisation of a vaccine in the country is decided by its authorities.

As part of its efforts to promote vaccination, the EU is also developing a broad information campaign on individual products, as well as encouraging their use and combating misinformation about them. It also provides support to national vaccination campaigns. The European Centre for Disease Prevention and Control additionally collects data and tracks vaccination progress and makes it available, including through the publication of information on weekly vaccination progress.

For the implementation of the COVID-19 activities to promote research on therapies and vaccines, diagnostics and treatments, the EU has also allocated additional funding of EUR 660 million from, among others, the Horizon 2020 research programme, the Innovative Medicines Initiative and the Accelerator programme of the European Innovation Council (EU Council: COVID-19: Public Health, 2021). The European Investment Bank funds have also been redirected for these purposes.

During the pandemic, the EU also launched a number of procedures to support the Member States' health systems and crisis management and emergency relief. In this regard, for example, the European Commission, through its Emergency Response Coordination Centre, at the request of a given Member State, coordinates and co-finances the supply of personal protective equipment and essential medical supplies to Member States, supports the organisation of transport of medical teams from one country to another, and, if necessary, organises repatriation flights to enable EU citizens temporarily in other Member States of the Union or outside Europe to return to their countries.

During the pandemic, the European Commission further developed the role of the coordinator for anti-crisis cross-border cooperation in healthcare (European Commission: Recommendations on Directive 2005/36/W). Indeed, transportation of patients from one Member State to another has been developed on an unprecedented scale, medical personnel has been enabled to provide assistance in other EU countries, and the basis for patient transfers has been established as part of support in situations of health system overload due to the pandemic (European Commission: Crisis Management and Solidarity, 2021). This cooperation is coordinated by the EC-chaired Health Security Committee and through the EU Early Warning and Response System (EWRS).

In addition, a large-scale emergency response uses the EC Civil Protection Mechanism, through which the EU helps coordinate and finance the distribution to requesting Member States of medical equipment, personal protective equipment, and disinfectants. In total, since the beginning of the pandemic, the Union has provided assistance through this channel to 30 EU and non-EU Member States by coordinating and co-financing the distribution of 15 million such resources (European Commission: Crisis Management and Solidarity: 2021). An important element in this regard was the creation of a strategic stockpile of medical equipment including ventilators, oxygen concentrators, protective masks, medical gloves, and laboratory equipment on 19 March 2020 within the "rescEU" network. This stock is 100% funded by the EC and is currently located in countries such as Germany, Romania, Denmark, Greece, Hungary, Sweden, Belgium, the Netherlands, and Slovenia. The distribution of the equipment in this case is handled by the EC Emergency Response Coordination Centre, while the procurement and replenishment of the equipment through the Commission is the responsibility of the countries where the warehouses are located (European Commission: Crisis Management and Solidarity, 2021).

An important instrument for supporting emergency response at the Union level is also the Emergency Support Instrument, which provides frameworks for joint actions and resources to respond rapidly to common strategic needs (e.g. vaccines, purchase of therapeutic agents, plasmapheresis equipment, clinical trials of repositioned medicines, transport of first aid supplies, medical professionals, patients, training of health professionals in intensive care skills, linking national contact tracking applications) (European Commission: Emergency Support Instrument, 2021).

Also, establishing the European Health Emergency Preparedness and Response Authority (HERA) is part of the effort to strengthen anti-crisis action. HERA will undertake tasks in the areas of: risk modelling, global surveillance, technology transfer, production capacity, supply chain risk mapping, identification of flexible production capacity, and development of vaccine and medical research. The European Commission has also prepared and is responsible for implementing a new bio-defence preparedness plan, in the form of the HERA Incubator (European Commission: Public Health, 2021).

An important part of supporting the EU's efforts to contain the spread of SARS-CoV-2 is building a coordinated approach to travel within the EU. Although these measures have been introduced to protect the health and lives of the EU citizens, they have serious implications for the functioning of the economy and civil rights. Among the key measures in this regard is the EU Council Recommendation on a coordinated approach to the restrictions of free movement in response to the COVID-19 pandemic (Council of the EU: Council Recommendation (EU) 2020/1475) of 13 October 2020, which is continuously updated according to the epidemiological situation, vaccination progress, etc. The Recommendation was last updated on 14 June 2021. On the basis of the Recommendation, the following were introduced: a common mapping system of zones based on a colour code, common criteria for Member States when deciding to introduce travel restrictions, more transparency on measures applied to travellers from high-risk areas and rules to inform the EU public quickly and clearly about restrictions. The launch in December 2020 of the Re-open EU portal, which provides key information on travel restrictions, public health, and safety measures applied by individual countries and the epidemiological situation in individual countries, was also important from this perspective. It also provides maps produced by the European Centre for Disease Prevention and Control.

The development of guidelines on travellers who should be exempted from temporary travel restrictions and the updating of the EU Council Recommendation on the temporary restriction on non-essential travel into the EU (Council of the European Union: Council Recommendation 9208/20) are also important reinforcements of the principles of a coordinated approach to travel in the EU. A very important additional endeavour in laying the foundations for a common approach to travel within the EU is the introduction of the EU digital COVID-19 Certificate issued to people who have been vaccinated, are recovered, or have tested negative. The certificate facilitates safe travel within the EU and is recognised by all EU Member States plus Switzerland, Liechtenstein, Norway, and Iceland. The proposal to introduce this type of certificate was announced by the EC on 17 March 2021, and on 14 June 2021 the regulation on this issue (European Commission, Proposal: EP and Council Regulation, COM(2021) 130 final) was signed by the presidents of the EU Council, the EC, and the EP. It entered into force within the EU on 1 July 2021.

It should be stressed that the EU, as part of the anti-crisis package for overcoming the medium- and long-term effects of the pandemic, has also taken a number of unprecedented decisions related to the financing of socio-economic recovery, with measures that go beyond the existing legal regulations in force in the EU strictly for healthcare. To this end, the EU Heads of State and Government agreed already on 23 April 2020 to set up a reconstruction fund with the main objective of overcoming the effects of the crisis. A project in this regard was presented on 27 May 2020 by the EC in the form of a *Recovery Plan for Europe* (Council of the EU: Recovery Plan for Europe, 2021), the implementation of which was to be linked to the Multiannual Financial Framework (MFF) of the EU for the years 2021–2027. The Recovery Plan, called Next Generation EU, was agreed on 21 July of the same year at the level of Heads of State and Government, amounting to a total of EUR 750 billion. Together with the EU Multiannual Financial Framework 2021–2027, finally adopted on 17 December 2020, amounting to EUR 1,074.3 billion, and the additional EUR 540 billion for the EU's 3 assigned COVID-19 securities for workers, companies, and Member States, this makes a total package of EUR 2,364.3 billion, which can largely be used for post-pandemic socio-economic recovery. The most significant element of the Recovery Plan for Europe is the Recovery and Resilience Facility adopted as a regulation on 11 February 2021 with a total amount of EUR 672.5 billion, which will be mainly used for realising the objectives of strengthening health systems and resilience, as well as for post-pandemic digital and green transformation and inclusive and sustainable employment policies, social and territorial cohesion, and the development of activities for the next generation through education and skills enhancement (EP and Council Regulation (EU) 2021/241).

In conclusion, the European Union has not avoided, in the fight against the COVID-19 pandemic, the problems associated with the initial difficulties in adapting to the situation and planning the necessary actions. Admittedly, as early as 9 January 2020, the Directorate-General for Health and Food Safety (DG SANTE) activated the first alert notification in the Early Warning and Response System established by the 2013 Decision (EP and Council Decision No. 1082/2013/EU), and on 17 January 2020, the EU Security Committee convened its first meeting on a new variant of coronavirus, which also formed the basis for the activation of the EU Civil Protection Mechanism for the first time on COVID-19 on 28 January 2020, but these were not actions that would tangibly and sufficiently support Member States in their fight against the pandemic. The Union has therefore not escaped serious accusations by the Member States of a lack of dynamism in the measures taken, particularly in the early months of the pandemic (spring 2020) and, inter alia, on the flawed negotiation of vaccine supply agreements with key vaccine manufacturers whose products were authorised for distribution globally and within the EU in the first place. Faced with this situation, EU Member States therefore began to negotiate, in parallel and separately from the EU's action, the supply of vaccines with their key manufacturers, such as BioNTech, AstraZeneca, or Moderna, while a few, such as Hungary, began to use in their countries Chinese and Russian vaccines not officially authorised for distribution in the EU.

Nevertheless, it must be said that over time, i.e. on the verge of the second wave of the pandemic in Europe, with the development of research on COVID-19 and the activation of the necessary structures, mechanisms, and capacities at its level, as well as under the influence of the growing needs of the Member States, the Union began to perform the tasks of managing the pandemic at its level with increasing success within the limits of the assigned competences. This is evidenced both by the pandemic management approaches developed at its own level and by the initiation and promotion of various forms of international cooperation to combat COVID-19. The most important examples of activities in this area within the Union include: the elaboration of the financial package for 2021–2027 with the Recovery Plan for Europe creating incomparably greater opportunities than in previous periods for the EU Member States to finance socio-economic development and overcome the consequences of the pandemic, the increasing coordination of the supply of vaccines to the EU Member States, and securing 2.6 billion doses for the needs of the EU citizens, the development of recommendations on the COVID-19 case testing system, EU-wide synchronisation of the introduction and then gradual lifting of travel restrictions in connection with the pandemic, or the development of broad information activities at its level on the risks associated with the pandemic. Crucially, the Union has also been at the forefront of many of the most innovative international solutions in this area and is mobilising the international community to implement them. Key examples of such engagement include the EU's participation in the ACT-Accelerator for the development of vaccines and medicines for COVID-19, or the COVAX international network for the supply of vaccines to countries most in need; the initiation by the president of the European Council of discussions on an international treaty on pandemic prevention and preparedness; the co-organisation together with Italy as part of the G20 of the Global Health Summit in Rome on 21 May 2021, and mobilisation during the summit of multimillion aid for the poorest countries to fight the pandemic.

7.4 The Visegrad Group and the pandemic

Activities to combat the COVID-19 pandemic are undertaken not only at the global and regional level, but also at the sub-regional level applying the specificity and nature of structures for the development of cooperation at this level. An example of such a structure is, among others, the Visegrad Group, which was established in 1991 as the Visegrad Triangle before the dissolution of Czechoslovakia, and after its dissolution into the Czech Republic and Slovakia it functions under its current name and serves to develop cooperation on issues important for the future of the Central European region and the EU, as well as in the field of science, culture, education, youth exchange, transport, and in strengthening energy security in the region. Except for the International Visegrad Fund, meetings within the Group are non-institutionalised and consist in coordinating positions and exchanging views at various levels, i.e. heads of state or government, ministers, parliaments, government institutions, non-governmental organisations, scientific centres and cultural institutions. The agreements within the Group usually take the form of non-legally binding declarations. From the point of view of the Group's activity and the scope of its activities, it is extremely important that since 1 May 2004 all its member states are EU Member States. This fact is also of fundamental importance from the point of view of coordination of initiatives in the fight against COVID-19, because it is at the EU level that the mainstream of cooperation in this field among the V4 member states takes place. Importantly, however, also the EU in the face of the threat pointed to the need to coordinate and exploit cross-border cooperation in this dimension using already existing sub-regional and regional arrangements and agreements.

Within the Group, the COVID-19 pandemic fell under the Slovak, Polish, and Hungarian presidencies, with issues related to it being first officially included in the programme of the Polish presidency running from 1 July 2020 to 30 June 2021. This is because Slovakia's presidency from 1 July 2019 to 30 June 2020 coincided with the initial period of the pandemic and Slovakia was not in a position to foresee such actions in the programme of its V4 presidency, but only to respond to the pandemic through ad hoc initiatives, while Hungary's presidency began on 1 July 2021 after the end of the Polish presidency.

At the start of the V4 presidency, Poland stressed that the European and global response to the pandemic would have a significant impact on the development of individual countries and regions, the EU and the world as a whole, and that the V4 countries would therefore have to actively cooperate to contain the impact of the pandemic and put social life in the Central European region and the EU on track. The four objectives of the presidency therefore included, among others, the objective of returning to normality in connection with combating the COVID-19 pandemic and its consequences, and within this framework cooperation of the V4 for returning to normality as soon as possible after the pandemic, and cooperation in the field of health and science. Other objectives were also largely linked to the pandemic issues. In terms of strengthening people-to-people contacts, restoring and strengthening cross-border cooperation and contacts was in fact identified as one of the most important objectives, and the goal of strengthening the collaboration in the digital sector, including, among others, digitisation, robotics, e-commerce, development of digitisation in administration, promotion of digital cross-border initiatives, and collaboration of this type among regional private and public entities was additionally connected to the anti-crisis response to the COVID-19 pandemic (Polish Presidency of the Visegrad Group: Presidency objectives, 2020).

Despite extensive plans of the V4 in the area of activities related to overcoming the pandemic and its consequences, in the first months of 2020, during both the Slovak and Polish presidencies, a rather serious problem was still the lack of appropriate mechanisms for information exchange and communication allowing coordination of initiatives in this area. An expression of such problems was, among others, the situation in border regions, where the lack of appropriate communication channels hindered cooperation related to the change of border regime, causing serious consequences primarily for cross-border employees. Striving for improvement in this dimension, on 11 September 2020, at the meeting of V4 prime ministers in Lublin, it was decided that a virtual V4 Centre for COVID-19 serving as a platform for the exchange of information on planned and undertaken activities, as well as knowledge, experiences, and good practices in order to ensure coordination and more effective cooperation in this area was going to be established. It was intended that contacts within the centre would complement those implemented at the level of the EU, WHO, and other international structures in the fight against the pandemic. The centre started its activities from 9 October 2020. Since its establishment, the centre's meetings have taken the form of cyclical weekly meetings of V4 ministerial experts, attended by representatives of the ministries of health and foreign ministries of the Group member states. They consult with other ministries before the meetings. The issues of the meetings mainly include an analysis of the current situation of border management and healthcare systems in the context of the fight against COVID-19. Transport issues, including air transport, and issues related to internal regulations and restrictions implemented in individual countries of the Group in connection with the pandemic are also subject of the exchange of information. Experts from other institutions may also participate in these meetings (Polish Presidency of the Visegrad Group, News: 09.10.2020). The activities of the centre are currently the primary platform for cooperation of V4 countries on pandemics at the sub-regional level.

In addition to the activities of the V4 Centre for COVID-19, which improves the response to changes in the situation caused by the pandemic, the Visegrad Group countries are also undertaking other activities aimed at overcoming its effects primarily in the area of economic and social cooperation. In this context, noteworthy are actions taken within the V4 to coordinate the positions of member states in the negotiations conducted at the EU level on the European Recovery Plan and the EU Multiannual Financial Framework for 2021–2027, which took place, inter alia, in May and June 2020. Additional agreements on economic issues within the V4 included, in particular: decisions on the need for joint action with regard to tax issues in the electronic economy and the fight against tax fraud in this dimension (Joint Declaration V4: September 4, 2020); decisions of the V4 prime ministers on the development of mutual cooperation on digital innovation and digital issues, aiming at the establishment of digital innovation centres, the joint development of artificial intelligence and the creation of a digital technology exchange network (Visegrad Group Joint Declaration: February 17, 2021); supporting the development of greater autonomy for the European pharmaceutical sector by, inter alia, formulating a call for greater independence from the supply of active ingredients for manufacturing medicines from non-European regions and increasing the production capacity of the EU countries, including the V4 countries, for vaccines (V4 Contribution to the Pharmaceutical Strategy for the EU, September 29, 2020); decisions on cooperation in support of the tourism sector particularly affected by the pandemic, e.g. through broader cooperation of tourism administration of V4 states, creation of coordinated legal regulations in this area, and promotion of incoming tourism to the countries of the Group from third countries, organised jointly by tourism organisations of the four states (Polish Presidency of the Visegrad Group: News, 27 April 2021).

It should be noted that as part of the COVID-19 control, the Visegrad Group has also developed cooperation in the V4+ formula, which now primarily includes support to the Eastern Partnership and the Western Balkan countries. As for the Eastern Partnership countries, on 29 April 2021, readiness to develop cooperation to overcome the economic and social consequences of the pandemic using the V4 East Solidarity Programme implemented under the Visegrad Fund was declared. The decision to supply vaccines to the Eastern Partnership countries through the international instrument of solidarity in this area – COVAX (Joint Statement on the Eastern Partnership: 29 April 2021) – was also supported. The Visegrad Group also expressed its readiness to develop cooperation for overcoming the socio-economic effects of the pandemic with the countries of the Western Balkans, using as a basis of the post-COVID reconstruction the *Economic and Investment Plan for the Western Balkans* adopted by the EU, as well as supporting the Western Balkans Fund modelled on the Visegrad Fund and implementing the programme for the development of start-ups for the Western Balkans (Joint Statement on the Western Balkans: 28 June 2021).

From the perspective of the continuation of the COVID-19 cooperation, important decisions were also taken during the V4 Summit organised on the occasion of the Group's 30th anniversary, on 17 February 2021 in Krakow. At that time, a continuation of activities for the development of capabilities in civil protection, risk management, and crisis management of the V4 based on the experience of the V4 Centre for COVID-19 was declared (Declaration on the Occasion of the 30th Anniversary of the Visegrad Group: 17 February 2021).

In conclusion, during the first phase of the pandemic, the V4 member states mainly focused on national level activities. The first more consolidated actions of the V4 to combat COVID-19 and its consequences were designed only by the Polish presidency, which was also due to the emergence of increasingly serious problems resulting from the lack of systematised cooperation on cross-border issues, such as the movement of employees, goods or services among the states of the sub-region. The most tangible result of the V4 cooperation to date in the fight against the pandemic is the improvement of the system for exchanging information on planned and implemented actions in this area, the institutional expression of which was the establishment in October 2020 of the V4 Centre for COVID-19. Thanks to the activities of the Centre, the system of border management among the V4 countries and cooperation among their healthcare services has been improved. Initiatives to overcome the socio-economic consequences of the pandemic in the region are also starting to take shape in an increasingly real way, manifested primarily by closer coordination among V4 countries in the movement of people, services (e.g. transport and tourism), and goods. Although these are important undertakings, it should be stressed that the EU remains the main multilateral forum for V4 member states' cooperation in tackling the pandemic, and initiatives undertaken at the sub-regional level are either complementary in this context, or aim to mark the specificity of the V4 countries' approach to individual issues within the framework of broader EU initiatives (e.g. in developing the EU Pharmaceutical Strategy taking into account the needs of current and future pandemics).

References

2019 Novel Coronavirus (2019-nCoV): Strategic and Response Plan: Drafts as of 3 February 2020. Available from: https://www.who.int/docs/default-source/coronaviruse/srp-04022020.pdf, 21 April 2020, p. 5, accessed: 10.06.2021.

A UN Framework for the Immediate Socio-Economic Response to COVID-19. Available from: https://unsdg.un.org/resources/un-framework-immediate-socio-economic-response-covid-19, accessed: 29.07.2021.

ACT Accelerator & COVAX, World Health Organisation. Available from: https://www.who.int/initiatives/act-accelerator/about/, accessed: 12.06.2021.

Commission Recommendation of 18.11.2020 on the Use of Rapid Antigen Tests for the Diagnosis of SARS-CoV-2 Infection, C(2020) 8037, Brussels, 18.11.202.

Commission Recommendation of 28.10.2020 on COVID-19 Testing Strategies, Including the Use of Rapid Antigen Tests, C(2020) 7502 final, Brussels, 28.10.2020.

Communication from the Commission to the European Parliament, the European Council, the Council and the European Investment Bank: EU Strategy for COVID-19 Vaccines, COM(2020) 245 final, Brussels, 17.6.2020.

Considerations on the Use of Self-Tests for COVID-19 in the EU/EEA. Available from: https://www.ecdc.europa.eu/en/publications-data/considerations-use-self-tests-covid-19-eueea, accessed: 15.06.2021.

Constitution of the World Health Organisation, Journal of Laws 1948, 61.477, Item 477, p. 1232.

Coronavirus Disease (COVID-19) Advice for the Public, World Health Organisation. Available from: https://www.who.int/emergencies/diseases/novel-coronavirus-2019/advice-for-public, accessed: 10.06.2021.

Council of the European Union. Available from: https://www.consilium.europa.eu/pl/press/press-releases/2021/05/20/eu-supports-start-of-who-process-for-establishment-of-pandemic-treaty-council-decision/, accessed: 10.06.2021.

Council of the European Union: Council Recommendation on the Temporary Restriction on Non-Essential Travel into the EU and the Possible Lifting of Such Restriction, 9208/20, Brussels, 30 June 2020. Available from: https://data.consilium.europa.eu/doc/document/ST-9208-2020-INIT/en/pdf, accessed: 20.06.2021.

Council of the European Union: COVID-19: Public Health. Available from: https://www.consilium.europa.eu/pl/policies/coronavirus/covid-19-research-and-vaccines/, accessed: 10.06.2021.

Council of the European Union, The EU's Recovery Plan, Available from: https://www.consilium.europa.eu/pl/policies/coronavirus/covid-19-economy/, accessed: 20.06.2021.

Council Recommendation on a Common Framework for the Use and Validation of Rapid Antigen Tests and the Mutual Recognition of COVID-19 Test Results in the EU, 5451/21, Brussels, 20 January 2021 (OR.en).

Council Recommendation (EU) 2020/1475 of 13 October 2020 on a Coordinated Approach to the Restriction of Free Movement in Response to the COVID-19 Pandemic, Official Journal of the European Union, L 337, 14.10.2020.

Country & Technical Guidance – Coronavirus Disease (COVID-19), World Health Organisation, Available from: https://www.who.int/emergencies/diseases/novel-coronavirus-2019/technical-guidance, accessed: 10.06.2021 .

COVID-19 Response Fund, World Health Organisation. Available from: https://www.who.int/emergencies/diseases/novel-coronavirus-2019/donors-and-partners/funding, accessed: 29.07.2021.

COVID-19 Strategic Preparedness and Response Plan (SPRP): Looking Back at a Year that Changed the World, World Health Organisation, 22 January 2021. Available from: https://www.who.int/emergencies/diseases/novel-coronavirus-2019/strategies-and-plans, accessed: 10.06.2021.

COVID-19 Strategic Preparedness and Response Plan, 1 February 2021 to 31 January 2022, World Health Organisation. Available from: https://www.who.int/emergencies/diseases/novel-coronavirus-2019/strategies-and-plans, accessed: 10.06.2021.

COVID-19 Strategic Preparedness and Response Plan. Operational Planning Guideline, 1 February 2021–31 January 2022. Available from: https://www.who.int/emergencies/diseases/novel-coronavirus-2019/strategies-and-plans, accessed: 10.06.2021.

COVID-19 Supply Chain System. Available from: https://www.who.int/emergencies/diseases/novel-coronavirus-2019/covid-19-operations, accessed: 10.06.2020.

Decision No. 1082/2013/EU of the European Parliament and of the Council of 22 October 2013 on serious cross-border threats to health and repealing Decision No. 2119/98/EC, Official Journal of the European Union, L 293.

Declaration of the Prime Ministers of the Czech Republic, Hungary, the Republic of Poland and the Slovak Republic on the Occasion of the 30th Anniversary of the

Visegrad Group. Available from: https://www.visegardgroup.eu/calendar/2021/declaration-of-the-prime, Krakow, 17 February 2021, accessed: 20.06.2021.

EU Health Preparedness: A Common List of COVID-19 Rapid Antigen Tests and a Common Standardised Set of Data to be Included in COVID-19 Test Result Certificates, Agreed by the Health Security Committee, 17 February 2021.

European Commission: Crisis Management and Solidarity. Available from: https://ec.europa.eu/info/live-work-travel-eu/coronavirus-response/crisis-management-and-solidarity_pl, accessed: 14.06.2021.

European Commission: Emergency Support Instrument. Available from: https://ec.europa.eu/info/live-work-travel-eu/coronavirus-response/emergency-support-instrument_pl, accessed: 15.06.2021.

European Commission: Guidelines on Freedom of Movement of Health Professionals and Minimum Harmonisation of Training in Relation to COVID-19 Emergency Measures – Recommendations in Relation to Directive 2005/36/EC. Available from: https://eur-lex.europa.eu/legal-content/PL?TXT/?uri=CELEX%3A5202XC0508%2801%29, accessed: 15.06.2021.

European Commission: Public Health. Available from: https://ec.europa.eu/info/live-work-travel-eu/coronavirus-response/public-health_pl, pp. 7–8, accessed: 15.06.2021.

European Medicines Agency. Available from: https://www.ema.europa.eu/en/about-us/legal-notice, accessed: 30.05.2021.

Executive Board. Available from: https://www.who.int/about/governance/executive-board, accessed: 20.06.2021.

Global Outbreak Alert and Response Network – GOARN. Available from: https://extranet.who.int/goarn/, accessed: 15.06.2021.

Joanna Starzyk-Sulejewska a, 2021 They concerned drug issues three times and once HIV/AIDS.

Joanna Starzyk-Sulejewska b, 2021 The UN system units involved in the UN system's global response to the pandemic include: FAO, IAEA, ICAO, IFAD, ILO, IMF, IMO, IOM, ITU, UN Women, UNAIDS, UNCTAD, UNDP, UNEP, UNESCO, UNFPA, UN HABITAT, UNHCR, UNICEF, UNIDO, UNITAR, UNODOC, UNDRR, UNOPS, UNRWA, UNWTO, UPU, WB, WFP, WHO, WIPO, and WMO.

Joint Declaration of V4 Finance Ministers on the Cooperation In the Financial Area, 4 September 2020. Available from: https://www.visegradgroup.eu/calendar/events-in-2020/joint -declaration-of-v4, accessed: 15.06.2021.

Joint Statement of the Foreign Ministers of the Visegrad Group on the Eastern Partnership. Available from: https://www.visegardgroup.eu/calendar/2021/joint-statement-of-the, Warsaw, 29 April 2021, accessed: 18.06.2021.

Joint Statement of the Ministers of Foreign Affairs of the Visegrad Group Countries on the Western Balkans, Rogalin, June 28, 2021. Available from: https://www.visegradgroup.eu/calendar/2021/joint-statement-of-the-210629, accessed: 1 July 2021.

Polish Presidency of the Visegrad Group, Meeting Inaugurating the Creation of the Virtual V4 Center for COVID-19. Available from: https://www.gov.pl/web/V4prezydencja/spotkanie-inaugurujace-powstanie-wirtualnego-centrum-v4-ds-covid-19, 09.10.2020, accessed: 15.06.2021.

Polish Presidency of the Visegrad Group, Presidency Objectives, July 2020 – June 2021. Available from: https://www.gov.pl/web/V4prezydencja/priorytety-polskiej-prezydencji, p. 3–4, accessed: 15.06.2021.

Polish Presidency of the Visegrad Group, The Polish Presidency Wants to Rebuild the Tourism Sector after the Pandemic. Available from: https://www.gov.pl/web/V4prezydencja/grupa-wyszehradzka-chce-odbudowywac-sektor-turystyczny-po-pandemii, 27.04.2021, accessed: 20.06.2021.

Proposal for a Regulation of the European Parliament and of the Council on a Framework for the Issuance, Verification and Acceptance of Interoperable Certificates on Vaccination, Testing and Recovery to Facilitate Free Movement during the COVID-19 Pandemic (Digital Green Certificate), COM/2021/130 final, Brussels, 17.03.2021.

Regulation (EC) 851/2004 of the European Parliament and of the Council of 21 April 2004 Establishing a European Centre for Disease Prevention and Control, Official Journal of the European Union, L 142, 30.4.2004.

Regulation (EU) 2021/241 of the European Parliament and of the Council of 12 February 2021 Establishing the Recovery and Resilience Facility, Official Journal of the European Union, L 57, 18.2.21021.

Regulation (EU) 2021/522 of the European Parliament and of the Council of 24 March 2021 establishing a Programme for the Union's Action in the Field of Health ('EU4Health Programme') for the Period 2021–2027, and Repealing Regulation (EU) 282/2014, Official Journal of the European Union, L 107, 26.3.2021.

Regulation (EU) 282/2014 of the European Parliament and of the Council of 11 March 2014 on the Establishment of a third Programme for the Union's Action in the Field of Health (2014–2020) and Repealing Decision No. 1350/2007/EC, Official Journal of the European Union, L/86, 21.3.2014.

Resolution 2532 Adopted by the Security Council on 1 July 2020, S/RES/2532(2020).

Resolution adopted by the General Assembly on 11 September 2020, Comprehensive and Coordinated Response to the Coronavirus Disease (COVID-19) Pandemic, A/RES/74/306, 74th session.

Resolution adopted by the General Assembly on 11 September 2020, United Response Against Global Health Threats: Combating COVID-19, A/RES/74/307, 74th session.

Resolution Adopted by the General Assembly on 2 April 2020, Global Solidarity to Fight the Coronavirus Disease 2019 (COVID-19), A/RES/74/270, 74th session.

Resolution Adopted by the General Assembly on 20 April 2020, International Cooperation to Ensure Global Access to Medicines, Vaccines and Medical Equipment to face COVID-19, A/RES/74/274, 74th session.

Resolution Adopted by the General Assembly on 5 November 2020, Special Session of the General Assembly in Response to the Coronavirus Disease (COVID-19) Pandemic, A/RES/75/4, 75th session.

Resolution Adopted by the General Assembly on 16 December 2020, Strengthening National and International Rapid Response to the Impact of the Coronavirus Disease (COVID-19) on Women and Girls, A/RES/75/156, 75th session.

Resolution Adopted by the General Assembly on 16 December 2020, Women and Girls and the Response to the Coronavirus Disease (COVID-19), A/RES/75/157, 75th session.

Revision of the International Health Regulations, The Fifty-eighth World Health Assembly, Doc. WHA58.3.

Special Session of the General Assembly in Response to the Coronavirus Disease (COVID-19), United Nations Headquarter. Summary of the President of the General Assembly, 3–4 December 2020, in: Treaty on the Functioning of the European Union, in: Official Journal of the European Union C 326, 26.10.2012.

United Nations Charter. Available from: https://www.un.org/en/about-us/un-charter/full-text

United Nations Comprehensive Response to COVID-19: Saving Lives, Protecting Societies, Recovering Better, September 2020,United Nations, p. 8. Available from: https://www.un.org/sites/un2.un.org/files/un-comprehensive-response-to-covid-19.pdf, accessed: 10.06.2030.

V4 contribution to the Pharmaceutical Strategy for the EU. Available from: https://www.visegardgroup.eu/documents/official-statements/v4-contribution-to-the, 29 September 2020, accessed: 15.06.2021.

Visegrad Group Joint Declaration on Mutual Cooperation in Digital Projects, Krakow, 17 February 2021. Available from: https://www.visegradgroup.eu/download.php?docID=458, accessed: 15.06.2021.

Summary

Jolanta Itrich-Drabarek

In the history of the state there are constant actions aimed at strengthening it against visible and invisible enemies. Armies are being armed, hospitals are being built, enormous resources are being spent both on preparation and on development of a strategy of action. Then comes the moment of crisis and the moment of checking how the state has actually coped with the challenge.

Contemporary states, due to their political system and regime, have adopted different models of fighting the SARS-CoV-2 virus and have achieved different results, because state resources have a decisive influence on the choice of measures taken by governments in the fight against SARS-CoV-2.

Regardless of their political system and regime, today's countries have been affected by the same economic problems caused by the SARS-CoV-2 pandemic, and its effects will be important for the direction of the global economy after the pandemic ends. In the short term, definitely negative, but in the long term, they will contribute to the development of the information society and the development of ITC tools, acceleration of pro-environmental activities, and integration of national economies.

The Visegrad Group countries, in addition to the problems associated with the SARS-CoV-2 pandemic, which are universal in nature, are characterised by a greater susceptibility to breaking and circumventing the law in force, because there is an increased number of irregularities and abuses of power associated with the previous level of socio-economic development, governments due to political connotations have a greater tendency to manage through restrictions, and the effects of the pandemic will be more profound than in other EU countries.

Authorities in developed democracies, through a system of developed human and civil rights, are constrained in their decision-making on pandemics, but will still be able to enjoy public trust in the long term. The authorities of authoritarian states are more effective in managing the causes, course, and effects of the pandemic, but in the long term this will not improve their standing with the public.

DOI: 10.4324/9781003353805-9

Undoubtedly, in crisis situations the state as the central reference point is often the only remedy. Opponents of its omnipotence get quiet or are silenced because it's impossible to solve the problem at hand without the participation of the state. The ability of state authorities to make effective decisions related to the protection of human life, maintaining stable functioning of all institutions was and still is crucial in any crisis situation.

The outbreak of the SARS-CoV-2 pandemic proved to be an extremely serious challenge and test for the entire international community, including not only states, but also the effectiveness of international institutions operating at global, regional, and also sub-regional levels. As the presented analysis indicates, in reaction to this unprecedented situation, international organisations such as the UN, WHO, the EU, and sub-regional cooperation structures such as the Visegrad Group were forced to:

- stimulate their activities and expand their scope on an unprecedented scale;
- make maximum use of their powers in the field of health and health-related areas;
- use almost all existing instruments, mechanisms and procedures within their scope;
- use in many cases their existing forms of cooperation in an innovative way;
- develop, at times completely new, ways of action adapted to the scope and dynamics of the current pandemic; and
- undertake international cooperation in much broader forms than in their previous activities.

The analysis clearly shows that each of the discussed organisations, despite initial great difficulties in adapting to the situation and planning necessary actions, is currently fulfilling tasks in the scope of pandemic management at their level with increasingly better results, within the limits of the granted competences. However, the overall assessment seems to be in favour of the EU, which, among international organisations, has emerged over the last year as the leader of European solutions in this field due to the way in which the pandemic has been dealt with at its level in many areas, as well as the fact that it has been at the forefront of many of the most innovative international solutions in this field and is mobilising the international community to implement them. Key examples of such engagement include the EU's participation in the (ACT) Accelerator or the COVAX international delivery network, the president of the European Council's initiation of discussions on an international treaty on pandemic prevention and preparedness, the development of the 2021–2027 financial package with the recovery plan for Europe, and the co-organisation of the Global Health Summit in May 2021 in Rome as part of the G20. Cooperation at the level of international organisations such as the UN, WHO, and the EU also demonstrates that they have served to develop, on an unprecedented scale, the foundations and mechanisms for scientific and research cooperation on an international scale, as demonstrated by the development and production of vaccines for SARS-CoV-2 at an extraordinary rate, and that with their strong participation the cooperation among the health administrations of many countries has been tightened.

Activities to mitigate the effects of the SARS-CoV-2 pandemic are also undertaken at the sub-regional level. In the case of the analysed Visegrad Group (V4), however, they are of a limited nature and mainly involve coordinating and organising cooperation on the most relevant immediate problems resulting mostly from difficulties in the movement of people, services, and goods in connection with the pandemic and cross-border cooperation. These activities complement actions primarily at the EU level in the area of border management and strengthening cooperation among health services of its Member States.

A certain amount of political correctness certainly triumphed during the pandemic – instead of the term "Chinese virus" the name SARS-CoV-2 was used.

However, the phenomenon of politicisation of the pandemic found its dimension in the initiation by governments of institutional transformations (normative, structural, related to the organisation of the state apparatus, introduction of legal solutions favourable to the ruling parties), which eroded the democratic system.

The situation within the Visegrad countries determined specific features of the politicisation of the pandemic. For example, in Poland, it took on the form of an umbrella syndrome, behind which the central government camouflaged the true purpose of its actions by introducing legal changes which violated the constitutional principles of presidential elections or the so-called abortion compromise, while in Slovakia, the government's crisis management policy became the main criterion for assessment of its efficiency and effectiveness and led to the resignation of the prime minister. Meanwhile, in Hungary, it exposed the main interest group, which is foreign capital, and the actions taken indicated that the stability of the internal government depends on its support, which was reflected in solutions promoting large companies and corporations.

In a very complicated situation, bearing in mind the recent crises (financial and refugee) and the current ones (fight against climate change, for minority rights, for the right to abortion, against the rise of the populist wave), the pandemic has triggered political processes whose effects will be felt for many years.

The pandemic exposed, on the one hand, the weakness of the nation-state, as none of the states in the world was able to cope with the effects of the pandemic on their own, but on the other hand, it also pointed to the latent power of nation-state egoisms and attempts to build new spheres of influence (China, Russia, Great Britain).

The pandemic revealed inconsistent legal solutions or a lack of procedures and mechanisms for effective cooperation between states. Lack of mechanisms for knowledge and information exchange. Lack of adequate infrastructural resources.

The pandemic overturned the belief in crisis management plans, as it turned out that none of the countries was sufficiently prepared for it; it only depended on their general resources, the structure of their health care organisations, or the wisdom of their leaders to cope with the challenges brought by the virus.

The pandemic deepened the popularity of populists in Central Europe, who were able to use apparent methods (controlling and closing borders, building temporary hospitals, never mind that they were ill-equipped and overpaid) to strengthen and confirm their electorate in the belief that they were doing well, despite the fact that during the peak phase, around 700 people a day were dying in Poland.

The pandemic exposed the problem of relations between scientists and politicians. It has emerged that in many countries, political decision-makers do not regard the results of scientists' work as relevant to the decision-making process. Results of work presented by the scientific world that are incompatible with the objectives and interests of policymakers are questioned or dismissed as false. This, in turn, results in social consent to question the findings of science by the public. This problem has taken on a particular dimension in the context of the activities of the anti-vaccine movement.

The pandemic revealed a new face of corruption and extended the phenomenon of letaprivation. During the pandemic, loopholes were exploited or laws were created for the benefit of a group of politicians associated with the ruling team, who took advantage of the crisis situation to seize some public assets.

It should be remembered, however, that in the numerous statements evaluating ways of dealing with the effects of the pandemic and attempts to implement strategies counteracting the intensification of illnesses and deaths, it was not large corporations but states that came to the fore. The network of power constructed around states and political systems proved to be irreplaceable once again, as in the crisis of 2008, when government interventions ultimately proved absolutely necessary.

Due to the specificity of pandemic threats, the increasing risk of their occurrence, and the difficulty of combating them, a society-wide discussion on changing existing security and health care strategies and reconfiguring security systems is urgently needed. If responsible health and security policies are not to remain mere postulates, responsibility cannot simply consist of restricting individual rights and freedoms, isolating the infected and quarantining the suspected, spending billions of dollars on unreliable vaccines, and ad hoc anti-crisis measures aimed only at protecting critical systems for the security and functioning of the state from a fatal overload.

Index